Can't Your Child See?

Can't Your Child See?

A Guide for Parents and Professionals About Young Children Who Are Visually Impaired

THIRD EDITION

Eileen P. Scott

James E. Jan

Roger D. Freeman

pro·ed

8700 Shoal Creek Boulevard
Austin, Texas 78757-6897

pro·ed

© 1995, 1985 by PRO-ED, Inc.
8700 Shoal Creek Boulevard
Austin, Texas 78757-6897

Library of Congress Cataloging-in-Publication Data

Scott, Eileen P.
    Can't your child see? : a guide for parents and professionals
about young visually impaired children / Eileen P. Scott, James E.
Jan, Roger D. Freeman. — 3rd ed.
      p.   cm.
    Includes bibliographical references and index.
    ISBN 0-89079-604-1
    1. Children, Blind.   2. Visually handicapped children.
3. Children, Blind—Family relationships.   4. Children, Blind-
-Education.   I. Jan, James E.   II. Freeman, Roger D.   III. Title.
HV1596.2.S35   1995
362.4′1′083—dc20   94-9262
                                                   CIP

This book is designed in Caledonia and Gill Sans.

Production Manager: Alan Grimes
Production Coordinator: Adrienne Booth
Art Director: Lori Kopp
Reprints Buyer: Alicia Woods
Editor: Tracy Sergo
Editorial Assistant: Claudette Landry

Printed in the United States of America

2   3   4   5   6   7   8   9   10   99   98   97

*To all the parents of
children with visual impairments*

Contents

Foreword

Books written for parents of visually handicapped children are so few in number that any new one is a welcome publication event, provided it is well conceived, based on sound experience, and competently executed. All that and more can be said in favor of this book.

It often is asserted that blind children are just like other children, only they cannot see. But it is this "only they cannot see" that upsets the parents emotionally and makes their task of bringing up a visually handicapped child more difficult and more challenging. The authors of *Can't Your Child See?* recognize this, and they approach their goal of assisting such parents with optimism and with confidence in the power of individuals—parents and children—to overcome obstacles.

Guidebooks for parents of visually handicapped children have a function that goes beyond that of books written for parents in general. Most parents can discuss their problems with each other at home, on the playground, or wherever there is an opportunity. Parents of visually handicapped children feel that they cannot do this because their children's problems are so different from those of other children. They feel that they are alone in their task and must cope without the support that other parents gain from each other. In this situation a guidebook for parents plays a much more important role. It has not only an informative but also a supportive function.

Eileen Scott, the primary author of the book, has more than 35 years of experience in dealing with parents of visually handicapped children and, directly or indirectly, with the children themselves. This enables her to illustrate any point she wants to make with practical and often amusing or touching examples. Her approach is practical and realistic, and she explains in easily understandable terms the reasons for what she recommends as sound procedures. But she is too experienced a professional not to know that what may be right for one child, one parent, one environment is not necessarily the best or even good for another. Thus she avoids being dogmatic and gives parents a choice whenever that seems wise. Above all she stresses that visually handicapped children, like all others, are quite resilient to mistakes in methods, provided they are sure of and secure in their parental affection.

The authors, recognizing the importance of the early years of life as a truly formative period, deal more extensively with that age. They consider the needs of all visually handicapped children and also have included a chapter on children with multiple disabilities, whose preponderance among the visually handicapped is increasing.

The book is eminently practice oriented, with factual information and examples and concrete advice. Thus it will be most useful to parents but also can serve as a supplement to other available publications for concerned professionals.

A German writer once said: "If books do not make people good or bad they do make them better or worse." This book will certainly help to make parents more competent in raising their young visually handicapped child and more aware and understanding of the child's special needs.

Berthold Lowenfeld, PhD

Preface

◆ ◆ ◆ ◆ ◆ ◆

What are children with little or no sight really like?" "Can they grow and develop like other children?" "Where do they go to school?" "Do blind people ever get married?" "Can they work and earn a living?" "Do they live in a world of darkness?" "Can they be happy?"

These are the questions usually asked of the counselor by each new family of a blind or partially sighted baby on a first get-acquainted visit. At some stage in the conversation the mother wants to know whether "they" get married and the father inquires about what kinds of employment are open to blind people, despite the fact that their baby is only a few months old. The scope of the questions is an indication of how bewildered and apprehensive parents feel about the awesome responsibility with which they are suddenly faced. Certainly most visually handicapped children do grow up to be normally happy and productive adults, many do get married and find employment, and best of all their parents do survive the experience and grow to feel great pride in their children.

Most new parents feel overwhelmed when they think of the long years ahead in which they will have to cope with what seems to be an insurmountable number of problems involved in raising a visually impaired child. They may feel it would be a lot better for the child and easier for themselves if they could hand the child over to specially trained people who would know just what to do. Perhaps it would be easier for the parents, but past experience has shown that loving, informed parents can provide a child with a much more positive climate for growth than can any institution full of so-called experts.

There are so many "experts" on child care these days, writing in books and magazines and talking on the radio and television, that parents can become confused and more uncertain, especially since the experts do not always agree with one another. One young mother summed it up neatly when she said, "I have read three books and taken a night class in child care, and everybody tells me something different. How am I supposed to decide who is right? I think I will ignore them all and do my own thing."

There is a good deal of wisdom in her decision. Each set of parents is different, has different cultural backgrounds and personalities, and brings to its marriage different experiences. Hence their views on child rearing will vary from those of other couples. Concerned parents will want their children to grow and mature physically, mentally, socially, and emotionally. They will want them to learn courage and independence, to be curious about the world around them, to be friendly to people, and to be happy within themselves.

A number of good books on child development are readily available. Parents are well advised to find one they like and refer to it for basic information about things like sequence of development, the approximate age at which children can be expected to reach a specific level of development, and the common problems (and their solutions) that may arise along the way. It can be very comforting to parents of a blind child to discover that what they had considered to be a problem exclusively related to impaired vision is a problem that arises with most sighted children too—in other words, it is normal. It also helps parents to know approximately when a child should be taught a specific skill, since children will learn it then much more readily than they will several years later. If you know when to look you will be better able to tell when the child is ready to learn.

In this book, we hope to provide parents and teachers with that additional specialized information that they seek when faced with the task of raising a child with little or no vision. Most of the material in the book has been distilled from a long and close working relationship with the parents of more than 700 children who are blind or partially sighted. These parents have been actively involved in helping to determine the form and content of this book, and we are tremendously grateful for their help and cooperation over the years. All cases mentioned are actual, but names of families and individuals have been changed.

Parents and teachers reading this book should feel free to change and adapt the suggested techniques or to improvise new solutions of their own. After all, there is no *one* right way to teach a child. If parents believe their children are ready and able to learn, and they receive that message, then the children will learn in their own good time. Parents can become the experts for their own very special children.

For all parents of children who are visually impaired we hope that *Can't Your Child See?* will provide comfort, reassurance, practical information, and hope for the future.

Note

Since the first edition of *Can't Your Child See?* was published in 1977, there have been far-reaching changes in the educational services available to visually impaired children, particularly in Canada and the United States. This third edition reflects changes in current medical information about diagnostic procedures and treatment, as well as changes in many family situations involving working mothers, single-parent homes, and alternate care.

Chapter 1

Diagnosis and Implications

◆ ◆ ◆ ◆ ◆ ◆

Blind is the one word that parents hear and react to when first discussing their child's eye condition with the doctors. To most people it is a frightening word meaning total absence of sight, and it is loaded with emotional and cultural implications. It is important to understand that the term blindness does not always mean the same thing to medical personnel as it does to parents, and that a person who is considered to be medically or legally blind actually can have a good deal of useful vision. Chapter 2 provides information about the meaning of the various medical terms, the measurement of visual acuity, and descriptions of various kinds of partial sight.

The diagnosis of a severe visual defect may be made at birth, later in the first year, or even later if the child has relatively good partial sight or when a child who is born with normal vision loses it. Diagnosing blindness or partial sight in a newborn infant is not always a straightforward procedure. If the baby's eye condition is one in which there is a marked abnormality in the appearance of the eyes or the eye movements are abnormal, the attending physician usually will call in an ophthalmologist (eye specialist) to examine the baby's eyes shortly after birth to determine what is wrong. Some diagnoses (such as congenital cataracts, retinopathy of prematurity, or corneal scarring) usually are made early, while the baby is still in the hospital. The parents have not yet had time to get to know and love their new baby. For these parents the child starts out in life as a blind baby. Sometimes the damage to the eyes seems to obscure the baby, and grief and worry surround the child from the very beginning.

Some other eye conditions that result in severe visual defects are not so readily detected at birth because the eyes appear to be normal. The damage may be at the back of the eye and may not be apparent except to a skilled ophthalmologist. It is only when the parents begin to notice that they cannot establish eye contact with the baby during play or when they observe that the child does not seem to follow brightly colored objects that they begin to wonder if something is wrong. If the child has some remaining vision, it becomes even more puzzling for parents, because the baby sees things sometimes but other times does not seem to be aware of them. It is usually around the age of 3 to 4 months that the "invisible" eye conditions are first noticed by the parents and later confirmed by the doctors. The parents of these children have had some time to get to know and love their baby before they have to cope with a visual disability. They also have to live through a period of almost unbearable suspense until the diagnosis is finally confirmed.

The whole diagnostic procedure can be an exhausting experience for parents, both physically and emotionally. It may involve numerous medical appointments with the family doctor, the pediatrician, and one or more ophthalmologists, office examinations, and hospital examinations, all requiring a good deal of running around and waiting for appointments. Then there is the problem of which doctor is going to discuss the diagnosis and its implications with the parents. Sometimes it is the ophthalmologist and sometimes it is the family doctor. It is helpful to parents if they ask the family doctor to arrange for the ophthalmologist to explain the eye condition to them, as well as sending his or her report to the family doctor.

WHAT DO PARENTS WANT TO KNOW?

Many parents of visually handicapped children are frustrated by their own lack of information about the child's eye condition. Some doctors routinely provide full information about the diagnosis to parents, and the great majority will do so on request. A few leading questions from the parents will assist the doctor in telling them things such as what is actually wrong with the eye (explained in lay terms); what the cause is; how severe the condition is; whether there is any effective treatment available in the area or elsewhere; what changes, if any, may occur in the future; what long-range expenses, if any, may be involved; and where help for parents can be found. Parents have a right to this information. Sometimes it is not possible for the doctors to reach an exact diagnosis when the child is very young, in which case they should tell parents that it will be necessary to do further investigation as the child grows older. They may have determined which part of the eye is not functioning, but they may not know the reason why. In this type of situation the doctor may wish to refer the baby to a university medical center for further investigation. Finding out the exact diagnosis will not restore the child's vision, but until they can put a name to it they cannot determine what caused it to happen. Sometimes, however, the cause remains unknown.

Early intervention is a term used by professionals to describe the supportive and educational services available to parents of children who are blind or partially sighted. These services are provided by a variety of governmental and private agencies. The services are designed to assist parents in minimizing the effects of visual impairment on their child's development. We urge parents to seek out such help as early as possible, for their own sakes as well as their children's. Developmental delay and uneven development are more common in visually impaired children whose parents do not have access to such programs.

Whenever possible family doctors should be asked to refer the child to a good pediatric diagnostic center or clinic where the staff is familiar with visually impaired children for a full diagnostic assessment. Many of these centers are associated with university medical schools, and there is a trend to include parents as an integral part of the diagnostic team. At such a clinic the parents should learn why their child cannot see, the cause of the impairment, the presence of any other physical or mental problems, and whether any treatment is indicated.

EMOTIONAL EFFECT ON PARENTS

All family members need to have a clear understanding of the cause, the nature, and the extent of the child's disability and to come to terms with their own feelings about it before they can effectively relate to the child. Professional people are just beginning to recognize that, since medical treatment seldom can cure blindness in infants, it becomes a parent problem rather than a child problem. Parents should expect the doctors to recognize that there is a realistic basis for their anxiety, that there are heavy physical and emotional demands on them, and that they need a good deal of support at the beginning if they are to function as good parents to their child.

Parents awaiting the birth of their child naturally assume that their baby will be healthy, handsome, and wise and have a winning personality. They do not let themselves even think about the possibility that something might be wrong with the baby. As soon as the baby is born they seek immediate reassurance that their new son or daughter is "normal" and at their first opportunity fondly check to see if the baby has the regular complement of fingers and toes.

When parents are informed that their baby is not the hoped-for perfect child but has a serious physical or mental disability, their feelings of pride and happiness are replaced by shock, grief, anger, despair, and anxiety about the future. Sometimes parents are so shocked that they cannot remember anything the doctor said about the baby's eyes except that the sight was impaired. Others remember in vivid detail years later every word that was spoken on that day. They say that nothing in their previous experience had prepared them to cope with that kind of situation, and they were completely overwhelmed by what they felt was the enormity of the problem confronting them. This reaction of shock may be nature's way of helping us survive such traumatic experiences and giving us a little time to get used to the new situation and marshal our resources so that we will be better able to cope.

In talking about the grief and sorrow they felt after receiving the diagnosis, some parents say they felt almost as if their long-awaited perfect baby had died. And yet they could not really mourn for him or her because their baby *was* living. They felt sad and disappointed for themselves, and they also felt sad for the baby because he or she would never be able to do all the things they had hoped for. Mr. and Mrs. Baron had waited for many years for the birth of their first son Tom, who was diagnosed as blind one day after his birth. Mr. Baron was desperately upset. An avid sportsman, he had been happily planning on teaching his new son to ski and hike and play football. He said he felt as if his whole world had collapsed around him, and he was frightened that he might do something drastic. Three years later, having become actively involved in helping to raise his young son, he confided that he never would have believed that it was possible for him to feel the great joy and satisfaction he was experiencing through watching his nearly blind young son grow and develop into a happy, active boy.

Grief is almost as immobilizing for parents as the initial shock, and it is fortunate that in the first few weeks the needs of visually handicapped babies, like others, are pretty well limited to being kept clean, fed, and warm, which gives the mother and father badly needed time to recover their emotional equilibrium before they must get busy meeting the special needs of their baby. This is a time when the sharing of feelings of grief and disappointment between the parents is almost essential, albeit difficult. When each parent feels that he or she is literally struggling to survive under the weight of the troubles, it is easy to forget that the other parent may be feeling the same way. Each one is in need of loving comfort and reassurance from the other, and when it is not offered its absence may be interpreted as a lack of love and understanding, or even as rejection. To hear a young mother say, "He doesn't care about me or the baby," while the young husband sits at home silently, unable to bring himself to go to work and face the solicitude of "the guys," is not that unusual. If they could only reach out to comfort each other and to talk about their grief and disappointment, they would begin to realize that they are not alone and that if they share the load they might just make it.

After shock and grief the next stage for most parents is one of anger and resentment. Feelings such as "Why me? I don't want a blind child . . . make it all go away . . . it is too much" are perfectly normal reactions under the circumstances but somewhat frightening to the parents.

Visiting the Thomas home, the parent counselor was concerned about Mrs. Thomas's apparent lack of reaction to the fact that her one-month-old son was totally blind. She appeared very controlled and somewhat impersonal in talking about the baby until the counselor said, "I am surprised that you don't seem to feel very upset about having a blind baby." With that Mrs. Thomas blurted out, "You don't know that I lie in bed every night and think of ways that I could kill this baby so nobody would find out. I haven't told anyone that." When the counselor replied, "Thank goodness you are reacting. I was beginning to think you weren't normal; you seemed so cool. Can you think of anyone in their right mind who would choose to have a blind baby?" Mrs. Thomas looked startled and said, "You mean other parents feel this way? What a relief! I thought I was some kind of monster!" Then she gave a little smile and said quietly, "You knew I wouldn't really kill him, didn't you, because he is sort of cute, isn't he?"

Some parents feel very angry at what has happened to them. They tend to blame the doctor who informed them of the diagnosis, calling him cruel, callous, and impersonal, and they frequently may change doctors. Mr. and Mrs. Anthony haven't had a good word to say about Dr. Lopez, who broke the news to them, but think that Dr. Yardley is most compassionate and kind, while Mr. and Mrs. Bronson, who started out with Dr. Yardley, have nothing but praise for Dr. Lopez. That is not to say that all doctors are automatically endowed with the concern, compassion, frankness, and optimism we hope to find. Of course they are not, and some do the very difficult job of informing parents about their baby's eye condition better than others.

Angry feelings can be very useful if parents are able to use them constructively. Being angry makes them feel like doing something about the situation. Parents of a visually handicapped child can decide to pick up the pieces and give the child the best upbringing possible. If they are not too sure just how to do it, they will be moved to find out how.

When Mrs. Powell returned to her ophthalmologist for the final confirmation of her son's diagnosis (Craig had only light perception, that is, he was only able to see bright lights), she was told that the parent counselor would be asked to phone her to arrange a home visit. The counselor tried and tried but was unable to reach Mrs. Powell at the number given her by the doctor, and unfortunately the Powells had an unlisted phone number. After a week Mrs. Powell phoned and most indignantly berated the counselor for not phoning. She continued her scolding throughout the first visit. She said that she was told that she would have help and that if her child couldn't see then there was no time to waste and she wanted to get started right away. By the second visit she had cooled down enough to realize that, since Craig was only 6 weeks old, she didn't have to teach him everything that day. She shamefacedly confessed that she had driven past the agency several times while waiting for the phone call that didn't come and had been very tempted to stop and throw a few rocks through the windows. She did not want to have anything to do with "that blind place," and yet she needed help from it that had not yet come. This reluctance to accept help from an agency for the visually impaired while wanting it at the same time is a common reaction among new parents, particularly if they have not personally been acquainted with a blind child or adult. Such an acquaintance can make a big difference.

Mr. and Mrs. Rozinski, both under 20, were remarkably unperturbed when they learned that Neil would never see. When questioned about it, Mr. Rozinski replied, "Blindness is no big deal. We went all through school with Brian Lunn. You know him, he was the smartest kid in the school—president of the school council, editor of the paper, and he played lead in that rock band. He didn't miss out on a thing." They had concluded from their own personal acquaintance with Brian (a brilliant student) that blindness does not necessarily limit all of a child's activities and accomplishments and that a blind child can live a fairly normal life. Fortunately, Neil, by age 4, proved to be a bright child who stayed very busy getting into all kinds of mischief at nursery school.

WHAT ABOUT THE RELATIVES?

Young parents not only have to cope with their own emotional reaction to the diagnosis but also have the very difficult job of dealing with the reaction of their own parents, the baby's two sets of grandparents. It is usually a lot easier if the grandparents live at a distance and the parents have time to get their own feelings sorted out before trying to cope with them. In-laws may comment, "We never had anything like this on our side of the family; it must come from yours." Words that are not meant for comfort but rather seek to place blame on someone else are hurtful. Young Mrs. Kay tearfully said she could face the fact that her son would not be able to see and she thought she and her husband would manage well. What really distressed her was the dreadful thing she had done to her parents by giving them a blind child as their only grandson. Their disappointment was made most evident to her every time they came to visit, with the result that she believed she was a complete failure as a daughter. This belief was adversely affecting her functioning as a wife and as a mother. Many grandparents, on the other hand, are a tremendous source of emotional support for new parents, and many families have been helped over some very rough times by their love and support.

Sympathetic and well-meaning advice from friends and relatives is sometimes hard to refuse without hurting feelings. Recommendations about the gifted doctor who successfully removed Great Aunt Nellie's cataracts and who could without doubt fix the baby's eyes are hard to turn down politely. So are the prescriptions for miracle diets, vitamins, and unorthodox treatments. The Fell family drove 300 miles each weekend at the insistence of relatives to take their son, who had a degenerating brain condition, for treatment by a quack who blew air up the boy's nose, on the theory that it would stretch the skull and his brain would have more room to grow. Hope springs eternal and can be fanned by misguided advice from friends and relatives who mean well. Parents have a hard enough time accepting the reality that their child has an irreversible eye condition without having their hopes raised and dashed again and again. The best solution is for parents to be sure of their doctor and trust him or her to keep them informed of any new type of treatment that might benefit their child and for them to make this fact clear to those offering advice.

ETHNIC ATTITUDES

Different cultures have different attitudes toward blindness and how blind people should fit into society, and these may be a source of misunderstandings.

Mrs. Freberg, who emigrated from Austria with her husband soon after their marriage, has two children who are blind. She has found it hard to reconcile her parents' view that blind children should be raised in institutions with the North American philosophy of blind children living at home and being a part of their community. Her mother repeatedly comments that "there are places for children like that" and wants them hidden away.

Mr. and Mrs. Santos returned to Spain with their blind son to visit relatives. The grandparents, uncles, aunts, and cousins all accused the parents of being cruel in demanding that the child sit up at the table and eat properly with the family. Mr. Santos said they seemed to believe that because the child could not see he should be waited on hand and foot. They did not think he was capable of learning to be independent in any way; they thought he was helpless and hopeless.

It is, in other words, that much harder for parents who have been raised in one country and live in another to agree on how they want to raise their visually impaired child. One parent may have stronger emotional ties to the "Old Country," and the other parent needs to be aware of this should they happen to disagree on a question of management. The new country's way does not necessarily have to be all good; probably a compromise would be most comfortable for the whole family.

WHAT DO YOU TELL PEOPLE?

One of the questions confronting the parents of a visually handicapped baby is what to tell people when they ask about the baby. Word does get around, and the parents are not sure who knows and who doesn't know about the eye condition or how they should deal with it.

Mrs. Miller announced with great indignation that they were going to sell their brand new house and move out of "that horrible neighborhood." She said that their next-door neighbors had come over the previous evening and had not asked to see the baby, Cheryl, or even asked how she was. It was suggested that the neighbors had really come to express their concern and affection but were waiting for her to let them know if it was all right to talk about Cheryl's lack of sight. When she had not done so, they had assumed that it was still too painful for her to discuss it and had respected her feelings. When asked how she could have let them know that she did want to talk about Cheryl, she said that perhaps she might have made them comfortable by saying, "Would you like to see the baby? Even if she can't see, we think she is beautiful!" Then they would have been able to talk openly instead of waiting for a signal that never came.

Friends and relatives also may look to the parents for cues as to how they should react, not only to the baby but to the parents as well. When parents send them the message that they consider the child's visual disability to be the greatest of all tragedies, the relatives tend to react accordingly, with pity for the poor little blind child who will never have a chance in life and with condolences to the poor parents who must shoulder this great burden. If, however, the parents can send the message, through words and actions, that although they are disappointed and sad about the fact that their child cannot see normally, they are going to do their best to continue their former lifestyle and they expect their blind child to grow into a happy and independent person, it will help their friends and relatives to react in a more positive way. When the parents are feeling depressed and upset it is very easy for them to misinterpret what other people say and do and to feel that the whole world is aware of and reacting to their problem.

Writing about her early reactions to her daughter's blindness, Mrs. Barry said, "When Betty was first born and we were told that she was blind, I experienced that first feeling of despair and defeat that I am sure confronts all mothers when they are made aware of the baby's blindness. First of all, I hated people for their thoughtlessness, their unkind stares and whispered remarks. This was overcome by facing and realizing that Betty was blind, and it was a matter of ridding myself of my own self-consciousness. Having a blind child, I felt at first, was something to hide, rather than face the endless questions of unthinking strangers. When I finally faced it, it wasn't half so bad. I decided to concentrate on the development of Betty into a happy, contented, and good-natured child, and I am proud of the spirit she shows." That was written over 25 years ago, and Betty is now a beautiful and charming university graduate, married and working part-time in adult education—solid evidence that her parents achieved their goal.

There are bound to be times when some tactless but well-meaning person will say something upsetting about your child. The best defense is to grow a thick hide and develop a sense of humor, to laugh instead of cry. One parents' group had a running contest for years to see who had the worst thing said to them. The winner to date is the mother who, when shopping with her baby, was stopped by an elderly woman who looked into the baby carriage and said, "My, my, so this is that little blind baby I've heard about. Too bad she didn't die, isn't it?" Indignation, the usual reaction, unfortunately interferes with parents' ability to come up with a devastating reply.

Whenever parents start feeling depressed and sorry for the baby because he or she cannot see, it helps to remember that the child does not know what normal sight is. The baby has not lost anything and so will feel no loss and will never really understand what normal sight means. In the early years the child will not be particularly aware of any difference from the rest of the family *unless the child is made to feel a difference.* Once parents realize this, it will be much easier to cope with their own feelings about blindness and to deal with the reactions of other people.

LEARNING TO COPE

New parents of a child with a disability are apt to feel overwhelmed at what appears to them as a future loaded with problems, and they may wonder how they are going to survive. There is no denying that raising a visually impaired child will tax ingenuity, energy, and emotions, but most families will be constantly amazed at their ability to manage. If parents can force themselves to live one day or one week at a time, it will be easier. Worrying about all the things that might happen in the future uses up time and energy in a wasteful way. Some of those problems disappear on their own, and as parents gain in knowledge and firsthand experience they will be so much more competent that they will easily cope with many situations that currently may seem to be insoluble. Parents can grow along with their child to reach their own unrealized potential. Mrs. Davenport, the spoiled daughter of a wealthy family, became the mother of premature twins who were blind and had to learn how to keep house and care for the twins all at once. After a particularly tough day when the furnace broke down, the twins had the measles, and her husband was out of town, she said, "I just wish my parents could see me coping with this mess. They always said I had no inner strength and that I should marry a rich man who could look after me, and here I am able to handle all kinds of emergencies that I never thought I could. I feel good about myself!"

WHAT ABOUT THE OTHER CHILDREN IN THE FAMILY?

How other children in the family will react to learning that their brother or sister cannot see normally will depend, first, on whether they are old enough to understand fully the implications of blindness or severely impaired vision and, second, on how aware they are of their parents' grief and worry. Very young children are more apt to be upset if frequent medical appointments and hospitalization for the baby keep the parents away from home a good deal and preoccupied when they are home. Siblings may feel angry at the baby for disrupting their routine and taking too much of their parents' attention away from them. If the diagnosis of impaired vision is not made until the baby is a few months old, it can reactivate the feelings of jealousy and resentment that sometimes occur in young children after the birth of a new baby, just when things had begun to settle down. The same kind of reassurance and extra attention that most parents know is needed then will have to be given all over again to convince the other children that the baby has not supplanted them in their parents' affections. Small children tend to be self-centered and worry mainly about things that affect them directly and more or less ignore the things that affect others. If the baby is blind their reaction will tend to be one of curiosity rather than sorrow. They may even bring their friends in to see this quite remarkable baby that everyone seems to be so concerned about, acting almost as if the baby is their claim to fame and somewhat of a status symbol.

If the brothers and sisters are older or if the child loses his or her sight after infancy, the impact on the children in the family can be much greater. The most common reaction is for them to fear that they, too, might lose their sight. They worry about this possibility, sometimes becoming fearful and anxious in the daytime and having bad dreams at night. Brothers and sisters should be given a factual explanation (appropriate for their age) of what has happened to their sibling's eyes and why they cannot be fixed. Other children should be reassured that it will not happen to their eyes too. It helps them if they can be enlisted to help the visually impaired child learn to function as independently as possible.

WHAT ABOUT HAVING MORE CHILDREN?

The question of whether or not to have more children seems to confront many parents at the time or just after their child's eye condition has been diagnosed. Despite the fact that they may not have been planning to have another child immediately, it nevertheless may become one more serious problem confronting the new parents of a child who is visually impaired. Some parents react immediately with the decision that they will never have another child, like young Mrs. Keel, who still felt so negative about the whole situation 3 months after the birth of Ted that she became hysterical if her husband even touched her. As a rule, couples are not in any state to make a rational decision about future children until they have had several months to get used to the idea of having a child with little or no sight and have worked out their best way of coping with their own reactions to the disability and the physical routine of providing good care.

Before parents can make an informed decision about having more children, they should know whether the baby's eye condition is a genetic one, one that has been transmitted from one or both parents. If it is genetic, they will want to know the chances of their next child also inheriting it. Will it be a one in four chance, or a one in two, and if so are they prepared to take the chance of having a second visually impaired child? There are some families who literally do not care whether their children have normal vision or not, for example, the Turlock family. Both parents have partial sight from two different genetic eye conditions, and to date they have produced six children, three of whom have defective vision, and they firmly intend to have more, despite counseling to the contrary.

GENETIC COUNSELING

All parents want to know the cause of their child's eye condition. Was it simply one of nature's accidents? Was it due to something that happened to the baby before birth (the damage that can result to the baby from the mother's exposure to rubella early in the pregnancy is well known)? Was it something that happened to the baby during birth or in the first few days of life? Finally, was the eye condition inherited by the child from his or her ancestors? Could it be hereditary even without a family history of the condition? Genetic counseling will help to provide information to parents about familial eye conditions, the odds for the condition occurring again in any future children, whether brothers and sisters may transmit it to their children, and whether the visually handicapped child can pass it on to his or her descendants. The family doctor should refer the parents to a medical specialist in genetic counseling. The timing of the referral should be delayed until the parents are ready for such a discussion or until they plan to have other children.

If the cause of a child's eye condition is readily apparent, the parents' questions about why it happened can be answered by their eye specialist or family doctor. For example, if a mother is exposed to rubella early in her pregnancy and her baby is born with cataracts, or if a sick, premature baby who has been in an incubator for a long time develops impaired vision, it will be obvious that the eye was damaged by something specific and genetic counseling will not be called for. The parents run little or no risk of producing another affected child, and the child runs little risk of passing on the condition to his or her children in the future.

On the other hand, if the eye condition is diagnosed as genetic, or inherited, then parents should find genetic counseling both informative and reassuring. It helps to answer many of those so-far-unanswered questions about how and what we can inherit from our ancestors. Genetic information was not readily available in the past, and most families were totally unaware of the risk factor involved. Whether one of their children might inherit Aunt Mabel's poor sight or Grandfather Smith's blindness was simply not known. Genetic counseling is best done by a specialist who has been trained in this field and who has made a study of the inheritance patterns of various diseases and defects. The geneticist will want to know, first of all, as much as possible about the parents' family trees on both sides of the family. Information about the sight of relatives is very important. The information is sometimes difficult to track down, especially when families have moved from one country or region to another, but older relatives frequently will provide useful information. In a few eye conditions, particularly when there is some doubt about the precise diagnosis, further tests need to be done. If the eye disorder is obviously an inherited one, the geneticist will explain the inheritance pattern, the chances of it recurring if the parents have more children, the possibility of their unaffected children transmitting it to their children, and how they should counsel the visually handicapped child when he or she is old enough to think about having children. Most parents find that genetic counseling takes some of the mystery out of the situation, and they state that it is easier to live with facts, no matter how unpleasant, than to hang in suspense, not knowing.

When it has been determined that the eye disorder is not due to genetic or inherited causes, those parents who have previously had a sighted child find it easy to decide about having another baby because they already have proved to themselves that they can have a child without disabilities. Young parents whose first infant is visually impaired often are reluctant to try again, and yet they are the ones who have the most to gain. There is nothing quite like having a baby with regular vision after having a visually impaired one to make them feel good about themselves, and they will be amazed at how easy and rewarding it is to raise a sighted child, who just seems to learn to do things independently. This is quite a contrast to the hard work they have invested in teaching the visually impaired child to function independently. An additional child dilutes all that parental concern and anxiety formerly centered on the only son or daughter, who is also disabled. It also provides them with someone to play with, to fight with, and to teach all sorts of interesting things. The visually impaired child who is an only child is usually lonely, spending far too much time with adults. If parents for good reasons choose not to have more babies, they might consider adopting or providing foster care or day care for one or two children of an age to be companionable to their own child.

LOSS OF SIGHT

The parents of a child who has had normal sight but lost it through accident or illness must cope with a different set of circumstances. It is only natural for them to grieve for a beloved child's loss of sight and for all those pleasures he or she may miss in the future and to mourn for the loss of the parental hopes and aspirations vested in the child. On the positive side is the fact that they have had time to learn to know and love the child as a "normal" child and a functioning member of the family before the loss of sight, and their reaction to the blindness does not obscure the child, as can sometimes happen when a baby is born blind. Everything the child has learned while sighted can be a base on which to build for the future. If the child is encouraged to do all those things he or she could do while sighted, he or she should continue to make steady progress. It is hard at first for a parent not to want to do everything for a child who has just lost all or most of his or her sight for fear of harm or failure. Unfortunately, that only teaches the child that he or she is helpless and does not encourage him or her to learn to function competently again.

There are a few children, born with normal vision, who through accidents, brain tumors, or other severe illnesses lose their sight after infancy. Parents and professionals are continually amazed at how calmly small children react to the loss of sight and how quickly they are able to resume their normal daily activities. The adjustment is much more painful for their parents.

Children are remarkably tough and have an inner drive to grow and learn if only their parents will encourage them to do so. Very young children adapt quickly to impaired vision and do not seem to be preoccupied with how their lack of sight will affect them in the future. They are much more concerned about reestablishing themselves in the here and now. The older the child is the more aware he or she will be of the loss of sight and its implications. For example, the school-age child will realize immediately that he or she cannot see to read and will require reassurance that some plan can be worked out for continuing with schooling.

The child who had sight and lost it after turning a year old is certainly aware that things are different. The older the child is the more aware he or she will be of the effect of the loss on his or her functioning and the implications for the future. If the parents can send good, positive messages that they still love the child, that they expect him or her to continue to grow and learn even if eyesight has become a problem, it will help the child get through a rough time more easily. Questions should be answered truthfully in easily understandable terms. For example, a parent can say, "When you had that bad pain in your head and had to go to the hospital, the doctor tried very hard to make you all better. He did make the pain go away, but he just couldn't fix your eyes so they would work properly. You are going to learn how to do things without looking with your eyes and we will help you learn how. Pretty soon you will be able to walk all around the house and yard and ride your trike just like you did before. I bet you already know what this toy is. Of course, it is your old teddy bear." It is hard for parents who are feeling sad about what has happened to their child to sound confident and reassuring when talking to the child, but if they send the message by words, tone, and behavior that the child is poor and helpless and cannot do anything on his or her own, then that is exactly how the child will act. Parents

Figure 1.1. "My best friend is so soft." (5 years)

should try to do their grieving when the child is not there and present to him or her a happy demeanor and voice.

The older the child is when the loss of sight occurs, the greater the emotional and physical impact will be, the longer he or she will take to adjust to living with impaired vision, and the more support he or she will need from the family. The helpful parent will admit that it is a hard job to learn to do things without normal sight but will express faith that the child will manage to do it very well.

GRADUAL LOSS OF SIGHT

With some eye conditions children may lose their sight over a period of time. Sometimes the loss in one eye occurs more rapidly than in the other. In such situations the child and the family may be unaware of the visual loss until the child happens to close one eye to look at something and finds the sight almost gone in the other. Naturally this can be a great shock for everyone, but it also illustrates how well the child has adapted to having just one useful eye without even being aware of it.

In other instances a child may experience a narrowing of the field of vision, that is, he or she sees as though looking through a narrow pipe and has no side vision. The children usually are unaware of the loss and the families cannot understand why the children are getting so clumsy and constantly running into the sides of doorways and knocking things over. One teenage boy with this type of vision was called to the principal's office and accused of trying to pick fights in the halls by shouldering other boys. Since he was a rather quiet boy no one could explain his behavior until he went to get his glasses changed. The ophthalmologist found the boy had only a small spot of central vision left. The boy actually was relieved to learn why he was bumping into the kids and doors and falling into ditches on his paper route, as he also had lost his night vision. He found the diagnosis reassuring, while his parents found it hard to accept.

Chapter 2

Eyes and What Can Go Wrong

◆ ◆ ◆ ◆ ◆ ◆

For those parents who vaguely remember from their school days how an eye functions, a simple diagram will refresh their memories (see Figure 2.1). For those who have completely forgotten or who have never learned about the mechanics of seeing, the public library or local health department probably can provide a book or pamphlet giving basic information about the normal eye.

Figure 2.1 is a greatly simplified version of how the eye functions and will serve as a base for discussing the different eye conditions that can result in impaired vision. Light rays pass through the transparent front of the eye (the cornea); then through the hole (pupil) in the iris (the blue or brown part); then through the lens, which is suspended behind the pupil. The lens focuses the rays on the retina (the lining at the back of the eye). The retina is composed of thousands of photo-electric cells, and messages are carried from these cells by the optic nerve (like a big cable made up of many small nerve fibers) to the visual center of the brain, where the message is decoded to tell us what the eye sees. If there is structural damage to any part of the eye, the visual efficiency of the eye can be affected; how much will depend on the extent of the damage and the function of that specific part of the eye.

We will try to describe what happens to the eye and what parts are affected by the different eye conditions that can cause blindness or partial sight in children. We also will explain in lay terms some of the more commonly used medical terms.

VISUAL ACUITY

In determining visual acuity, the ophthalmologist measures how much an eye sees under controlled circumstances, using a set distance of 20 ft for distance vision and 16 in. for near vision. She or he will measure without glasses and with glasses (if they improve the vision). Distance vision is usually determined by what can be seen on the Snellen chart (the long charts with letters on them). Normal vision is stated as 20/20, which means that a person can see at 20 ft what is supposed to be seen at 20 ft with that eye. If vision is stated as 20/40 it means that person can only see at 20 ft what a normal eye can see at 40 ft. If vision is stated as 20/200 it means that person can only see at 20 ft what a normal eye can see at 200 ft. Below the measure of 20/400 the vision is usually measured by counting fingers. For example, *C.F.* @ 5′ on an eye report means the person can count fingers at 5 ft, etc. *L.P.* on an eye report means light perception; in other words, the person is aware of light. What a person can perceive when passing a hand between closed eyes and a bright light approximates how much a person with light perception can see.

PREFERENTIAL LOOKING TEST

How far a young child can see should influence the decisions on management and treatment. Until a few years ago it was difficult to estimate accurately the visual acuity of preverbal or multidisabled children, which caused the parents a good deal of anxiety. The development of the *Preferential Looking Acuity Test*[1] was most welcome.

---

[1]Teller, D. Y., McDonald, M. A., Preston, K., Sebris, S. L., & Dobson, V. (1986). Assessment of visual acuity in infants and children: The acuity card procedure. *Developmental Medicine and Child Neurology, 28,* 779–789.

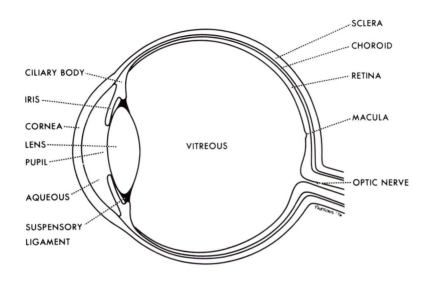

Figure 2.1. Diagram of human eye.

This test is administered in a few minutes by simultaneously presenting two targets on cards to the child. One target has a series of black and white vertical stripes, and the other has a blank gray area. Since the child's eyes immediately focus on the stripes, it is possible to determine when the child can or cannot see them. There are a number of cards, each with progressively smaller stripes. When the child no longer focuses on the stripes, the severity of the visual loss is determined. Some practitioners offer a reward after a correct response to encourage the child's participation in the test. The results are not identical to those from the Snellen charts, but the *Preferential Looking Test* is a great help in assessing the vision of the very young.

VISUAL FUNCTIONING OR VISUAL EFFICIENCY

The term *visual function* means what a child does with the vision he or she has. Two children both could be described as having 20/200 visual acuity, but they might function very differently depending on

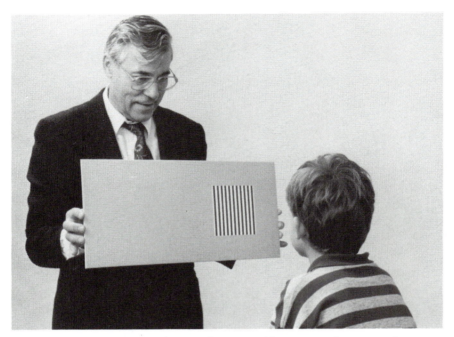

Figure 2.2. Preferential looking cards can quickly measure the vision of preverbal and disabled children who cannot read. This is a very useful test.

Figure 2.3. Low visual acuity—mother's face (courtesy Dr. B. Huntsman).

Figure 2.4. Low visual acuity—traffic scene (courtesy
Dr. B. Huntsman).

Figure 2.5. Restricted field, central vision—traffic scene (courtesy
Dr. B. Huntsman).

Figure 2.6. Restricted field, central vision—newspaper (courtesy
Dr. B. Huntsman).

Figure 2.7. Peripheral vision—traffic scene (courtesy
Dr. B. Huntsman).

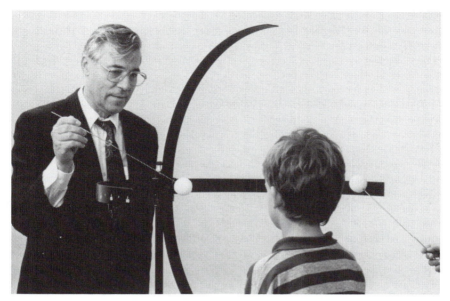

Figure 2.8. Peripheral visual field testing is important to obtain in most visually impaired children. It can be done quite accurately even with disabled individuals. The examiner is shaking a small white ball in the center as the child intently looks at it. Then a second shaking ball is introduced gradually from the side (above and below). When the child first notices the second ball, the measurements are noted on the bars.

the kind of residual vision they have. Are they, for example, very near-sighted and able to see everything up close but not much in the distance, or is the field of vision impaired or limited? How much practice and opportunity has the child had to use his or her remaining sight? While visual acuity tends to remain the same, visual efficiency can improve as the child gets older and more adept at using what vision remains.

LEGAL BLINDNESS

Any person whose vision in the better eye cannot be corrected with glasses to more than 20/200 or whose field of vision is restricted to an angle of 20° or less is considered legally blind in most countries. This category does not mean total blindness, as many people think. Children who are classified as legally blind may have useful vision.

Field testing in young children is difficult to do and in fact is rarely done. Vision is a very complex sense, and how far a child can see does not describe the residual vision. Thus the term *legal blindness* by itself has relatively little practical significance.

COMMON EYE CONDITIONS

The majority of children with visual impairments are born with their eye disorders (congenital disorders), while only one quarter acquire their visual loss later in life. Some of the more common eye disorders are described in Appendix A at the back of the book. It is suggested that parents use Appendix A as a reference and simply read the part that discusses the eye condition of their child.

THE EFFICIENT USE OF PARTIAL SIGHT

Residual Vision—How Much, What Kind

Most children who are visually impaired have some residual (remaining) vision, which may range from an awareness of bright light to the ability to see everything but fine print. The type and amount of residual vision is determined by the kind of structural damage present in the eyes. The child's doctor should explain in lay terms what and where the damage is and whether there is any vision remaining. Then the parents and child will know just what they have to work with. The parents will want to know if the child has any remaining central vision (i.e., the ability to see fine detail). This visual function is located in a small (2%) central portion of the retina (the seeing part of the back of the eye). The balance of the retina provides what is called peripheral vision and objects seen by it are only vaguely defined. In a normal eye peripheral vision is used to locate an object and determine if it is moving, whereas the central vision's function is to determine what that object is.

While the natural reflex is to try to look directly at an object with one's central vision, that is, to fix on it, a child with damaged or no central vision has to learn to look, or fixate, off center and to use peripheral vision. This off-center fixing is hard to do and takes a good deal of practice but must be mastered if the child is to make maximum use of residual vision. Many children with impaired vision also have to cope with the constant moving of their eyes (nystagmus), which makes it more difficult to fixate on an object.

It is almost impossible to assess just how much a visually impaired baby can see and even more difficult to forecast what he or she will be able to see in the future, so the parents will not get any actual measurements from their doctor. Occasionally parents are mistakenly told their child has no useful sight, but then they notice that the baby turns toward a bright light, the sun, or a light moving object. Obviously there is some residual sight in these cases, and the parents will want to teach the child to use it consciously to advantage. Recent research has shown that even children with severely impaired vision learn to use that tiny bit remarkably well. The most effective use results from early visual training and lots of practice.

Visual Training

Babies with normal eyes have limited vision at birth, but under ordinary circumstances their visual systems mature and develop with constant use over the first few years of life. If for some reason there is no opportunity to use an eye, as in lazy eye, the sight in that eye does not develop normally but remains relatively poor. When parents have been told their child has no useful vision or very little vision, they tend to be unsure about what to do and often treat the child as if he or she cannot see anything.

The vision of newborns is often less than 20/600. As they grow, their eyes, the visual pathways, and the visual centers rapidly develop, and within a few years their sight becomes like that of normal adults. The development of vision is almost entirely dependent on constant visual experience. Without visual stimulation the parts of the brain that deal with sight do not develop. They remain immature and actually become structurally different. Areas of the brain that have nothing to do with vision also depend on sensory stimulation to reach normal function. The growth of the brain is stimulus dependent.

Visual learning for sighted children is largely spontaneous, but children with eye defects must be encouraged to use their remaining vision. Especially during their early life their visual environment should be rich and stimulating. It is important for parents and caregivers to know how important visual stimulation is and that they can actually reduce their child's disability and enhance his or her visual functioning.

Eye Contact

It is not easy to establish eye contact with babies who are visually impaired. Their parents say, "The baby looks past me, not at me." Such babies miss out on the tremendous amount of communication that can occur between a sighted baby and his or her mother and father. Parents talk toward a baby's eyes and watch for a response in the child's eyes. Holding your child a few inches from your face and moving him or her around so the child can see your teeth or your bright lipstick may enable him or her to catch a glimpse of your face or find your eyes and perhaps with practice learn to fixate for longer periods.

Suggestions from Other Parents

Opportunities to practice using partial sight do not happen spontaneously as a rule, but some do happen accidentally, as when the child reaches for a sunbeam or a bright piece of aluminum foil. A mirror fastened low on the side of the crib lets the baby see his or her face up close. A brightly colored mobile, with figures suspended horizontally, may attract the baby's attention if it is hung low over the crib. If the baby can see a flashlight beam slowly moving from the peripheral part of the eyes, he or she can learn to look for it and track it as it moves. Similarly, the baby can learn to reach and grab for the flashlight and other bright objects held close to his or her face. Twinkling Christmas lights, revolving colored lights, objects covered with foil or red and yellow fluorescent tape, shiny pot lids, spoons, and finger puppets over pen lights have all been useful in helping visually impaired children learn to track and look. Parents who are eager to help their child learn to use residual sight will find more and more bright objects to attract him or her. The whole exercise should be fun, with much praise and admiration and with no pressure and no dreary routine.

As the baby gets older, bright, clearly defined pictures may be visible. Test out where he or she can see them best. It may be as close as three or four inches. Help the child learn to recognize and name familiar objects. Kenny, a 2-year-old, was so excited to read books that he used to show everyone the picture of a big red tractor and say "baby." He was proud that he could find the page, even though he could only see the red color. Help the toddler to recognize and name pictures of familiar objects. It is the only way some children with limited vision will ever be able to see a whole house, a car, or an elephant. They can never get close enough to the real object to see it all at once.

The child may need extra opportunities and help in developing and practicing eye–hand coordination skills through the use of blocks for stacking, large pegboards, stacking rings, etc. While many visually impaired children learn to perform these skills by touch alone, some children may need extra encouragement to use both partial sight and touch. Good lighting, at the proper distance from the object, and bright colors may help the child do better.

The use of even minimal vision can enhance the learning of many basic concepts, such as relative size. It is easier and quicker to tell by looking than by feeling which block is smaller, which is larger, which is the same as another. Children with minimal vision should be encouraged to use their sight to match colors, sizes, and shapes and to decide which one has a missing part.

Naturally the child with a fair amount of sight will tend to use it quite spontaneously and will learn to work at seeing by finding the best position to hold his or her head and the object being viewed, but the child with minimal vision does not know what to do or how to do it. If there are no additional disabilities, he or she will learn to function reasonably well without using sight. If, however, the child learns to use sight efficiently, all kinds of new avenues of learning are opened, as they were for Rodney, who was considered to be totally blind as an infant. Around age 4 he was observed reaching for a dark light switch on a white wall in the clinic, and further testing showed that he had some residual vision, which he did not know how to use. His parents were advised to encourage him to use his sight, but since they had considered him blind for 4 years, they could not change their handling. He had started braille at school, but an itinerant teacher spent a great deal of time with him, and much to everyone's amazement, he was using print books by the seventh grade.

HOSPITALIZATION

Unfortunately it is often necessary for visually impaired babies or children to be hospitalized for investigation or for treatment, despite the fact that the experience can produce adverse effects. In a strange place an infant who is visually impaired tends to turn off the outside world because he or she is unable to receive any visual clues that either reassure that everything is all right or warn of impending pain or discomfort. In an unfamiliar place full of meaningless sounds, smells, and sensations, the child tends to withdraw.

A hospital stay can be made less traumatic if the child receives as much attention from the parents as possible under the new, more liberal visiting hours and care-by-parent arrangements available in many children's hospitals. A visually impaired infant should receive as much physical contact as can be managed. He or she should be held, stroked, rocked, and talked to even if he or she does not understand the words. It is only by touch and by the sound of voices that the infant can distinguish people from things. If the infant is held while being fed, he or she learns that food comes from people and not from a "good fairy." An infant should always be addressed by name before being touched or picked up so that he or she will not be startled by suddenly being grabbed.

The infant should be shown where to find familiar toys—whether they are tied to the left side rail or in the top right corner of the crib—and how to reach for and find them. The toys should always be kept in the same place so they can be found. If the child drops a toy or a cookie, he or she does not know that it is right in front of him or her. As far as the child is concerned it is gone and someone must help to retrieve it. Worries about spoiling the child are out of place; the hospitalized child needs all possible attention.

Some professionals suggest that a consistent signal, such as a gentle flick on the heel, be given before any unpleasant or painful procedure is administered. If the child can be forewarned, he or she will not become unnecessarily apprehensive when someone approaches.

The negative effects of hospitalization on a visually impaired preschooler can be reduced by a previous visit to the hospital to become acquainted with his or her bed and nurses. By talking calmly and playacting about what will happen at the hospital, parents can give the child a chance to discuss worries and misconceptions. The child of 4 or 5 may think that hospitals are places where people go to die, as Uncle Pete and Grandma did, and fear that he or she will die there too. When the child enters a hospital, family members should describe the room and show how to find the bed, the door, and the toilet and explain the meaning of all the weird noises. Hospitals are very noisy places.

The child who cannot see what is happening may be frightened by the crying of other children. To the child who is blind it may seem that these children are being hurt in ways that may happen to him or her too.

Staff should always call the child's name and describe what they are going to do before washing his or her face, taking temperature, or giving shots, so that the child will be prepared. Even if the child does not understand, a calm, matter-of-fact tone can be reassuring.

If it is absolutely essential to restrain a visually impaired child by a harness or crib bars, the reason for restraint should be explained frequently to the child so he or she will not feel like a trapped animal. The child should be taken from the crib and walked around the room and in the corridor as often as possible, thus allowing an opportunity to examine the strange objects, such as wheelchairs and stretchers, found there.

Lots of physical contact and reassuring conversation from parents and hospital staff can greatly reduce the negative effects of hospitalization on a child and can facilitate adjustment when he or she returns home.

Chapter 3

The Infant

The way parents think of their child—as a blind baby or as a baby who happens to be blind—makes a difference. If the infant is a "blind baby" then the blindness tends to obscure the baby and the parents react to the blindness. If the infant is a "baby who is blind" then the parents are able to think of him or her as a baby first and can consider how to meet those needs the baby shares with all other babies. Only after those needs are taken care of should the parents consider any special needs related to the fact that the child does not see normally.

BASIC NEEDS OF CHILDREN

There are certain basic needs common to all children, and the visually handicapped child is no exception. Every child not only needs but should have the right to be warm, clean, and well fed and to receive any required medical care. The child not only needs to be loved but to know that he or she is loved. Love is like a fertilizer that makes children grow and thrive. The child needs to be secure, to feel safe with familiar people in a familiar place in a familiar routine. He or she needs the opportunity to grow and a chance to learn from successes and failures. Finally, every child needs to be treated with courtesy and respect so that he or she will consider himself or herself a worthwhile person. These statements are very general and few parents of blind children would disagree with them. They would be more apt to say: "That's fine for all children, but how do I know what to do and when to do it with this special baby?" We will try to provide the answers to some of these questions about special needs and offer suggestions for meeting them. It is hoped parents will remember that their baby is like other babies and will try not to make him or her too "special."

EMOTIONAL DEVELOPMENT

Babies need to know they are well loved if they are to grow and flourish and feel good about themselves. Early communication with sighted babies is primarily visual—eye to eye. When there is no visual communication, parents may feel rebuffed and think that the baby does not like being played with and will tend to leave him or her alone.

Mrs. Booth, a quiet, reserved woman, was as efficient in caring for her 5-month-old blind son as she was in everything she did. She kept him beautifully dressed and fed him a well-balanced diet. She bathed and changed him quickly and silently, with a minimum of fuss, and tucked him back into his crib upstairs where he would not be disturbed. We asked her if she loved Michael and she replied indignantly, "Of course I do. You know that." When we said that yes, we did know, but we didn't think Michael knew, she looked startled and began to wonder how she could tell him. Some parents just naturally know how to show their love for their baby; others have to learn.

How can parents convey their love to their visually impaired offspring? It really isn't too hard—lots of holding, cuddling, patting, stroking, rocking, and just plain enjoying. Parents can talk to the baby, tell the child how wonderful he or she is or discuss what is being cooked for dinner, what the weather is like, what a hard day it was at the office—anything at all, just talk. The child's name should be used a lot so that he or she learns it. The parents should hold the child upright and talk against a cheek so he or she can feel the puffs of breath. They should blow on the child's neck and stomach and bounce him or her a little. In short, they should try all the ways parents have played with babies for generations. Soon the baby will recognize them by the way they hold him or her, by their smell, by the sound of their voices and footsteps. The baby will welcome them with the same joyous wiggles that babies who can see use to greet their parents. Parents should not worry about spoiling the baby with too much loving.

Whenever the baby is awake the parents should carry it from room to room as they go about the daily household routine and talk to and touch the child with little pats, hugs, and kisses so he or she knows they are there. At this early age, touching is a most important form of communication. The child has not yet learned that hearing the parent's voice means he or she is there. That comes later, near the end of the first year. The baby can lie on a blanket on the floor while a

Figure 3.1. "Love."

parent cooks, sit propped up in the clothes basket while the laundry is done, and sit on the parent's lap while he or she is watching TV. Parents should pretend they are radio commentators and do a play-by-play broadcast of what they are doing. Talking not only lets the child know they are paying attention to him or her but also teaches what many of the words such as *bottle, drink, cookie, bath,* etc., mean as they are repeated and associated with real experiences.

If a child has too little vision to see a person approaching, it is only good manners on the adult's part to avoid startling the child by speaking before suddenly picking him or her up. The child will soon know what *up* means. The baby should have an opportunity to know and trust people other than the parents. Grandparents, friends, and neighbors all sound and feel strange at first, but the baby can learn to feel safe and enjoy their attention.

Early communication with normal infants is largely visual. A baby learns to fix his or her gaze on the parent's face; the parent looks fondly at the baby, who soon learns to respond to smiles with smiles. A baby's smile is a very heartwarming experience. Parents will laugh and talk and play with a baby and are rewarded by a smile. The baby learns to recognize their faces and reacts when they approach. This is the beginning of communication between the parents and the baby. They both receive and send messages of love.

If a baby has little or no sight, he or she does not look at the parent's face. When there is no eye contact, the parents may feel rebuffed or rejected and deprived of one of the joys of parenting. If the parents think the child is indifferent, their ability to express their love may be impaired. The parents may handle and play with the child less because it is not rewarding for them, with the result that communication between parent and baby never gets started.

If the parents know that lack of eye contact does not mean the baby is unaware of them, they will be alert for signs that the child is responding to talking and touching by little squirms and wiggles or by holding still when they are talking to him or her. If they look for these messages, they will know the baby is reacting and will be encouraged to continue to talk and play with the baby, and, in good time, the baby will start to respond by making sounds. The baby will learn to recognize the family's voices from across the room and react to them.

Babies who are left alone tend to become tuned out and to ignore people and sounds around them. Often after a period in the hospital, a child will seem unhappy about being held and will resist cuddling. If the child is permitted to remain in this isolation, development can be affected or delayed and the child will get stuck at that level. It is vitally important for the parents gently but firmly to help the baby learn to like cuddling, rocking, and singing. Even though he or she resists strongly at first, the child gradually will discover that being with people is more pleasant than being alone.

SMILING

Parents sometimes wonder if their visually impaired child will learn to smile at them. It may take him or her a few weeks longer than it did sighted siblings. It is harder for this baby to recognize parents and the rest of the family when he or she cannot see them. With lots of loving attention, the baby should be smiling sometime between 2 and 3 months of age. The baby will not return a silent smile when unaware that the parents are smiling but will learn to smile with pleasure when he or she learns to know the parents' voices and when they play with him or her.

BODY MOVEMENT AND CONTROL

Vision plays a vital role in learning body movement and control by small infants, especially in the first few months—a much more important role than most parents realize. When a sighted baby accidentally lifts his or her head, he or she discovers all sorts of interesting moving and brightly colored objects. The sighted baby finds these much more entertaining than the ceiling or the sheet, so he or she quickly learns what we call head control. If placed on the stomach the sighted baby will lift his or her head and gaze around the room. Even lying on his or her back the sighted baby tries to lift his or her head. By 5 or 6 months, a baby wants to sit up to look around and, later, will pull himself or herself up to see even more. By 9 or 10 months, the sighted baby will be attempting to crawl across the room to look more closely at those strange objects stored in the stereo cabinet and will notice and pick up toys in the playpen and crumbs from the carpet with equal skill. All these activities are triggered by sight.

The baby who has little or no sight is not aware that all those interesting things are out there waiting to be discovered and so has no motivation to move his or her body purposely. The visually impaired baby does not learn spontaneously to hold up his or her head, to sit, to reach and grasp, and to crawl and walk but can learn these motor skills and learn them in the same sequence and at roughly the same age as a sighted child if the parents know how to teach him or her. They must know how to make it pleasurable for the baby to practice the activity until it is learned.

A visually handicapped baby left lying on his or her back in the crib will not learn much except to like being undisturbed in a warm nest. These babies tend to be so good and undemanding that it is easy for busy parents to leave them there as long as they seem happy. A few months go by and then, suddenly, everyone is concerned because little Manuel is not progressing like the sighted child next door. It is not unusual to find blind babies of 7 or 8 months who are unable to hold up their heads, to sit, or to hold a toy, simply because their parents did not know they had to be taught. Too often, babies with defective vision and delayed motor development are labeled as re-tarded and incapable of learning when they are potentially normal but lack the opportunity to learn.

When the baby is lying in a crib, the parents should try to change the position frequently so that he or she will not get used to lying on the front or the back or a particular side. Children who are used to lying only on their backs are reluctant to go front side down when it comes time to learn to crawl. Those who have slept only on their stomachs think they are expected to go to sleep when placed that way on the floor at crawling time.

Many parents are experimenting with various substitutes for the many kinds of mobiles to hang over babies' cribs. If a baby has any residual vision, a low-hanging, brightly colored mobile will be in-triguing as it moves in the air currents. If a baby has no sight, small, light objects that make a sound when accidentally touched can be hung within reach across the top of the crib. Bells, rattles, beads, or wind chimes can provide a start; they later can be augmented by other gadgets that are appealing to touch or that do something when pulled. One totally blind little boy who also had severe cerebral palsy learned to twirl with his toes a large musical ball that was hung above his crib, and his family was sometimes awakened in the night by the tinkling sounds as he played happily with it.

Parents can make their own mobiles, which can be changed periodically to provide a little variety. Hang the mobile low enough so the baby can reach it. A rotating mobile with four objects is the easiest to make. Balloons with small bells inside, small bunches of metal keys, measuring spoons, in fact anything that makes a noise can be used.

For a change a young baby can lie on the couch with his or her feet against the arm. Place a newspaper or crackly cellophane against the arms so that it makes a noise when the child kicks it.

Small bells on socks make kicking the feet pleasurable. It will be some time before the baby connects the sound with what he or she is doing. Sighted children discover their feet by seeing them moving. We have to help babies with visual impairments become aware that they have feet, that they can be moved at will, and later that they are for standing. Remember that if a baby's vision is too limited to observe people walking around, he or she will not automatically know what feet are for.

Head Control

Parents can be most ingenious in finding ways to make holding up the head a pleasurable experience for the baby. Stroking a baby under the chin while the baby is being held vertically or lying on the stomach feels nice, and the baby reacts like a kitten. Stroking the back while the baby is lying facedown on a firm surface also makes lying in that position pleasurable, and the baby soon will be lifting his or her head and turning it from side to side. We all like to be caressed and stroked—it not only feels good, it also tells us that someone likes us. Snuggling up cheek to cheek with the parents while they talk and hearing and feeling the vibrations of their voices is very nice for everybody and babies soon experiment with moving the head away and back again. Holding the baby upright close to the parent's face and having a long, animated conversation about the weather and how smart and beautiful the infant is can be much more entertaining than lying in the crib, and it also can encourage head control and togetherness. If a parent places the baby on his or her lap with the infant facedown, the baby can practice holding his or her head up while being stroked and talked to. If the baby is put facedown on the parent's chest while the parent is lying down, the baby will raise his or her head when talked to.

Mr. Anderson, an avid hockey fan, regularly discussed the relative merits of the Montreal Canadiens and the Chicago Blackhawks with his blind infant son while he held and played with Robbie. Robbie not only learned to hold his head up but also developed such a keen interest in hockey that by age 5 he knew the names of the players on all the National Hockey League teams and which teams were ahead.

It is not too early to start the baby learning head control at 4 weeks of age. Sometimes parents feel their blind baby is too fragile to hold up his or her own head, and they continue to provide support for it when they pick the child up until 10 or 12 months. The parents seem to feel that if they do not hold up the child's head it will snap off at the neck and roll on the floor. Babies are actually quite tough—just think of all the babies with small, wobbly heads who are carried around quite safely in backpacks. Backpacks or frontpacks present a

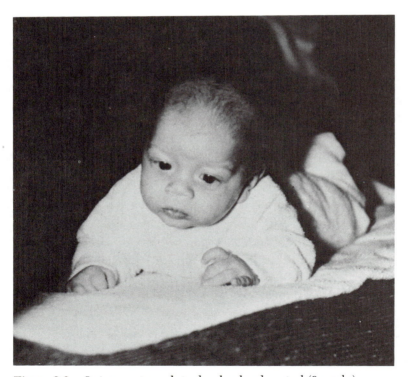

Figure 3.2. Lying on stomach to develop head control (6 weeks).

good way for parents to keep the baby with them in order to acquaint the infant with the parents' feel, smells, and sounds.

When changing the baby, parents can take the opportunity to do exercises and play with her or him a little. They should hold the baby's hands and slowly pull him or her up to a sitting position, pausing when the head is about 6 in. above the table so the baby can become organized, and then pulling the baby all the way to a sitting position. They should say "up" each time they raise the baby, and "down" as they ease him or her down. Very soon they will notice stiffening of the arms and slight bending as they pull. Before long the child will stiffen at the hips and they will be able to pull him or her to standing for a few seconds. The baby then will have to learn to sit down and then lie down. This routine should be fun for everyone and not looked upon as a duty.

From the age of 3 months, the baby should spend two or three short periods each day lying on a blanket on the floor, most of the time on the stomach with short rests on the back. The baby should be encouraged to lift his or her head and to raise himself or herself onto the elbows. This is much easier on a firm floor than in the crib. The family should talk to the baby and play and make being on the floor enjoyable. A collection of small, light, interesting toys can be placed within reach so that the baby can encounter them as he or she moves around.

Turning Over

Visually handicapped babies frequently seem to be late in learning to turn over. These are usually children who have been permitted to lie only on their backs and are quite content to stay in that position. Just as a turtle is helpless when turned on its back, so a baby is more mobile when placed on his or her stomach rather than on the back. The baby learns to wiggle and squirm and move around by thrusting with his or her feet. When the baby gets too tired of lying on the stomach he or she will try to turn over onto the back, and by 6 or 7 months, the baby should manage this but may need a little help in finding out what to do to get his or her arms out of the way. Once that problem is solved, the baby will turn from back to front at will. It will take about another month before the baby can go from front to back.

Sitting

Visually handicapped children are not a bit enthusiastic about sitting up. They don't really understand why the parents want them to try to balance a heavy head and shoulders on a narrow little bottom when it is much more comfortable to lie flat on the floor. Their sighted brothers or sisters struggled to learn to sit up at around 6 months of age because they discovered they could see all kinds of exciting things when they sat, so it was well worth the effort. We have to find ways to help children with visual impairments learn to enjoy sitting even though they cannot see any more by doing so.

Vertical balance is something we learn by noticing that when we lean to one side the floors, walls, and people all seem to tilt. When we receive this information visually, we react by straightening up, or else we get a bump on the head. Blind babies do not get any visual feedback about which way is up. They have to learn by the feel of gravity, and that is difficult. Before a baby can sit up unsupported he or she has to learn how to balance by the feel of his or her muscles and without visual clues. When the baby is very young (6 to 8 weeks), a parent can sit him or her propped on the parent's lap, with the baby's back to the parent. In this way the baby gets used to being in a sitting position. Once the baby has head control he or she can be propped up in the corner of the couch while the parent reads the paper or takes half an hour to watch TV. The parents should let the baby know they are there by touching and talking. A 4-month-old baby usually will enjoy sitting on a lap facing the parent and maintaining balance while the parent holds him or her by the wrists and playfully bounces the baby. As the baby grows more skilled at balancing, progress will go from gentle bouncing to vigorous rides on the parent's foot.

By 6 months, the baby can sit propped up for a short time in the corner of a carton on the floor, toys can be put in the carton or the baby can be dragged around in a make-believe car by an older sibling.

At 7 or 8 months, a good time to practice sitting is at mealtime. A blind baby will not sit patiently in a high chair waiting for food. For the first few weeks, the baby should be tied securely to the back of the chair with a diaper or towel across the chest and under the arms. Otherwise, he or she may fall facedown into the food! As soon as the baby finishes he or she should be taken out of the chair. By the time the baby is anywhere from 8 to 11 months old, he or she should be able to sit unsupported on the floor and will learn to sit up and get

Figure 3.3. Learning to sit (8 months).

down unaided. A visually impaired baby will not sit happily alone for long unless she or he is busy playing with toys or eating a cookie.

The plastic infant seat, or baby recliner, in which the child is propped in a semisitting position, is very popular with young parents. As soon as the sighted child has the strength, he or she will struggle to lift the head and lean forward to see more. The baby with little or no sight will have no motivation to do this and will lie passively with his or her head fully supported, effectively trapped in a position from which it is difficult to learn how to hold up the head or to develop the neck and back muscles. With babies who have visual impairments, infant seats should be used only for short periods so motor development will not be unnecessarily delayed.

On phoning Mrs. McLaughlin, a newly referred mother, the worker could hear Tiger (a very small premature baby, just home after 8 months in the hospital intensive care nursery). When asked about it, Mrs. McLaughlin said, "Yes, I have him propped in his infant seat on the kitchen counter while I do the dishes. We are just getting acquainted." Pleased that things were going so well, the worker visited a few days later and several times subsequently and found Tiger in the infant seat every time she visited, even though she emphasized the need for him to be encouraged to lie on his stomach on a firm surface so he could learn to hold his head up, to wiggle, and to roll over. Tiger felt secure in his familiar infant seat and objected to being anywhere else. Anxious to keep him happy, his mother did not persist in making any changes, and 6 months later, although tests showed no physical reason, Tiger still could not hold his head up or sit unsupported. He was able to hold and eat biscuits and seemed alert and responsive in other ways.

Infant seats are fine for having the baby join the family at dinner, but opportunities to sit on rocking horses, in the corner of a carton, in high chairs, in doorway swings, and on the floor also must be provided, with appropriate accompanying admiration and enjoyment. Toys tied to the high chair by strings can be thrown off and hauled back up again.

Using the Hands

Parents of a sighted baby can remember that, at around 4 months of age, the baby suddenly discovered his or her hands. For a while they were fascinating. Then, one day, the baby accidentally discovered clapping two hands together. This opened up a whole new experience, and the baby had lots of fun playing with both hands together, opening, closing, or grasping the hands and waving the arms. Some babies who are blind find their hands on their own, but a little encouragement may hasten the discovery. Parents can play pat-a-cake with the baby on their laps and sing or talk to him or her. In the bath the baby can learn about hands by splashing, patting the stomach, or clasping hands. While feeding, the baby's hands can be placed on the bottle.

Little rattles shaped like dumbbells are easy to hold, as are the plastic disks strung on a chain. Too big or too heavy a rattle can hurt when banged on the face and may discourage grasping. Rattles often have been overrated as infant toys, as the visually impaired infant cannot see the bright color or make the connection between the movement and the sound of the rattle. Far more interesting are things that feel interesting or smell or taste good, such as metal chains or beads, a leather key case, a rubber sink stopper, or a good chicken drumstick bone. A child who is blind will be much more likely to hold and gnaw on one of these non-toys than some brightly colored plastic toy that has no taste, no smell, and no texture to invite further investigation.

Parents should keep a variety of toys near the baby so that they can be found as he or she moves arms and hands. They should show the baby how to hunt for a dropped toy by putting their hands over his or hers and moving the hands back and forth until they encounter the toy and say, "Here is the duck! You found it." If this technique is repeated long enough, the child realizes that the dropped toy is still nearby and can be found by searching for it. Parents need to remind themselves that the only way for young blind children to be aware of the presence of any object, such as a toy, is to touch it or hear it. Touching and searching are basic skills that are essential for learning about the world in which we live. As soon as the baby starts to put toys in his or her mouth, which will be around 7 or 8 months of age, he or she should be encouraged to hold and taste a cookie or a cracker.

Visually handicapped children do not learn to pick up and play with toys or any other objects unless they are taught to do so. The toy will not entertain them because of its bright, shiny color or funny face. It may entertain them because it makes a sound if shaken or banged, or it may have an intriguing taste or smell, or it may just feel interesting. Parents have been most ingenious in providing playthings that their blind infants enjoy so much that they will hunt for them by tossing aside other toys until the favorite one is located. Chains seem to have great appeal. One father came home from the pet department with a dog leash that his young son played with for months. He chewed on the leather loop forming the collar, which had a smokey flavor, sucked on the chain, ran it through his fingers, banged it on the table, hung it around his neck, and later on dragged it on the floor as he walked. That dog leash met all the criteria for a good toy. It had an interesting smell, taste, and texture and could be played with in any number of different ways determined by the child.

Most of the children we have known do not like furry or fuzzy toys; in fact, they do not like to touch them at all. Loving grandparents and friends are apt to turn up with a beautiful woolly lamb as a gift, which, unfortunately, is greeted with screams from the child. By the time the child is 4 or 5 he or she may tolerate teddy bears and other furry beasts, but they seldom become the well-loved nighttime cuddle toys they are for the sighted child.

Small, light rattles, large pop-it beads, plastic shapes such as disks on a short chain, small and large rubber squeaky toys, strings of beads, windup musical toys, cradle gyms, vegetable brushes, and measuring spoons all encourage the use of hands for picking up, identifying, and handling in a purposeful way.

Feeding

For the first few months, feeding a child with little or no sight presents no special problems to parents. Lack of sight alone will not affect the ability to suck. Because we want the child to understand what is happening and is going to happen, the parents should say, "It's time to eat, and here comes your bottle." From the time the baby is 2 months old, his or her hands should be placed gently on the bottle so he or she will learn to hold it. The child will have to be shown this skill many times.

Most babies dislike any change in their food and at first tend to spit it out, but if the parent persists for a few days, the baby starts eating and enjoying. When a child is disabled it is harder for a parent to insist that he or she learn to like new foods. Sometimes the parent goes so far as to put all the food into the bottle; thus the child doesn't learn to take it from a spoon. This can go on indefinitely, and the longer the delay in eating a variety of foods, the more resistant the child will become. There is no law that says peaches can't be mixed with liver if that makes the food more palatable to the baby, since later the proportion of peaches gradually can be reduced. A Chinese Canadian mother suggested to other parents in her support group that they try mixing a teaspoonful of boiled rice into their child's food at around 5 or 6 months to get the baby used to a different texture. The rice added texture to a familiar food but did not introduce a new flavor or smell to which the child could object.

Since a baby who is blind tends to droop his or her head while sitting, it is helpful if the parent gently lifts up the child's chin as the spoon nears, at the same time saying "open." In a relatively short time, the child will learn to open his or her mouth for the next bite as soon as the first has been swallowed. Before long, the child's head will come up when the smell of food is apparent. The smell of food is very important to blind children, who usually are reluctant to try a new food. The children smell the food before tasting it and thus learn to recognize different foods and to accept or reject them according to their past experience with that food. Parents should introduce new flavors gradually so that there is a good variety by the time the child is one year old. If the visually impaired child is not as active as other children, he or she may eat less food. Parents of children with disabilities sometimes are overanxious about having a well-nourished child, and their anxiety is communicated to the child. Mrs. Keel, a tense and anxious mother, approached meal times with great trepidation. This was the usual routine: She expected Ted to be uncooperative and, of course, he got the message. First, she coaxed him in a syrupy sweet voice to eat his nice dinner. Nothing doing. Then she scolded him. Nothing doing. Then she got angry and slapped him. Mr. Keel then jumped into the fray and yelled at her for slapping Ted, and Mrs. Keel fled from the room in tears. Ted enjoyed this performance far more than he could possibly have enjoyed his lunch, and he knew someone would feed him eventually anyway.

Drinking from a cup can be introduced gradually at around 5 or 6 months of age. A small, light, plastic cup or glass is a better choice than a cup with a spout, since the child will have to get used to drinking without the spout later on anyway and might as well move from bottle to cup in one step instead of two.

Hand Feeding. A baby who has had lots of opportunity to use his or her hands by 6 or 7 months will begin to suck and bite and taste anything that can be picked up. That is the time to teach the child to pick up food and put it in his or her mouth. The parent should first get the child used to the taste of a cookie while the adult holds it, then should put the cookie in the child's hand and guide it to the mouth while gently describing how good it tastes. It may be several weeks before the child becomes adept. When the visually impaired child drops food, it is gone, and the parent must show how to hunt and find it.

Children who do not see others eating are more apt to feed themselves by hand if the foods offered have a strong smell and flavor. Chocolate chip or peanut butter cookies, dry room-temperature pieces of celery, stalks of raw rhubarb, a nongreasy piece of bacon, a piece of dry garlic sausage, and cheese crackers all have been used successfully by parents in convincing their children that food in the hand is much more tasty than canned baby food. Hand feeding is messy, but it is a skill that should be mastered before the child can be expected to use a spoon.

Finger Feeding and Fine Motor Development.   For children who cannot see with their eyes it is most important that they develop the skillful and dexterous use of their hands because they will be depending on those hands and fingers to explore their world. Sighted babies see crumbs, threads, buttons, and dust bunnies on the floor as they play and promptly pick them up and put them in their mouths to see if they taste good. In doing so they learn to oppose their thumbs and forefingers in a pincer movement to pick up the goodies. No one has to show them how, and they get lots of practice picking up small objects.

Children with visual impairments do not see these tempting bits and have no incentive to pick them up and thus learn to use their thumbs and forefingers for that purpose. Here again parents can intercede by placing some small, dry pieces of food that tastes good (e.g., Cheerios, puffed rice, cheesies, and raisins or other dried fruit) where the children can accidentally encounter them. They will in time get picked up and tasted. Once the children show interest in such treats, the food can be placed in a small bowl or a tin pie plate. Brothers and sisters can be a great help in convincing the children that they will enjoy the treats. Regular foods, dishes, and high chairs should not be used for this exercise in case there are eating battles going on at mealtimes. This should be a treat that the children can eat or not. Finger dexterity, not good nutrition, is the goal.

Standing

Learning to stand starts very early in a baby's life; usually by 3 or 4 months parents are holding the baby upright on their laps, talking and playing. All the while the child's feet are bearing a little weight. Usually by around 7 months the child can bear full weight. A child with sight likes to stand up to see more, but children with little or no sight need encouragement to get them to stand. Teaching the blind baby to stand on the parent's lap or on the floor supported by the parent's knees can be part of the evening routine.

Mr. Martinez and 10-month-old Paul regularly read the paper before dinner each night. Mr. Martinez commented on the latest international crisis and the price of gold to Paul, who was firmly held between his father's knees, trying to grasp the bottom of the paper whenever it touched him.

If toys are strewn along a couch, the baby can be placed in a standing position on the floor with the parent's hand holding the child's knees straight against the couch. Some of the weight is being borne by the baby's chest on the couch. The baby can be encouraged to seek and find all the interesting things waiting to be played with and often will forget he or she is standing up. This works well with children who are very late in standing.

Standing beside a low window permits the partially sighted child to look out; the child with light perception can enjoy the sun or sunbeams, and the child who is blind is intrigued by feeling and tasting the cool, smooth glass.

It is a long time before a child who has just learned to stand is ready to walk, and this child will resist if the parents try to hurry him or her. After all, the child still has to learn to crawl and find his or her way around before being ready to walk. Standing comes before crawling and crawling comes before walking in the usual scheme of things, although a few children skip the crawling.

Pulling Up to Stand

Visually handicapped children will need help in learning how to get up on their feet once they have learned to enjoy standing up. They have to be shown how first to find, then to hang on with their hands, and then to pull up on the edge of a chair, the coffee table, or crib railings. If the children are first taught how to kneel, the parents can help them put one foot flat on the floor and lift up on their bottoms so they will move up to standing. If this is repeated a few times, they quickly should learn to do it on their own.

Getting down to sitting from standing beside a chair can be taught by bending and gently pulling down one of the child's legs until he or she is kneeling on it, and then bringing the other leg down. Then the child can get down into a full sitting position on his or her own.

Crawling

People used to think—and some still do—that babies who are blind do not crawl. Of course they will not crawl if no one provides the

Figure 3.4.   Happy Birthday! (1 year).

opportunity or sends them the message that they are expected to crawl. They can and do crawl, however, and from our observation of a large number of children, those who crawl seem to have better coordination and gait and are able to move about more confidently later on. Crawling is much less scary than walking into unknown space. If a baby has been down on the floor for a few months, he or she already knows about wriggling and squirming and rolling underneath the coffee table. Next the baby needs to learn to do it at will. When the baby is lying on his or her stomach on a nice, smooth tile or wood floor, and a parent pushes the baby's two feet up as far as possible and holds them there, the baby will automatically thrust against the adult's hand and spurt ahead on the slippery floor. After they both master this trick, the parent can show the baby how to thrust with his or her feet alternately and then turn the baby loose and call him or her to come.

Ten-month-old Sonya had been almost glued to the shag carpeting by her corduroy overalls and was not crawling at all. When her mother put her on the kitchen floor, she propelled herself across the room that first day, being very intrigued by the humming of the refrigerator, and she was all over the house by the end of the week.

A child with no useful vision will learn to put the rear end up, then put the front end up on the elbows, and eventually will get up on all fours. Then the child will rock back and forth without going anywhere. The child does not know he or she can move independently until the parents send the message.

Each family works out its own way to get the baby moving. Some try several techniques simultaneously and then are not sure which one did the trick. Touching the baby's hand with a favorite toy and drawing it away a few inches may encourage the child to reach for it. "Come to Mother" or "Come to Daddy" works with some. Other parents have used food. Five-year-old Mary taught her little brother to crawl by holding a chocolate chip cookie just in front of his nose where he could smell it; she had him crawling all over the house trying to get a bite. Mrs. Walker, on being asked how she taught her daughter, Jean, to crawl so well, replied, "Oh, it's very simple. We put her in the living room; then the rest of the family went out to the kitchen and had a good time out loud. Jean couldn't stand to be out of things, so she came to join us."

Figure 3.5. Blind children can crawl (12 months).

It's usually about 4 weeks from the time the baby is up on all fours until he or she starts moving. Mr. Otis phoned long distance to say Jimmy had been on all fours for 6 weeks and still had not moved. The counselor suddenly remembered that the Otis family lived in a trailer, and when the mother, father, and Jimmy were in the living room section, there literally was no place for him to go—he was already there. She suggested they put Jimmy at the far end of the hall and see what happened. Sure enough, Mr. Otis phoned in a couple of days to say that Jimmy not only had crawled but also was spending all his time exploring the hall—brand new territory.

Showing a crawling baby how to crawl up and down stairs provides lots of exercise and practice in lifting his or her body weight. The baby will have to be shown how to crawl up frontwards and how to back down. When her energetic daughter became bored with her usual routine, Mrs. Rooney found a happy solution. She would ensconce herself on the fourth step from the bottom of the stairs with a magazine and Melanie would spend 15 or 20 minutes busily climbing up and down the first three steps. Safety gates at the top and bottom of stairs are needed until a child knows his or her way around the house and is smart enough to avoid stepping off into space at the top of the stairs.

Walking

To learn to walk, a sighted child must be physically ready and must be motivated to walk. This fact also holds true for a child with little or no vision, but the situation is more complicated. The visually impaired child has more things to learn than a sighted child, and some of these things are hard. For example, take vertical balance. Try standing on one foot with your eyes open, then try with your eyes closed. Surprising the difference it makes, isn't it? When a person can see, there is continual and automatic visual feedback to show when one is leaning to one side or the other. It takes much more practice, if one cannot see, to learn which way is straight up by the feel of gravity. This is the reason we have put so much emphasis on teaching the visually impaired child to learn to stand up early so that, by the time the child is ready for walking, he or she will have developed good balance. Until the child can stand comfortably without any support, he or she is not ready to walk.

Figure 3.6. First steps (13 months).

The child who has never seen how other people walk also has to learn how to move his or her feet alternately. Parents have come up with a number of ways to show babies how to alternate their feet, such as standing on a parent's feet while the adult walks or having a sibling push the child's feet alternately while a parent holds his or her hands. One suggestion, however: it does seem to make more sense to a blind child to walk toward a parent's voice rather than away from it. The parent, thus, should face the child and walk backward while they practice walking.

Orienting

Walking around the outside of a playpen, along the front of a couch, or along the coffee table provides security and a chance to explore the furniture. A nice long wall or the kitchen cupboards provide space for walking and interesting handles, radiators, etc., for feeling and tasting. A child who uses the furniture and walls for support also is using them to help form a mental map of the house for later reference. For that reason, it is important to attach names to what the child touches. "That is Daddy's chair, that is the TV, that is the coffee table, that is the fridge." No map is any good unless the places on it have names. The child learns that first there is Daddy's chair, then the curtain, then the window, then another curtain, and then the bookcase with all those things to pull onto the floor, a maneuver that gets an immediate reaction from the parents.

It takes a tremendous amount of courage to step off into space and walk across a room unless a child is thoroughly familiar with it. After the child can walk he or she may still crawl across the room if he or she is in a hurry but may carefully walk all around the edge touching all the familiar things if there is time. Then one day, after the route has been learned, the child will suddenly let go and walk all the way out to the kitchen, not bumping into a thing. It helps if, instead of being carried, the child is encouraged to walk to the kitchen, the bathroom, and the bedroom. The idea that the parents expect the child to walk thus is established. Children with impaired vision vary in the length of time they take to get ready to walk alone. A few manage to walk freely before 13 or 14 months of age, but the majority are walking by 20 months. How early a child will walk unsupported depends on physical mobility, temperament, and the opportunity and encouragement received from the rest of the family. If they feel strongly that they want the child to live as normally as possible, they will be able to risk an occasional bump and bruise as the child learns to become independent. If the parents act as if the child is too fragile and are afraid of harm, the child will be reluctant to strike out on his or her own.

If small children are encouraged to go barefoot indoors it will help them learn to recognize the different floor surfaces like rugs, tile, linoleum, hardwood, and small mats. Familiarity with the different surfaces will help them establish landmarks as they make a mental map of the house.

Playpens

Playpens should be used sparingly for a visually impaired child because they tend to restrict mobility. We want the child to be curious, to explore, and to move around and become familiar with the whole house. There simply is not room in the playpen for a child to learn to crawl, and the visually impaired child can become used to being confined in a small, safe area and later be reluctant to venture into strange places. It is convenient to have a safe place to leave the baby while the parents are distracted, but the child should not be fenced in. A child with impaired vision needs freedom to move around more than other children do.

Jumpers or Canvas Swings

Jumpers or canvas swings can provide a pleasant change from lying on the floor or in the crib. If they are hung in such a way that the child's feet can be flat on the floor, he or she can practice holding his or her head erect, moving the feet, and bearing a little weight on the feet. It also gives the child a chance to get used to the feeling of being in a vertical position and to learn a little about balancing. Some children become very deft, particularly if they are barefoot, at moving the swing or jumper by walking up the side of the doorjamb and then giving a big push. These devices should be used for relatively short periods to provide a variety of experiences but should not be used as baby-sitters for prolonged periods.

Walkers

The use of walkers for children who are blind can result in a marked delay in their learning to walk independently and, for that reason, should be avoided. The walkers interfere with the development of vertical balance, which, at best, is difficult for children who are blind to master, but which is essential before they can stand and walk unsupported. The sale of walkers is prohibited in some regions because they are considered to be unsafe.

Crawlers

Crawlers were first used for orthopedically disabled children but are appearing in toy departments for normal children. They are small, low platforms mounted on wheels, something like a mechanic's dolly. Children lie on their stomachs and propel themselves around by pushing with their hands and feet. Crawlers encourage curiosity and provide mobility to explore new and interesting places.

DELAYED DEVELOPMENT

If, for any reason, a baby who is visually impaired has reached 8 or 10 months of age before the parents learn that he or she needs special teaching because of visual problems, the child may be considerably behind the norm in development. The 8- or 10-month-old may still be functioning almost like a newborn—unable to hold the head erect, unable to sit or grasp or stand. In turn, parents tend to treat the child like a newborn. The child and the parents have worked out a reasonably comfortable way of getting along together. The baby is content and does not know any other way of life and probably would be happy to carry on this way indefinitely. The parents are waiting for the baby to show them he or she is ready, while the baby is waiting for them to show that they expect growth and learning and for them to show how to do things. When nothing happens, parents gradually reach the conclusion that the child is incapable of learning and stop hoping. It is extremely difficult for a family physician who is not familiar with the needs of blind children to tell the difference between a blind child who has not been taught and one who is mentally retarded or cerebral palsied and incapable of learning at a normal rate. If it is at all possible, parents should request a full assessment of the child at a diagnostic clinic where the staff is familiar with the development of children who are visually impaired.

In the meantime, it is never too late to start the baby moving. A child who has been permitted to do as he or she liked for months will object loudly and fiercely to attempts to change. The parents should get the child down on the floor on his or her stomach and sell him or her on the idea of learning. The child will insist on lying on his or her back and doing nothing, so the parents must make lying on the back

Figure 3.7. Identifying body parts (14 months).

very uncomfortable by fastening to the back of the shirt various objects such as clothespins, small hard balls, etc., which will poke into the child when he or she is lying on the back. Babies are very smart about wiggling just enough to twist the clothing so that the hard ball is moved under the arm and away from the back.

Isaac was 18 months old when we first met him and his family. He was the typical limp, passive, understimulated blind infant. His parents were most eager to make up for lost time, but Isaac was not as happy about the new routine and preferred to lie on his back forever. He lay happily on clothespins, golf balls, and even some building blocks fastened to his back to make it uncomfortable for him just to lie there. Then his father tied a toy telephone to Isaac's back that actually rolled him over onto his side every time he tried to lie on his back. This was too much for Isaac and he gave up the struggle and learned to lie on his stomach. Six weeks later he was crawling, and eventually he walked at 2 years, putting up token resistance at every new demand that he become independent. Finally he learned that life could be more fun if he moved around than it had ever been lying on his back in one spot.

The important principle to remember is that motor development has a definite sequence of stages, and even late starters do best if they start at the beginning and go through all the stages in the right order. Late starters often can cover more stages in a shorter time. Isaac, for instance, went from about a 3-month level to a 10-month level in 6 weeks. It can be very exciting for the family of a late starter when they see such amazing progress in a relatively short period. However, they must realize that, as the child's development gets closer to that of chronological age, learning speed will drop to a more normal rate, provided, of course, that the child has normal potential. If the pleasure and admiration of the parents at the child's newfound skills are clearly communicated to the baby, the parents will help the child give up the old passive way of life. The child will learn only for rewards, and it takes patience and optimism to convince him or her that the effort is worthwhile.

This is a tough period for parents: trying to change their handling, with the baby unhappily resisting and nothing apparently happening. If they give up, however, they will be teaching the child that passive resistance or screaming works beautifully and that he or she will not have to learn.

Chapter 4

A Different World

◆ ◆ ◆ ◆ ◆ ◆

Not too long ago, the assumption that impaired vision automatically meant impaired intellectual ability was held by far too many professionals who were unaware of the impact lack of sight could have on normal development. Consequently no one expected much from blind children, no demands were made on them, and no one taught them in ways they could understand. The children failed to develop well, with many of them remaining limp and unresponsive, thus fulfilling the earlier prophecy of mental deficiency. Now we know that if the families can replace the stimulus of vision with other stimuli, give lots of encouragement, practice, and love, and convince the children they expect them to learn, children who are blind (without other disabilities) can develop within normal limits.

Dozens of parents of visually handicapped children have complained that the hardest thing they had to learn to cope with was what at first appeared to be the utter passivity and lack of initiative of their children. "Why does he just lie there when he has all those toys to play with? Why do I always have to tell him what to do, even to ride his kiddycar, which he loves?"

To understand why, and before we get involved with teaching specific skills such as feeding, toileting, etc., let us consider exactly what kind of world the child with visual impairments is living in, how lack of sight can affect development, and what parents can do about it.

Our awareness of the world around us depends primarily on visual imagery. We can see the relative size, shape, color, and location of objects around us. We can recognize an object at a distance simply by looking at it. We know where we are in relation to our immediate environment. The child who has little or no vision can understand the world only by touching, smelling, tasting, and listening. These four senses combined give the child much less information about the environment than does sight alone. There are many things that cannot be touched either, because they are too far away, too hot, too fragile, too big, too small, or too complex (for example, a flame or a mosquito).

We can all remember the old tale about the three blind men describing an elephant. The first said an elephant was like a tree, because he had felt a leg; the second said an elephant was like a wall, because he had felt its side; and the third said an elephant was like a rope, because he had felt its tail. It is incredibly difficult, without good sight, to learn about concepts like space, direction, similarities, and differences.

Children with partial sight may see the world as a hazy blur or in fragments, and it is only as they grow older and become articulate that parents discover how limited their awareness of the environment is.

The child who is visually impaired becomes familiar with an object only through personal experience with that object, not through the secondhand experience of someone describing it. To the child, a cat is soft and warm and has sharp things on the ends of its legs that can hurt. The child soon learns to be gentle with it so it will buzz when touched and lick the child's hand with its scratchy tongue. Is that the way most people would describe a cat to a child?

There is a myth that when one sense is missing or impaired, the other four senses automatically become more sensitive to compensate. Many scientifically valid tests have proved that children who are blind do not have more sensitive touch, hearing, taste, or smell; but we have observed that they do learn to pay more attention to information received through their remaining senses, and they do learn to use their memories well.

A SEA OF SOUNDS

It may help the parents to understand their child's world if they blindfold themselves from time to time and start to listen to all the sounds around the house. Clocks tick, taps drip, kettles sing, furnaces and refrigerators hum, doors and drawers open and close, feet walk, dishes clatter, radios and TVs play, phones ring. As each sound is heard and recognized, it provides information about where the listener is and what is happening. When one is reading a very exciting mystery and the radio is giving the news, the radio does not register because the reader tunes out sounds that are not relevant at the time. The child who does not see is surrounded by a sea of sound—all of it irrelevant until he or she is taught what it means. In the first year, the child can learn to recognize a good number of sounds—the parents' voices and the sound of a favorite squeaky toy or music box, voices of brothers and sisters, and the meaning of a few words such as *mommy, daddy, bottle, cookie, up, bed, car.*

To become independently mobile, the child will have to learn to use the household sounds to find his or her way around. The parents should learn to say, "That is the fridge; hear it hum?" or "This is the window. Feel how cold it is. Be gentle and don't break it." "Feel that warm air. That is the heater." "Oh, did you bump your head? You forgot about the coffee table." The child will need help in learning to recognize where he or she is and more help in learning how to get to where he or she wants to go. What landmarks are there to mark the route for the infant to crawl from the bedroom to the kitchen or for the teenager to travel alone to the community center?

If the television or radio is left on all the time, the toddler who is just learning to map his or her home will have more difficulty. Sounds like the ticking of a clock, the humming of the refrigerator, the clinks and clanks of heating pipes and registers or radiators, which could be used as landmarks, are not audible. If given the freedom to roam around the house, the toddler who is visually impaired will learn to stop before bumping into a large obstacle like a wall or big easy chair. When we questioned teenagers who were blind (and who were very pleased to enlighten us about this and other mysteries), they told us they actually heard the object when close to it. They said what they heard was most likely the echo of their breathing, their footsteps, the rustle of their clothing, their cane taps, or their voices. They reached this conclusion after much heated discussion within the group, as most of them had never tried to analyze it before. They just knew when something was there.

So did Barry, a 4-year-old farm child, when he was sent out to play wearing a new, leather winter helmet with large ear flaps. After taking a few steps he screamed, "Take it off! Take it off! I can't see a thing."

A person who is blind uses sound to give him or her information about the environment being traversed, and it is particularly useful when traveling alone.

Peggy, an 18-year-old university student who is totally blind, told us she could travel all around the campus safely as long as she was alone. Only when she was alone was she able to concentrate on all the auditory and other clues, such as traffic sounds, the rustle of the leaves of the maple tree on the corner where she had to turn right, the clatter of dishes and the smell of cooking as she neared the cafeteria, and the different sounds her footsteps made as she walked on concrete, blacktop, grass, and gravel. When asked how she could find the entrances to the various buildings, she said that all the doors happened to be recessed and the echo of her cane and footsteps sounded different as she passed the doorway. Also, at the ends of buildings she could hear the difference and also feel the air currents.

Peggy said she had found that she could not concentrate on her clues if someone walked and talked with her. Then she relied on the voice and footsteps of the other student as a guide. However, if that student offered her an arm she could relax and let her friend steer the course.

COMMUNICATION

Children who are visually impaired do not reach out to explore their world but depend on their parents to bring the world to them and to interpret it for them. Therefore it is extremely important that communication between the infant and the parents be established as soon as possible. All the information and skills that the child acquires in the first 3 or 4 years of life will have to be taught by the child's family. Before any teaching or learning can occur they all must learn how to communicate with each other.

The blind children that we have known who have done well all had close, loving relationships with their parents or caregivers from soon after birth. A young sighted baby can see when the mother is present and soon learns to recognize her face, but the visually impaired infant does not even know if the mother is in the room until she speaks or picks the baby up. That baby cannot see the smiles and doting looks of a loving mother and has to depend on her cuddling, stroking, patting, rubbing, rocking, and sweet talking to receive her message of love and to feel loved. In turn the child who is blind will come to know the voices of other members of the family and to react to them.

When a child feels loved he or she will respond and communication begins. If parents talk to the infant while dressing, feeding, bathing, and playing, the words will begin to have meaning. Use phrases like "Let's put your left arm in your shirt sleeve" or "Here is your bottle. You hold it like this." Soon the child will come to understand simple directions and statements and will begin to cooperate, eventually learning the meaning of hundreds of words as they relate to actual experience.

Facial expression and body language enhance communication between two people who can see each other. Children who cannot see a nod, a smile, a wink, a frown, or a gesture are at a disadvantage and may not accurately receive the message the speaker sent. A smiling father who is in a hurry may speak abruptly, and the child who is blind may think his or her dad is mad at him or her for some unknown reason. In turn, the lack of expression on the face of a blind child who seems to be looking out the window can send the wrong message to the mother, even though the child actually is listening intently.

Adults sometimes forget that children who are blind do not know when other people are present in the room unless they are told. For example, 5-year-old Glen came home from a church-run kindergarten one day and said, "Mom, can God talk?" Slightly at a loss, his mother asked him why he wanted to know. Glen explained, "Well, every day we thank God for our food and the nice day, and he has never once said 'You're welcome'."

One young father said it helped him to think of his 6-month-old blind son as a brand new computer, one with unlimited potential, that could not function until it had been programmed.

He and his wife were very busy putting data into their little computer every minute they could spend with their son ("Here is your nose, and these are your toes") with the firm conviction that their son in the future would be able to access and use the skills and facts stored in his data base. While it sounds a little cold and mechanical, the father, mother, and baby were all having lots of fun with their programming.

BODY AWARENESS AND USE

While it is fairly easy to understand that a child who does not have normal vision would have a harder time learning about the world around him, it may come as a surprise to find that he or she also has difficulty learning about his or her own body. Older blind children and partially sighted children frequently have very distorted ideas of what their own bodies are like and even less awareness of others'. Five-year-old Tina proudly told the counselor that she could count to a thousand. When the counselor asked how many hands she had, Tina said, "I'll count." She proceeded to count and replied, "I have two hands." When asked how many hands her mother had, she went over to her and counted, responding that she also had two hands. Then she repeated the same routine with her little brother. When asked how many hands her father had, Tina said, "He is at work so I can't count his hands. Maybe two? Say, do all people have two hands? I never knew that."

Such basic information is so readily available to children who see normally that parents and teachers may forget to provide the blind child with a chance to learn such obvious facts. He or she must be taught the names of body parts and their relative locations and functions. They do not know that feet are for walking.

Infants who are blind need to start learning about their bodies in the first few months of life. Passive exercises where the parents move the babies' arms above their heads, out to the side, across their chests, and down again, with appropriate comments like "Put your arms up over your head, now down, now clap your hands, patty cake, patty cake," will help babies learn all the things they can do with their arms and hands. Similar exercises with legs—straightening, flexing, standing, kicking, and finding their feet with their hands—will acquaint them with their legs and feet. The child can practice rolling from side to side, sitting up, and standing up with parental help. All these activities help the children learn to use their muscles and develop their muscle memory, which they can draw on to repeat certain movements at will.

Few people are aware that without useful vision children will not learn to hold up their heads, to reach and grasp, to crawl, to sit, or to walk spontaneously. Vision seems to be the trigger to all motor development. Sighted babies learn very early that when they lift up their heads they can see more than when they are lying flat, so the pleasurable action is repeated until good head control is mastered. Sighted babies will reach for and later grasp a bright toy that they see nearby; later they will crawl or walk to get it. Children who are blind do not even know that the toy exists. Parents must be sufficiently creative to motivate the infants to learn to move and control their bodies and must ensure that the activities are sufficiently rewarding that the children will want to repeat them. With repetition a motor skill will become automatic.

Once the children have learned to move and control their bodies and body parts, they will need to understand directions such as "Bend your knees, squat down, bend over, jump, take a big step, touch your nose, touch your knees, touch your toes." Verbal instructions alone will only confuse the children. Instructions should be accompanied by parents gently placing the children's bodies into the desired position so the children can actually feel what the action is like. Parents should do this with sufficient repetition until the action looks normal.

Loose or low muscle tone, along with poor posture, is common among visually impaired children who do not get enough exercise and who are not encouraged to be physically active. Both low muscle tone and poor posture can be prevented. Most parents can remember their mothers nagging them to stand or sit up straight. Blind children do not know what *straight* means. They will need help learning where to hold their heads and their shoulders until they learn the feel of it. Standing against a wall and pressing their heels, backs, and heads against it can be a way for them to check their posture. The child who is encouraged to move freely, to roll, to crawl, and to walk around his or her house and yard will have better posture and a better walking gait than one who is left to sit in a safe place.

AWARENESS AND INTERACTION WITH THE ENVIRONMENT

Sight gives quick and accurate information about objects both near and far, while information gained from touch, smell, hearing, and movement is limited and often inaccurate. No other sense can stimulate curiosity, integrate information, or invite exploration in the same way or as efficiently and fully as vision does.

Children with sight are exposed to a constant barrage of visual stimuli all their waking hours. All they have to do is sit there and file it away for future reference. Long before they can talk they are aware of hundreds of things like people, cats, dogs, floors, ceilings, doors, windows, bottles, and toys. On the other hand, children with little or no vision are only aware of those things within reach, and children with partial sight are only aware of things within a few feet. They cannot explore the world visually, and limited mobility makes it difficult to explore physically. If they do explore independently they may not understand what they encounter. Children who do not see cannot understand an experience without language and need the explanation of a sighted person about the names, properties, and functions of specific objects encountered. Then the object will have to be explored and the explanation repeated several times before the object becomes familiar.

Vision is much more efficient for information gathering than all the other senses combined. It provides comprehensive information about an object as a whole and provides the opportunity to compare that object with others as to color, shape, and function. Only if an object is small enough to be held in two hands can blind children form a realistic idea of its shape and texture. Any larger object has to be explored in sequence, with the pieces of information put together to form a whole (usually an inaccurate one). Everything new is scary, and most visually impaired children are reluctant to try new experiences (e.g., a new toy or food). Once reassured, the very young children will explore new objects with nose, tongue, lips, teeth, and hands, and they will bang, shake, and squeeze it in an effort to learn as much as possible about the strange new object.

Of course, there are many things in a home that are not readily encountered by a cruising blind child, as was discovered by one father. Mr. Greaves was replacing the light bulb in the hall ceiling fixture when he was called to the phone. On his return he found 6-year-old Jane on the stepladder feeling the ceiling. Before her father could say anything, Jane said, "Dad, I didn't know our hall had a lid on it."

Space and one's place in space is a great mystery to all blind children and many blind adults. Reality to them is the little area that they can actually touch, and without familiar landmarks they are lost. That is why it is important to regularly tell the toddlers cruising about the house or yard, "That's Daddy's chair; that is the coffee table; you are beside the TV; that is the gate, feel the slats; that is the apple tree, feel the rough bark" etc.

While learning the placement of landmarks the children also are registering other clues (e.g., sounds, echoes, air currents, odors, and underfoot textures like rugs, linoleum, or tile floors indoors and grass, concrete, or gravel outdoors. They also are filing away for future reference how many steps and how long it took to get from the back steps to the gate or from the bathroom to the kitchen through muscle memory. Think about coming into a dark house and knowing where the hall light switch is without having to feel around for it—that is muscle memory.

Sorting out movable and immovable objects is a real puzzle for blind children. Emily, age 7, surprised her mother by asking, "Where does my house go when I am not in it?"

When a family becomes actively involved in helping their visually impaired child become familiar with and comfortable with the people and objects in their home, that child will learn to recognize them and feel safe and secure there.

OBSERVATION AND IMITATION

Young sighted children learn many skills simply by watching how other people do things and then imitating them. They learn that feet are for walking, hairbrushes for brushing hair, spoons for putting food into the mouth. They learn how to sit on a chair, how to climb stairs, how to dig in the sand, and how to use buttons and zippers. The list is endless and overwhelming when we consider how many hundreds of different skills we expect children to have mastered by the age of 5 or 6. With great ingenuity and much patient encouragement, the families of visually impaired children must teach all those skills. It is a complicated and difficult undertaking for any family and, according to the individual family circumstances, different families will have varying degrees of success.

By the age of 2 the average sighted child will be familiar with the routine for washing hands simply from observing how other family members wash theirs, unlike the 3-year-old blind child who did not even know that water for washing came out of a tap. His mother always washed his hands with a wet washcloth.

Using a spoon or fork requires very delicate and quite complicated movements of the wrist, fingers, and arm and also requires the ability to locate the mouth while holding the spoon level so the food does not fall off. It could be compared to a sighted adult trying to eat noodles with chopsticks while blindfolded, a hard and frustrating task.

No matter how hard they try families cannot teach their visually impaired children all the skills their sighted children have acquired by observation and imitation. There are bound to be gaps, which often show up when the children go to preschool. For example, a teacher may tell the children to pretend they are robins and ask them to flap their wings and fly around the room. The sighted children soon will be cheeping and flapping, and some of the slower ones will copy the more flamboyant ones. But any blind children in the class will be totally mystified about what the teacher wants them to do. They have never seen a bird, may never have heard of a wing (unless on the Thanksgiving turkey), and don't know what *flap* means. But as soon as the teacher shows them what to do with their arms and how to trot and flap at the same time, they can fly with the rest of the robins.

COGNITIVE LEARNING

Some parents who read professional books on child rearing may be puzzled by the term *cognitive ability*. In simple terms it means the ability to learn, to know, and to think. A child receives information through the senses, and the information is then processed and stored in the brain. That stored information is knowledge and consists of all the child knows about the world and his or her relationship to it. For example, a small blind boy encounters a ball several times, examines it, manipulates it, and becomes familiar with it and the word *ball*. Later he encounters a bigger ball, a smaller ball, a furry ball, or a Nerf ball and discovers that, although they are all different in size and texture, they are all the same shape and all are called *ball*. He has formed his own concept of a ball.

For a new experience to have meaning the child must be able to hook the new information onto something already known. Sometimes it is hard to find a known fact to hook onto if the person is blind. Talking to Irene, a blind teenager, we mentioned having a fish pond in our garden. She asked about the shape of the pool and was told it was kidney-shaped. Irene replied that she did not know how a kidney was shaped. Then she was told the pool was shaped like the letter S with the ends snipped off. She did not know what a letter S was like. Finally when she was told the pool was shaped like a jelly bean, pinched in the middle with one end bent a little, Irene said, "Oh, now I get it."

The families of visually impaired children play a most important role in providing their children with a wide variety of experiences to gather information, interpreting when necessary to clarify any misconceptions. The knowledge gained from personal experience has much more significance to the child than the knowledge gained from hearing about it secondhand.

Think about a walk in the park on a fall day. It can be very boring for children who are blind to listen to their parents chatter about the beautiful fall colors. The parents instead should concentrate on making the experience an opportunity for their children to learn. They can encourage the children to feel the different bark on the different types of trees, to hug a tree to see how big it is, to pick a few leaves and find the little bump at the end of its stem that fastened it to the branch, to feel the difference between the soft leaves still on the tree and those that have fallen off and are dry and crisp, and finally to have fun making a big pile of leaves and running and jumping in them. The children will come home with a good deal more information to add to their concept of trees.

There are many things that are too big, too small, too fragile, too hot, or too far away to be handled and experienced firsthand, and information gathered secondhand may be fragmented or erroneous. The limitations of their information-gathering systems make it more difficult for children who are visually impaired to acquire accurate information. They get the information in bits and pieces and often form some strange conclusions. Donna, a very bright 6-year-old was asked how many legs birds have. She pondered a while and then replied, "Well, dogs have four legs, and cats have four legs, but people have two legs. Birds are not people so I guess they must have four legs."

Children who are visually impaired have less opportunity than sighted children to become familiar with numbers and number concepts. The 5-year-olds may have little in the way of mathematical skills beyond rote counting. They may not have learned from observation

Figure 4.1. Stop and smell the flowers (3 years).

that shoes come in twos, regardless of size and shape; that tables and chairs usually have four legs; that to set the table for three people one needs three forks, three knives, three spoons, three plates, and three cups. It is hard to visualize a group of objects if they cannot be seen, and to know how many there are without counting them individually. They need to learn what the number words actually mean from handling, sorting, counting, and arranging a variety of real objects before they can be expected to understand the most elementary number concepts. It is interesting to note that a number of totally blind students have gone on to excel in mathematics.

Raising a child who is blind is a big job but a very rewarding one. Parents do invest a great deal of time and effort in helping their children who are blind or partially sighted function up to their potentials. A number of parents have confided that they feel more pride in the accomplishments of a child with visual impairment because they know the child could not have been successful without their help.

Chapter 5

The Toddler

♦ ♦ ♦ ♦ ♦ ♦

HOW DO THESE CHILDREN LEARN?

It would be very comforting for parents if we were able to provide a nice, clear-cut book of instructions about how, when, and what to teach a child who is visually impaired. Unfortunately, it cannot be done, because each child is so different from all the other visually handicapped children, and each family is so different, that every situation is unique. It may be helpful to parents to think about some factors that will have a very definite effect on helping to determine how their child will develop.

Readiness

Obviously, a child is not going to learn any skill unless he or she is ready physically and mentally. A child of 6 months cannot walk, and one of 2 years cannot ride a two-wheeler. The difficulty lies in determining when a child is ready for a particular skill. The first thing the parents must know is at what age most children learn to do a particular thing. If they have other children, these siblings can be a handy reference guide; otherwise, they should try to find a good book on normal child development to which they can refer for a baseline. The parents will want to be sure their child is around the right age with a body physically mature enough to be able to do what they want to teach. Then they will want to look at the child's stage of development. For instance, walking comes after standing. There is a regular sequence with one stage following another, and most children follow this sequence. Does the child have enough understanding of language to comprehend the parents' meaning and enough emotional development to let go of baby ways?

Amount of Vision

Every little bit of sight helps in learning, so we can expect that the more residual (remaining) vision a child has, the more easily he or she will learn. Some things are harder without sight (for example, learning vertical balance), and those skills will take longer to master. Visually impaired children often are slower in learning to walk, feed, and dress independently. Of course, some children who are completely blind do walk earlier than some sighted children. The amount of sight is only one factor to be taken into account.

Additional Disabilities

The presence of any additional disabilities can impede development. If a child has impaired hearing or cerebral palsy, learning will be more difficult. If parents believe a child is not progressing as expected and the child has not had a complete assessment, the family doctor should refer them to a diagnostic clinic to find out the reason for the delay. Many doctors who are unfamiliar with blind children will not make a referral without being asked. Should any other condition be discovered, it is important to arrange early treatment and also to learn techniques of home management.

Motivation

Motivation is vital for learning; no child will learn without wanting to learn. If the child is not motivated, it does not matter how hard everyone else tries. The trick is for parents to help the child to want to learn. Suggestions are given throughout this book that should help solve this problem, but each parent and child is different and each solution will be unique.

Parental Attitudes

How parents feel and act toward their child most definitely affects how that child will develop. Some of this material will be discussed in more detail in other parts of the book. What parents really want for their child, whether it's to be independent or to be safe in their arms, is an important factor. Do they believe the child is capable of learning to be self-sufficient? If parents are not sure of exactly how they feel about the child's potential, they can communicate this doubt to the child, who will then be a mirror for their fear and uncertainty. The child will be receiving a mixed message: "Yes, you can learn to crawl up the stairs, but you are in mortal peril if you do." It is perfectly normal for any parents to feel anxious about their child taking risks, but the anxiety may be greater if the child is disabled. The trick is not to let the child know that you are anxious about him or her trying new things.

Sometimes learning is delayed because the visually impaired child does not understand what the parents want. Clear communication is necessary. Can parents patiently push and push, providing encouragement until the child discovers the satisfaction of doing things on his or her own? Or do they meet all the child's needs before he or she is aware of them? Parents who are too helpful prevent a child from learning to be independent. It may be because they do not realize that the child is ready to achieve on his or her own.

GETTING THE MESSAGE ACROSS

Human beings learn to communicate with one another in many different ways, and spoken language is only one of the methods used to send and receive messages. In any family, there is a tremendous amount of nonverbal communication going on all the time. By a smile, a frown, or a tender look, a clear message can be sent across a room. Waving a hand, crooking a finger, and shaking or nodding a head all convey messages. The sound of doors slamming, pots and pans banging, feet thumping, and singing, whistling, or sighing can tell us whether or not we should keep out of the way. We often can tell how a person is feeling from observing the way he or she sits—with drooping head and slumped shoulders or perched on the edge of a chair all set to go. Just think how much of this information would be missed or misunderstood if one could not see!

Children who cannot see facial expressions depend more on the words and the tone of voice a person uses in speaking to them than do sighted children. It is easy for a child to receive the wrong message, as happens when a parent in a hurry to get to work on time sounds angry because the child is in the way. To the sighted child a smile can soften a reprimand to mean, "I do not like what you are doing, but I still love you." A pat or a hug can say, "I love you," and a squeeze of the hand can replace a reassuring glance in a strange and scary place for the child who cannot see.

All small children seem to have a built-in antenna that tells them when their parents are most vulnerable. Children who are usually pleasant and cooperative can be perfect devils if they get the message that someone has a headache, company is coming for dinner, or the washing machine has broken down in the middle of a large wash. Children who are blind are equally sensitive to the moods of their parents and will react just like other children. It does not require vision to feel the anger or impatience in the hands that change or dress them or the strain in the voice tone or the sound of quick, angry footsteps. Nor does it require vision to receive the message parents send by cuddling, patting, rocking, and sweetly talking.

The amount of communication that can be carried on without language or sight is very limited and of poor quality. It is natural for parents to be impatient for their child to learn to talk so they can better understand each other. If a visually handicapped child is slow in talking, the parents may become anxious because, deep down, they fear that if the child cannot see normally he or she might not be able to develop normally, and the slowness in talking is taken as a bad sign. Many parents, exhausted by the constant talking of their blind 5-year-olds, often ruefully wonder why they were so desperate for the child to talk at 2 and why they failed to enjoy the peace and quiet while they could.

Speech and Language

A normal child must meet three prerequisites to be able to learn to use language for communication. First, the child should be exposed to others and have interactions with active, talking people to find out that people do communicate with one another by words. Second, the child needs help in developing a meaningful vocabulary; if he or she doesn't know any words, there will be no talk. Third, there must be opportunities to use language to send and receive messages. When these requirements are met, children who are blind or partially sighted can proceed at the normal rate in their language development; in fact, some of them are quite precocious. Increasing numbers of small visually handicapped children, however, seem to be having problems with delayed or impaired language. This development is not surprising when we examine how much harder we make it for the child who is visually impaired to learn to talk. Children who are visually impaired cannot observe and imitate how their parents move their tongues and lips to make specific sounds as they speak. It is only by trial and error as they lie and play with sounds in their babbling that they can discover how to make different sounds. This kind of learning usually takes a little more time than if they were simply able to imitate their parents.

Sometimes when children are learning to walk they will appear to lose interest in learning to talk, almost as if it is possible for them to concentrate on learning only one major skill at a time.

Exposure and Interaction.   Many children just do not hear that much two-way conversation. With young families moving all around the country there are seldom grandparents, uncles, aunts, and cousins around. One parent or both may be away at work all day, and when the whole family is together at night they may all watch television. Unfortunately, the TV personalities are only disembodied voices to the blind child and are ignored much like traffic noises. Conversation has almost disappeared in many modern families. When television is a parent's major companion, the baby is left alone and has no one to interact with.

Of course, some talking is necessary, and the child does receive lots of spoken instructions: "Eat your cereal." "Go to the toilet." "Leave the cat alone." "Pick up your toys." "Don't climb on the furniture with your boots on." It is easy to fall into this pattern and not so easy to climb out. Even though they are worried about a child not talking, many mothers and fathers find it hard to converse with a very young child; hence the child gets lots of practice in receiving but none in sending messages. It is important to try to have at least a few small chats every day in which the parent really listens to what the child has to say. Simple questions like "Whose boy are you?" will help the child to want to talk to the parents. If a parent has the real desire to be close to a child, and the child finds out that the parent wants to hear what he or she has to say, there can be some very intriguing conversations in the future, like this one: Mr. King came home from golf one Saturday to be greeted by David, age 4, with the sad news that the family cat had killed a robin. Incidentally, Mr. King was a Protestant and Mrs. King was a Catholic. David and his father had a long conversation about whether robins went to heaven. Mr. King said he was sure they did not, but David replied that if it was a Catholic robin it would, and there was no way his father could prove it was a Protestant robin. After due deliberation they proceeded to give the robin a very solemn funeral. As he carefully patted down the soil on the grave under the rosebush, David said, "Daddy, I think I will come back tomorrow and dig up this robin and see if it did go to heaven. No, I had better wait until Monday because I am not sure that God works on Sunday."

Vocabulary.   The young child with sight nearly drives his or her parents crazy with a constant, "Whazzat?" "Whazzat?" pointing all the time to all kinds of things. That, of course, is how the child learns the names of things. The child who does not see at all, or just a little, is not aware of all the interesting things around him or her and never asks what they are. When such a child is in a car, a big truck going by is only a noise. How can we expect a child to talk when he or she has no words to use or limited understanding of the meaning of common words? Five-year-old Ricky was being assessed by a psychologist before his admission to school, and she was checking on his understanding of some words. When she asked him, "What runs?" he replied, "The washing machine." When she asked, "What bites?" he said, "Theresa, the baby."

Opportunity.   Many children have no real need to talk because they communicate reasonably well with their parents by whining until the parents guess what they want and provide it. Other children are content to sit back like little kings and let the willing slaves provide for their every need. The trouble with this drama is that, in time, the willing slaves become unwilling to continue pampering the child and get angry because he or she is so dependent. The poor child, however, has never learned to use spoken language to let people know what he or she wants because it was never necessary.

Suggestions for Teaching a Child To Use Language

We have already mentioned in the section on infancy how important it is to talk to the visually impaired child during feeding, bathing, dressing, and play, so that the child learns the words that describe the daily routines. By one year, the child should have had enough language exposure to know his or her own name and to recognize the names of Mommy, Daddy, brothers and sisters, and a few favorite toys or foods. The child may also be making some effort to say these words. The next step is to help him or her learn more words, but they must be words that have some real, personal meaning if they are to be of use.

Mrs. Grice was very proud when the first thing she taught her 2-year-old David to say was "The smoke goes up the chimney" and "Electricity makes the lamps give light." To David, language had no real meaning beyond the intriguing sounds the words made and his mother's original pleasure at his precocity. She could not understand why David at 4 still could not carry on the simplest conversation. He became very competent at parroting all the radio and TV commercials, complete with music and other sound effects, but he did not know how to ask for a drink of water, and he would stand by the sink and whine until his mother guessed what he wanted.

Every opportunity should be used to teach the names of familiar objects. As the child cruises around the room, the parents should mention the furniture he or she touches, the food he or she eats, or the clock ticking. Most children enjoy pulling toys out of a box and flinging them aside. Parents should gather up assorted toys and common articles like shoes, hairbrushes, spoons, buttons, and cups and, as the child flings them out, say, "That's your teddy." "That is your shoe." "That is a block." As the child is fishing objects out of the box, the parents should ask for their names and explain them when the child does not know them. This can be made exciting and fun. If, however, the parents are too earnest, the child will not want to do it.

They should move around the house with the child, touching things like doors, taps, and tables, first telling the name and then asking for it. They should teach him or her how to find and name all the body parts, by first showing and then asking and by showing delight when the child points to his or her knee and says "knee." After the child knows the names of a lot of things, the next step is to teach some verbs ("Give me the ball." "Put the cup down on the table." "Come to daddy.") The parents should never say, "Put it here." How will the child know what "it" is and where "here" is? They must try to keep in mind that the child does not see where they are looking or pointing, so they must use specific words.

The first way a child uses language other than to say a word on request should be to make known what he or she wants. After learning to understand language, the child must learn to use it for his or her own purposes, to ask for things. It is normal for all children to go through a stage called *parroting* or *echolalia*, that is, repeating back what is said to them. A parent says, "Luis, do you want a drink?" and Luis replies, "Luis, do you want a drink?" This stage tends to persist longer in a child who does not see, probably because he or she is more dependent on the parents to teach what is called expressive language.

Parroting may be very rewarding for a child if the parents react by trying to force the child to give a straight answer by giving a reasonable explanation. Luis is not interested in a reasonable explanation, but he *is* interested in the fact that he gets a lot more attention from his parents when he replies, "Luis, do you want a drink?" than he would if he had merely said yes. If his parents would offer a choice ("Luis, would you like milk or Kool-Aid?") he would be more apt to reply. A similar technique has proved useful in coping with the child who tries to communicate without words. If such a child goes over and stands by the cookie jar and whines, the parents should play stupid and pretend not to understand. They might say, "I don't know what you want. Do you want to have a cookie or a nap?" One day the child will say, "I want a cookie!"

These techniques of choice or stupidity are far more effective in encouraging speech than trying to force a child to say, "I want a cookie." No adult can be as stubborn as a small child. Fortunately, parents are still smarter and can use their intelligence to outfox the child.

Providing Opportunities for Language

Once a child can talk, the parents will have to provide topics and opportunities to use the new skill. Small children enjoy "togetherness" with their parents. The small boy with sight can look up and see that his mother is there and can tell that she is aware of him because she smiles at him. The child who cannot see at all may constantly need reassurance that she has not disappeared by asking, "Mom, what are you doing?" every 5 minutes. The child with partial sight may ask less often because he or she can see the parents are there but cannot see if they are paying attention to him or her. Parents who talk to their child a good deal give the child no need to check if they are still there and, at the same time, provide practice in two-way conversation.

What should they talk about? The parent should try talking about what is happening at the moment: "I am washing the bathroom floor. Here is a rag, you wash the door." "What are you washing?" "What am I washing?" "What will we wash next?" A trip to the supermarket can be talked about in advance: "We are going to the supermarket to buy bananas and peanut butter." At the supermarket, the parent could talk about each article that the child puts in the cart. The trip can be recounted, with a little prompting, to other family members at home: "Tell Daddy where we went. Tell him what we bought."

Stories and Nursery Rhymes

Visually handicapped children enjoy all the old nursery rhymes and take great delight in the rhythm of the words. They also love television commercials. The pictures in books will be of interest only to those children who have a good deal of residual vision. Parents may dispense with the books unless they are needed to remember the words and should try to dramatize the story or verse by inventing some actions to go with the nursery rhymes, for example, a big jump in, "Jack *jump* over the candlestick." Children like to hear the same stories over and over without any alteration in the dialogue. A familiar story or nursery rhyme often will encourage a nonverbal child to speak if you stop suddenly before the last word, as in "Jack and Jill went up the . . ." or "The Papa Bear said, 'Who has been sleeping in my . . . ?'" The engrossed child often will fill in the missing word, whereas no amount of coaxing can get him or her to ask for a drink.

Some children will sing when they are too stubborn to talk, and so an ingenious parent can dream up unlimited verses to the tune of "Here We Go Round the Mulberry Bush" (e.g., "This is the way we wash our hands, brush our teeth, pick up the blocks," and so on). Some of the old standard finger plays are thoroughly enjoyed by visually handicapped children, for instance, "Here are the ladies' knives and forks." A child will not be particularly enthusiastic about talking when the learning of speech is fraught with anxiety, but if it is a time for togetherness with the mother or father, a time that they all enjoy, then talking should come very naturally.

After children who are blind are able to speak, they still may have difficulty in finding anything to talk about. Sometimes they happen to find a topic that seems to work well as a conversational opener and use it indiscriminately with all the people they meet. Ian greeted each adult with the question, "Do you have a car?" When the answer was affirmative, he proceeded with a long list of questions: "What kind of car is it? How many doors does it have? Does it have a trunk? A steering wheel? An ignition key? An engine? Two bumpers?" This procedure always impressed the first-time visitor, who immediately became involved in a long conversation about cars. After several visits to the home, the visitor, when met with identical questions, would realize that Ian was only mildly interested in cars; he was much more anxious to have the visitor pay attention to him by talking to him. Unlike a sighted child, Ian could not glance at the visitor's face, clothing, or purse or look around the room and have pertinent questions pop spontaneously into his mind. He could only rely on his old standby that had worked so well in the past.

Children who do not see must get used to the family using words they do not, and really will never, understand. Color is a good example; a child is told the duck is yellow and the tricycle is green. The child will then talk about colors without being aware of what they mean because they do have meaning for the rest of the family. In time, a little girl will be able to tell her pink silk dress from the blue flannel one, not by color but by texture. They feel different, and thus she has worked out her own way of recognizing her pink dress.

Three-year-old Dickie, who had no useful vision, was presented to a staff training session at a children's rehabilitation center by the parent counselor as an example of a competent blind child. One of the staff asserted that blind people could tell colors just by feeling them. When told that this was not so, she turned to Dickie and asked him what color his overalls were. Dickie promptly replied that they were red and everyone was most impressed. Then the counselor spoiled it all by asking Dickie how he knew that his new overalls were red. Quick as a flash, he said, "My mom told me!" In time, Dickie would learn that the overalls with the smooth buckles on the straps were the red ones and that his old brown ones had buttons on their straps. Then his mom would not have to tell him which ones he had on.

Bilingual Homes

Parents sometimes ask if it will harm or confuse a blind child to be taught two languages simultaneously. Results from an observation of a relatively small number of children in bilingual homes where the two parents consistently spoke two different languages to the child, or where the parents spoke their native language to each other and only English to the children right from birth, indicated that there were no problems. In all instances the children learned to understand and speak both languages. Even when very young they surprised everyone by using the appropriate language with each parent.

The children seemed to have no particular problems beyond a slight delay in talking for some. All became fluently bilingual, speaking English correctly even when the parents had very strong accents.

Immigrant Parents

Parents who do not speak English in their homes should be encouraged to take advantage of parent–child centers, meetings for parents of visually impaired children, and day-care centers where English is spoken. They should be encouraged to speak English in the home to the child so that the child will be able to understand and speak with people when he or she moves into preschool. A group of mothers of young children who were visually impaired were able to share in the pride of a young Portuguese mother who excitedly reported one day, "Oh, Mees Smit, my Fernando no fix pee on floor, he now fix pee in pot." That family persisted in speaking English to their totally blind son. By the time Fernando was 6 he spoke English without any accent, while his parents still spoke very fractured English. At 10 he was patiently correcting their grammar but for some reason not their pronunciation, and they were both very proud of him.

WALKING INDOORS

A child who can walk alone needs practice to learn how human beings move around under their own power. It is much quicker to pick the child up and carry him or her off to supper or to bed, but this practice does not encourage the child to walk alone. At first, the child can be encouraged to follow a parental voice guiding him or her along the bookcase, past the couch, through the door, and along the hall wall to the bedroom. Next, the child can hold a parent's hand and learn that one can walk without touching the landmarks. Finally, the child will find his or her own pathway and make the journey alone.

As the child learns to move around, he or she will stop from time to time and seem to be listening very intently while stamping feet or clapping hands, snapping fingers, clicking the tongue, or squeaking. The child is developing a way of using echoes to travel safely and learning a remarkably efficient way to avoid obstacles and become oriented. Very soon the child will be able to avoid walking into walls or large furniture by actually hearing them. Half-open doors with edges too narrow to send back an echo will still be a problem. Family members should keep doors fully open or fully closed.

Five-year-old Donald learned to use his sonar so skillfully that he could walk down a street and call out each time he passed a parked car or a lamppost without missing a single one. If we pay attention we can all hear the difference in the sounds of our footsteps as we walk along the side of a building compared to our footsteps as we walk in a vacant lot. That kind of information is very useful to a blind person but is ignored by those who see. It is not necessary to keep the floor clear for blind toddlers; for some strange reason they seem to enjoy walking across a room strewn with toys. Maybe the obstacles add a little suspense to an otherwise dull trip.

Since there is little incentive for the visually impaired child to walk around on his or her own, the ingenious parent will invent small, easy errands for the child to do. Parents can create requests like "Arturo, will you please put this book on the couch for me" or "Please give Daddy this paper; he is over in his easy chair." As the child becomes more mobile, the errands can become more complicated. Rory liked to help his mother put away the clean laundry. As she sorted and folded each item she would tell him what it was and where to take it. Then he would carefully carry each pair of socks, each T-shirt, each pair of pajamas to his brother's, his sister's, and his parents' bedrooms and carefully place them on the bed. His mother frequently told him what a big help he was and he felt very important.

Those toddlers who have even a tiny bit of residual vision are very leery of steps and may get down on all fours to creep from the edge of a carpet to the bare floor or even to the area where there is a change in the color of the floor tile. Stairways should be protected by gates until the child is obviously aware and old enough to be cautious. A small piece of carpet or rubber mat can be placed at the top and bottom of the stairs as a landmark. Bumping downstairs on the bottom or backing down on all fours seems to work equally well. Climbing up presents no special difficulties, except that the whole trip should be made without stopping. A child who is distracted partway down may forget he or she is on the stairs and step off into space. Otherwise, visually impaired children should learn to use stairs competently and carefully.

WALKING OUTDOORS

Children Who Live in Houses

Learning to walk outdoors can be rather hair-raising at first when one is blind and expects all floors to be made of tile or carpet. The grass is sharp and prickly, the gravel is wobbly and slips under one's feet, the ground is uneven and tips one over, and the sidewalks have edges for falling off. Worst of all, there are no walls for sending back echoes with information. It is not surprising that panic is often the first reaction of a blind or partially sighted child to outdoor travel. Encouragement, reassurance, and a friendly hand will help. If there is an enclosed yard, take the child around to explore and find a few easy landmarks. "Here is your swing. See, it is just beside this big apple tree with the rough bark. Now let's go back to the house and see if we can find your swing again." Later on, a journey all around the fence, past the gate, and back to the door again can lead to future expeditions into strange country. In his or her own good time, the child will move freely and competently all around the yard and go in and out of the house at will. It helps at first to keep the door or window open so the parents can call back and forth to the child periodically so he or she knows they are still there.

Children Who Live in Apartments

The visually impaired child whose family lives in a house will naturally become familiar with the outdoors as soon as he or she is mobile. In the backyard of the family's house the child can experience grass, mud, stones, plants, trees, and concrete and become a part of a familiar environment. But the child who lives in an apartment, particularly in the city, will not have ready access to these outdoor experiences unless the family seeks them out in nearby parks and play areas. The child will be uneasy and less than enthusiastic about the strange feel of grass and sandpiles and may be frightened at the strange sounds of birds chirping or dogs barking. What a terrifying experience! Only if the family can share their environment of nature and the strange smells and sounds of busy streets can the blind or partially sighted child learn to feel safe enough to begin to be curious and want to explore the wide world. A daily visit to the nearest playground can provide the opportunity for the child to make friends with other children, who later may be invited over to play. Both indoors and outdoors the visually handicapped child can learn so much from other children that helping the child to make friends should be one of the parents' primary goals.

Going for walks with a young blind child can be intriguing and challenging for an adult trying to introduce the wider world. Adults will find themselves feeling trees and hedges, hydrants and lampposts; listening to cars, trucks, children's voices, bus doors closing, and even the occasional siren; feeling the warmth of the sun and finding the direction it is coming from; and feeling the wind, rain, and snow. Snow muffles echoes and makes it more difficult for blind people to orient themselves, so the child may become disoriented, but confusion should not deter the child from learning to jump and roll and have fun in the snow.

Finding a small hill to climb and running down it is worth doing. Children with impaired vision seldom run on level ground. Their attempts are usually awkward, with lots of up and down motion but not much forward speed. Probably they would overrun their sonar if they moved more quickly. However, a hill provides the momentum necessary for a good run to the shelter of waiting arms at the bottom. Rolling down hills also can be enjoyable.

A child of $2\frac{1}{2}$ or 3 who is completely blind can walk along beside the parent without holding hands as long as the adult keeps talking. If the child hears the parent's voice he or she will know the parent is there, and the voice will help keep the child walking straight on the sidewalk. A child who is a little older can ride a kiddycar or tricycle along behind a parent by following voice sounds. For those parents who don't have the patience to wait for the child to make numerous stops and detours, a wooden handle can be fixed to the center of the handlebars.

TRIPODDING

Between the ages of 18 and 30 months, some children develop a rather strange-looking habit. If a child has the kind of partial sight that forces him or her to hold an object 2 or 3 inches from the eyes to see it, the child's arms get tired holding things. It just happens that, at this stage of development, the hip joints are equally far from the top of the head and the soles of the feet. The child can, thus, bend over with head on the floor and make a perfect tripod. Resting the fore-arms on the floor, the child can examine a plaything to heart's content in a comfortable and efficient position. Unfortunately, as the child grows older, the legs grow longer proportionately and tripodding becomes impossible.

EATING

Feeding problems are not unusual in blind and partially sighted children, but with a little foresight they can be prevented. Janet, age 2,

Figure 5.1. Tripodding (2 years).

efficiently cleaned up everything on her plate, using her fingers and spoon, chewing pieces of meat and crisp vegetables as well as soft food. Tony, age 4, gagged on every small lump and would eat only strained fruits and puddings spooned in by his mother. Why the difference? Janet was one of twins who were eighth and ninth in a family of 10. She learned very early that if she didn't eat her food quickly another child would do it for her. Tony was 7 years younger than his brother, and his mother devoted her whole day to fussing over him—effectively preventing him from learning that mealtimes are for eating and enjoying. It is natural for the parents of children with disabilities to want them to be at least well nourished, but they should not turn eating into a proving ground.

Keeping in mind that we are all conditioned in our early years to like and dislike certain foods, it might help to examine what kind of conditioning a blind child receives. First of all, the child misses out on watching what the rest of the family is eating and drinking. Sighted toddlers will drain their parents' empty beer bottles in order to taste and share anything that others seem to enjoy. The blind or partially sighted child doesn't see others enjoying food; all he or she hears is his or her mother saying to his or her brother, "Eat your spinach or no dessert," or his or her father saying, "You know I don't like fish, why do you cook it so often?" Scarcely anyone comments verbally on how good food is. The cook may know by the happy faces and the speed with which it disappears, but the child who is blind does not get any of the positive messages about the pleasures of eating unless the family deliberately sends them.

There can be a lot of emotion involved when a parent feeds a child. Giving food is one way of saying, "I love you," and when the child refuses the food the parent may interpret it as rejection and react with hurt feelings or anger. They can get very upset without understanding why their reaction is so strong over the child refusing to eat carrots. Naturally, the child will react to the parents' reaction, and the battle is on. Does it really matter if Travis doesn't want to eat his carrots today? Will it matter 6 months from now?

Parents of a child with a disability can be even more vulnerable than other parents. Some of them think other people may look down on them because they have not produced a perfect child, and they want to make sure that no one thinks that their child is undernourished. They may be inclined to press more food on the child than that child wants or needs. Of course, the children will react to parental anxiety at mealtime, which can become a time of stress for everybody.

Some parents, when faced with a child who won't eat, will try coaxing, sweet-talking, pleading, and bribing. Others will scold, threaten, yell and shout, and get very angry. Children are quick to catch on that it is well worth missing lunch if the parents will put on such a show, especially if they know that soft-hearted parents will give them a nice snack in an hour or so.

The solution, while obvious, is not so easy to carry out. If the parents can stop reacting when the child refuses to eat and act as if it does not bother them at all, that will take all the fun out of it. If they can say, "Oh, you're not hungry; that is too bad. But remember there will be no snacks until supper" and *stick to it*, no child will willingly starve himself or herself.

At a parents' meeting, Mrs. Todd was telling how her 3-year-old daughter, Jean, would only eat bacon and chocolate pudding at each meal. The other mothers were concerned and suggested various solutions, all of which Mrs. Todd rejected as having been tried and failed. Finally, Mrs. D'Angelo (all of 18 years old) asked, "Does Jean like ice cream?" Mrs. Todd replied, "Oh yes, she loves it." With that Mrs. D'Angelo said, "Well, that does it. We all know that no baby takes to ice cream at first. If you were able to convince Jean that ice cream is all that great just because you like it, then you had better start convincing her that you think meat and vegetables are just as great." There was a short, startled silence and then all the mothers began to talk about ways they could start selling their children on the joys of eating.

Figure 5.2. "Is this spoon loaded?" (2½ years)

Some Useful Tips from Other Parents

- Introduce a variety of flavors early. Let the baby have a taste of everything—just a taste so the child will learn that the rest of the family is enjoying food and wants to share it. Food with strong tastes like pickles, pizza, cheese, etc., will intrigue the small child.

- Introduce a variety of texture early—boiled rice in the strained food, a Ukranian sausage to gnaw on, or a stalk of rhubarb.

- French fries, while messy, are great finger foods and have enabled many small blind children to enjoy eating out with their families.

- Present several foods and let the child choose. Never say, "Do you want some nice cereal?" The answer is apt to be no. Instead ask, "Would you like Cheerios or Frosties this morning?" "Do you want apple juice or orange juice to drink?"

- When spoon-feeding use two spoons. If the child grabs one, use the other. It does not make sense to any child to have a hand slapped for wanting to hold the spoon one week and then being expected to hold it the following week.

- A dish with straight sides held steady with one hand keeps the food in one place, making it easier to load the spoon.

- Some children load their spoons by picking up the food with their fingers and putting it on the spoon. That is all right for a while, but they should be taught to "dip, slide, and into the mouth" soon after they understand that food gets from the dish into the mouth with a spoon.

- Soup is easier to eat if it is full of crumbled crackers or bread.

- Food will be touched and smelled until it becomes familiar. It helps to name the food as the child learns to recognize it.

- A parent standing behind a child and gently putting a hand over the child's hand can guide it in the correct movements for dip, slide, and into the mouth while saying the words.

- If a child does not want to eat or dawdles, after a reasonable amount of time the food and the child should be removed from the table and no snack given until the next mealtime. This should be done calmly and without any scolding.

- Crisp foods such as thin potato chips, crackers, and celery that cannot be swallowed whole but are tasty will encourage chewing.

- Any new food will be met with suspicion. Only require the child to eat one bite the first few times until it becomes familiar.

- It takes a little extra convincing before a child who is visually impaired will hold a cold, wet piece of orange or apple because it does not feel nice. It takes several tastings before a child is willing to pick up and eat a piece of fruit.

- Children who are blind or partially sighted dislike getting their fingers dirty or sticky and want them wiped clean as soon as they finish eating.

The tidy parent finds it difficult to tolerate the mess made by little children learning to feed themselves. A huge plastic sheet under the highchair may help, but it is not as efficient as the big labrador dog that regularly waited for every morsel under one blind child's chair. The neatest mother of all waited until spring to let her child (who was deaf and partially sighted) learn to eat on her own. Then she put Yolanda outside, let her go to it, and then turned the hose on, much to the delight of the little girl.

WASHING

A nursery school teacher observed that 4-year-old Eric, who had only light perception, seemed to be at a complete loss when the children were asked to wash their hands. She asked him how he washed his hands and face at home and he replied, "Oh, my dad does it with a washcloth." He did not know that water came out of taps for washing, thinking that you got water out of taps only for drinking.

In learning to wash, the child without useful vision will need to learn how to find the plug, put it in the hole, find the tap, turn on the tap, turn it off, find the soap, rub his or her hands on it (simpler than rubbing the soap on the hands), put the soap back, rinse the hands by wiggling them in the water, pull out the plug, find the towel, dry the hands, and then hang up the towel. Of course, this is too much to expect any small child to learn all at once, and it will take many months before it is mastered completely. As early as possible the children should have a chance to learn about taps and plugs and running water. Bath time is a pleasant time to start learning some of these skills. One word of caution on baths: occasionally a blind child will be afraid of going down the drain with the water, and wise parents will let such a child pull the plug just before or after being lifted out until the child feels more comfortable about the procedure.

A small stool to lift the child up to a comfortable height at the basin makes washing hands easier and tidier.

Cleaning teeth presents no special problems; a good-tasting toothpaste always helps. Some parents like electric toothbrushes for their small children.

The bath provides a great opportunity to find out about liquids, pouring, spilling, and filling various containers. An empty plastic squeeze bottle, the kind used for dishwashing detergents, can be good fun and can help the child learn a number of things.

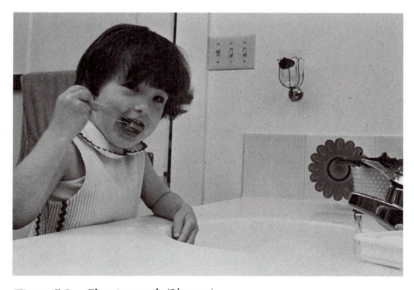

Figure 5.3. Cleaning teeth ($2\frac{1}{2}$ years).

DRESSING

Any parent who has ever tried to get dressed in the dark knows how hard it is to tell whether or not a T-shirt is on inside out and which hole in the slacks to put a foot through. At least sighted people know what the T-shirt and slacks look like and how they are supposed to go on.

It is no wonder that parents sometimes become impatient about how long it takes for their visually handicapped children to dress themselves. The secret is to start early. If the parent says, "Now let's put your right arm in the sleeve, now your left arm in the other sleeve, now we button it up," the infant becomes familiar with the routine, the names of body parts, and the action involved. By 12 months, many children are cooperating well in dressing by offering the appropriate arms or legs or lifting up their bottoms.

Simple clothing that is easy to take off and later put on makes dressing less of a problem. Unfortunately, the dressing and undressing of small children are done at times of the day when parents are

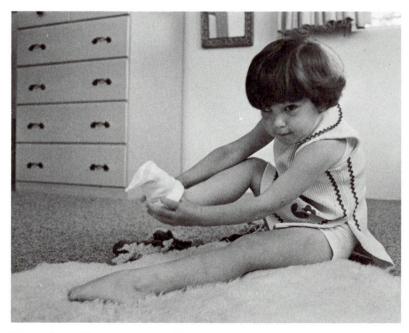

Figure 5.4. "I can dress myself!" ($2\frac{1}{2}$ years)

most apt to be rushed. This makes it difficult for them to be calm and patient. If the parents are not certain whether the child actually needs that much time to dress or whether he or she is deliberately dawdling, they will give up the struggle and dress the child. There is no easy solution to this problem—it all depends on how the parents feel on a particular day. Certainly, they can do it quicker and better, but do they want to dress the child forever? They must think of all the time they are going to save in the future if the child learns now to dress alone.

A play-by-play description of what is happening as the child is dressed or undressed will help the child to learn to do it alone later on. If the child's thumb is tucked under the elastic at the top of the training pants and he or she is told to hang on tight, it is easier to teach the child to pull them up and down. If the child learns to put

Figure 5.5. "Where is the top?" (2½ years)

clothes on a chair when they are taken off, it will be easier to find them in the morning and the child will become independent in dressing. Safety pins or tags should mark the back of a garment so the child can feel them. Socks are very hard to put on, because the heel always seems to end up on the instep. Show the child how to grasp the bulgy heel and pull it around under the foot, or, better yet, use heelless socks.

A child of 3 or 4 can learn to hang up a jacket on a low clothes hook and to find it there before going out. Orderly drawers and closets make it easier for a blind child to find clean clothes. The child can learn where the socks, pants, sweaters, and pajamas go if he or she helps put away the laundry.

TOILET TRAINING

There is no great mystery about what toilet training means to an adult. It consists, very simply, of first convincing a small child that it is more socially acceptable to urinate and defecate in the toilet than in his or her pants and, second, convincing the child to use speech to tell the parents about this need. The difficulties arise when the child in question either is not ready, has not been really sold on the idea, or, as often happens with visually handicapped children, has not the faintest idea what the parents want.

In addition to the standard advice about regular timing, secure seats, and no pressure, which applies to all children, parents of children who are blind have given us some useful suggestions. Placing the small pot in the corner of the bathroom rather than in the center of the floor makes it easier for the child to balance on it. Similarly, it is hard for the child to balance on the big toilet seat at first and he or she will need to be held securely until hanging onto the sides to keep from falling in becomes natural. After all, a child who is blind does not know how deep the toilet is. Having the child accompany each member of the family gets across the idea that everybody does this mysterious thing.

Myrna, a 4-year-old child who is deafblind, had exhausted the patience of her family and the staff at a child development center. When she was admitted to the hospital, the nurses, physiotherapists, and occupational therapists all had a try at toilet training, but Myrna still refused to use the toilet. It became obvious that there was more than stubbornness involved. It was suggested that maybe she did not know what was expected of her and perhaps one of the staff should take her hands and show her what to do. After one demonstration, Myrna, with a big grin, hopped on the toilet. She finally understood what all those people wanted her to do.

Once embarked on toilet training, the child should wear training pants. It does not make sense to the child that it has been permissible to wet a diaper for 2 years but, suddenly, it is no longer okay. It makes more sense to encourage the child to keep the nice new pants dry. When a small visually handicapped boy is taught to lift up the seat by the front and hang onto it, he won't spray all over the bathroom. A small box or stool may be needed to raise him up high enough.

Four-year-old Bobby's mother remarked one day that she was afraid her son would be ready for college before he learned to urinate standing up. She said she had asked her husband's help in teaching Bobby, but, although her husband tried, he was so modest that he could not bring himself to do it. A week later she phoned to say, "Everything is fine; my next-door neighbor showed him what to do."

Some children take longer than others, but there is no appreciable difference in the age at which visually handicapped children as a group are trained. It depends on the individual child and the child's parents. If the parents are relaxed about the business of toilet training, the child will not get trained any faster, but it will be a lot easier on all concerned.

SLEEPING

The sleeping patterns of children who are partially sighted or blind are much the same as those of the other children in the family, but most children with little or no sight require slightly less sleep than their brothers and sisters, probably because they expend less energy in vigorous play. They usually stop taking a morning nap around 12 to 14 months and stop taking an afternoon nap around their third birthday. Stopping any later is a bonus for the family.

If the child is not ready for bed until 10:00 or 11:00 at night, nap time during the day should be shortened or omitted. If the child is not sleepy when put to bed at the appropriate time, quiet play with a toy can be permitted in the bed. This is more apt to happen in the winter if the children cannot go outside to play.

Night prowling can become a real problem as soon as children are able to climb out of their beds. If they wake in the night, children who are blind do not need a light to find their way to the refrigerator, the TV, or the gas stove dials. This habit is easier to prevent than to eliminate. After Maria, an inveterate night prowler, broke a dozen eggs on the kitchen floor in the middle of the night, her father sawed the bedroom door in half and made it into a Dutch door. With a secure lock on the bottom half of the door, Maria was permitted to play quietly in her room when she awoke in the night, and her parents could sleep knowing that she could not get into mischief.

Parents occasionally report that a child is reversing night and day. A common story is that the child sleeps and naps off and on all day and then is full of pep all night, laughing and playing and demanding attention until dawn. Then the child sleeps until noon, while the family has to get up. In such cases, one parent may stay up feeding, rocking, and walking the child so that other members of the family can sleep. Other parents share the night watch, each staying up half the night. The result is the same—a well-rested child and two exhausted parents. Such a reversed sleep pattern can become firmly established if it is allowed to continue. Obviously the best way to control it is to nip it in the bud right from the start. A baby who is warm, dry, and well fed can be left alone to learn that parents will not fuss over him or her any more at night than they will in the daytime.

Most parents find it helpful to read books on how to handle their children's common sleep problems. One of the best is *Solve Your Child's Sleep Problems*, written in 1986 by R. Ferber (available from Simon and Schuster, New York).

While severe chronic sleep problems are rare in most children with visual impairments, they are common in children who have additional disabilities. Since sleep requires neurological control, it is not surprising that disorders of the brain may be associated with severe sleep disturbance. Children with multiple neurological disabilities can experience sleep difficulties that often respond poorly to strict bedtime schedules, various psychological measures, or sedatives. In fact, sedatives may cause agitation or provide the desired effect for only a few days. In many instances physicians cannot offer successful treatment. Some of these children have difficulty falling asleep; others have broken sleep, waking several times in the night, often for prolonged periods and often early in the morning. When they are awake they tend to fuss, cry, play, and demand attention from their exhausted parents, to the point where the sleep disturbance can become a major reason for parental burnout and for the introduction of foster care.

Recent research has shown that treatment with melatonin can help children with delayed sleep onset, fragmented night sleep, and free-running sleep disorders. Melatonin is normally released from the brain when we are ready to fall asleep. It plays an important role in the induction and maintenance of sleep. This substance has been chemically synthesized and can be given by mouth at the desired bedtime. It often induces sleep within 30 minutes. Melatonin appears to be able to stabilize sleep patterns of these children quite quickly. Unfortunately this drug is still under investigation and is not yet available for general use. It is not a sedative, but by working on the human "sleep clock" it controls the sleep patterns. There are no known side effects.

MANNERISMS OR BLINDISMS

Children who are blind or partially sighted frequently engage in what may seem to their parents to be rather strange and disturbing behavior. Self-stimulating activities are almost universally enjoyed by children who are blind and almost universally worried about by their parents, who feel their children look different and peculiar. The developing brain wants input, both visual and motor. If there is not enough meaningful input through normal activity, the child will use repetitive movements like twirling, rocking, or hand shaking to provide such input. This is why an active blind child has fewer mannerisms and the child who is inactive or has mental retardation has more.

"Eyes are buttons to push" was Cory's reply when asked what his eyes were for. Pressing on one or both eyes is the most common of what are known as *mannerisms*. Apparently, pressure on the eyeball results in a pleasurable sensation for the child, who finds it both entertaining and relaxing. When a child presses his or her eyes, electrical currents are produced in the retina. These travel to the occipital cortex (the area of the brain in the back of the head) where the visual information is decoded. Children with atrophy of the optic nerve or

Figure 5.6. The start of eye pressing (13 months).

cortical blindness never press their eyes because the messages are blocked. Interestingly, the children with retinal disorders are the most avid eye pressers.

Eye pressing is different from eye rubbing, which is seen in both sighted and visually impaired children when they are tired or sleepy.

When a visually impaired child is around 12 months of age, his or her parents may notice a lot of eye rubbing, and they naturally assume the child is sleepy or has uncomfortable eyes. By 18 months of age the habit is well established, and each child may practice three or four variations on the theme. The child may put the tip of the thumb up under the bone above the eye and press with a knuckle on the eye itself. A bent forefinger may be used in much the same way, or the child may like to lie on the floor with the head resting either on the back knuckles of both hands or on the closed fists. A child may favor one eye or press both of them. Few blind children have been observed sucking their thumbs, and the few who do are rarely eye pressers. Children press their eyes on the same occasions when others would suck their thumbs, that is, when they are tired, anxious, bored, or in any situation where they need comforting.

While it does not look strange to see a young child apparently rubbing or holding his hands on his eyes, it does look peculiar in an older child and is an extremely difficult habit to break once it has

Figure 5.7.   Well-established eye pressing (7 years).

become established. Many teenagers who are blind still revert to eye pressing when listening to music or when daydreaming. They say they are unaware of doing it, at the same time sheepishly admitting that it feels good. Unfortunately, there are some other negative effects of continued pressure on the eyes. Children who are habitual eye pressers commonly have deeply depressed eyes and considerable discoloration (almost like big black circles) around their eyes, which obviously detract from their appearance. The eyes seem to be literally pressed back into their heads.

Another very common mannerism is rocking, and like eye pressing it can develop unnoticed by parents and without being considered unusual behavior. Almost all babies like to rock back and forth when they first learn to sit up. They find that if they are put on an upholstered couch and rock vigorously against the back of the couch it shoots them forward and is lots of fun. As sighted children find other things to entertain them, they naturally give up rocking and busy themselves in other ways. The child who is visually impaired is much more limited in choosing alternative activities and, hence, tends to use rocking more often for entertainment. At first it is probably a consciously pleasurable activity, much like the pleasure most people get from swinging in a hammock: It feels good and is relaxing. The blind child tends to become hooked on it as a way of spending time when no one suggests a more attractive alternative. Since rocking is pleasurable the visually impaired child should be taught that while it is quite acceptable to rock on a spring horse or rocking chair or swing, banging the back of the couch or chair is not.

Spinning around and around in a circle is another mannerism that is more frequently observed in children who are totally blind than in those who are partially sighted. They report that it "feels nice," and they do not get dizzy and fall down. Four-year-old Susan wore a hole right through the dining room carpet by always spinning in the same place. Her 2-year-old sighted brother, who admired Susan greatly, did his best to learn to spin too but could never understand why he kept falling down and she did not.

Some children with limited partial sight are greatly attracted to bright lights and will spend hours gazing at the sun or fluorescent lights. Some become so hypnotized by the light that it is almost impossible to attract their attention without removing them from the light source. About half the light gazers will also play with shadows by waving their fingers in front of their eyes against the light.

There are a number of less common mannerisms, such as head turning or arm or hand flapping, and an individual child may engage in only one such repetitive activity or in several. Some repetitive behaviors should be separated from mannerisms. Occasionally visually impaired children with nystagmus will exhibit rapid horizontal and pendular head shaking during intense looking. This appears to be a compensatory mechanism to improve visual acuity, although the improvement is marginal. Studies have shown that head shaking counteracts the nystagmus, making the image more stable on the retina.

Visually handicapped children also may exhibit eye poking, which is different from eye pressing. Poking is diagnosed when children exert intense pressure with their fingertips on the side of one or both eyeballs. When this is done it can cause self-directed pain and eventual damage to the eye. Eye poking is seen mainly in severely multi-disabled children who are visually impaired. The majority of these children also exhibit hand biting, scratching, head hitting, face slapping, hair pulling, pinching, and other self-injurious behavior. Frus-

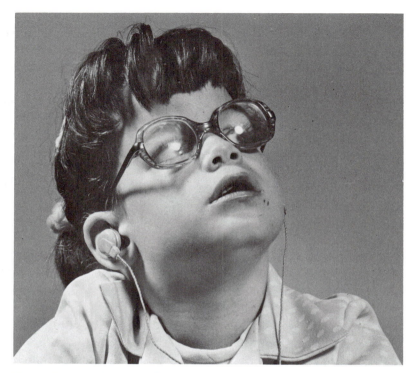

Figure 5.8. Light gazing (5 years).

tration, anxiety, fatigue, overstimulation, an unfamiliar environment, or a change in routine appear to be common triggering factors.

Other repetitive behaviors that are not related to blindness may occasionally occur in some visually impaired children who have unrelated disorders such as Tourette's Syndrome, a chronic tic disorder. The tics can take the form of eye blinking, grimaces, coughing, hissing, explosive utterances, and jerking different parts of the body. There are effective medications for this condition. Another example is a blind child who is also autistic; his or her mannerisms might take the form of rocking, spinning, preoccupation with shiny objects, etc.

There is a natural desire in most children to conform, and enrollment in a nursery school or preschool can provide a good incentive for a visually impaired child to give up mannerisms. There the child will find a greater choice of alternative pleasing activities and will also be motivated by the desire to do things just like the rest of the class if he or she is made aware of how and what the other children are doing.

Naturally, it is embarrassing for parents when their visually impaired children engage in behavior that sets them apart and makes them look strange. The usual pattern is for the parents unwittingly to let the habit develop for a few years and then start to nag about it. The more they nag the more their children press their eyes or rock, perhaps because the nagging makes them anxious and sad and they need to comfort themselves. As usual, hindsight is better than foresight, and most parents wish they had known enough to prevent the unpleasant mannerisms from developing when the child was very young.

Parents who were alerted early have been most successful in minimizing the mannerisms by ensuring that their children were distracted and offered more interesting replacement activities. Then they did not need to fall back on their own bodies for entertainment and comfort. Some parents actually encouraged their blind children to learn to suck their thumbs or a pacifier so they would leave their eyes alone. A few parents believed that their children were actually experiencing pain in their eyes and that the pressing made them feel better. This is seldom so. If there is any indication of discomfort it is a much better plan to have the ophthalmologist examine the eyes, thereby relieving the parents' anxiety on this score, rather than to permit children to develop the habit of eye pressing. When children have already been pressing their eyes for a few years, it will be a difficult battle to overcome the habit. Somehow the parents will have to convince these children that they want to have handsome faces, that they do not want to look silly and have the kids laugh at them at school, and that the parents will be very proud when they let go of such a babyish habit. Since the children are usually unaware that they are putting their hands to their eyes, the parents will have to find a way of alerting them without seeming to nag. Some children like to have a secret code with their parents, instead of being told to take their hands down. A child might like to invent a code word and may come up with anything from "peanuts" to "Flintstones" to serve as a reminder.

Before becoming too upset about their children's mannerisms, parents should pause and take a close look at themselves to see if they have any interesting little habits of their own that serve the same purpose as eye pressing or rocking. Nail biting, hair twirling, and key clicking all fall into this category but, because they are not associated with blindness, are less cause for anxiety.

SEX EDUCATION

Masturbation

Those parents who have children older than their visually hand-icapped child will realize that masturbation is a normal part of the growing up process and will not be overly concerned about it. When the first child is blind or partially sighted, however, parents tend to worry more about everything, including masturbation. If the child is left on his or her own a great deal, there will be more self-stimulating activity than there would be if the child were out playing with the other children or were helping around the house. Young children who are blind probably do not masturbate any more than other children; their problem is that they do not usually know when they are being observed by parents they cannot see. The wise parent is continuously teaching the child what kinds of behavior are appropriate and inap-propriate in public and what kinds should be considered private and confidential.

Sex Information

To some parents any discussion of sex education for preschoolers may seem premature, but the visually impaired child may be totally un-aware of the sex differences that are readily apparent to the sighted child. Mrs. Pine, the foster mother of a totally blind 5-year-old girl and mother of a 20-year-old blind girl, commented that when her daughter Sarah was in nursery school she could tell the boys from the girls by feeling the backs of the children's heads. If the hair was short and bristly it was a boy, if longish and soft it was a girl. Hair styles have changed and her foster child Marie found that this system no longer worked. In a group where the children seemed to have rather exotic names and all wore jeans or slacks she did not have any clues to tell her which was which unless she asked the child. It is doubtful that Marie even was aware that boys and girls were made differently, since her foster family is most conservative and not one to encourage ques-tions about sex, including gender differences.

If there are both boys and girls in a family it is much easier for a child with impaired vision to learn about sexual differences through natural curiosity, for example, by sharing a bath with the other children, if the parents understand that the only way the child can learn is by hearing and touch. If there are no brothers and sisters, perhaps young visiting relatives or neighbors might be available if the problem was explained to their parents.

Before the family cat has kittens or the dog has puppies, the young blind child can feel the swollen abdomen and, later, the babies. A pregnant relative might be happy to let the child feel the baby both before and after birth. Sighted children will ask questions about "a big tummy," but the blind child is unaware of such obvious physical changes unless someone shows him or her and explains what is happening.

It is advisable to provide a preschool child who is blind with opportunities to learn that boys and girls are made differently and to learn where babies come from. If the parents do not do this, it will become more difficult as the child grows older because of our taboos about touching and the natural reticence that primary school children have about their bodies. It is important that the child have such information, which is readily available to sighted children, in order to understand what the other children are discussing.

Chapter 6

Living with a Visually Handicapped Child

◆ ◆ ◆ ◆ ◆ ◆

What every visually handicapped child needs most is a set of parents who are intelligent, emotionally mature, socially competent, financially secure, and just crazy about small children. A child whose parents do not fit this description, however, has lots of company. It is hard for anyone to be a parent these days, with so many experts on child care sounding off in magazines, on television and radio programs, each one giving conflicting advice. Values in our society are changing and the old ways are being questioned. It is vital for the well-being of a child for the parents to agree about what their goals for the child are and what method they are going to use to help achieve those goals.

WHAT KIND OF PARENT ARE YOU?

In any discussion about children with disabilities the focus tends to be on the needs of the child, completely overlooking the fact that parents have needs too. Professionals, such as doctors, nurses, physiotherapists, and social workers, sometimes forget that parents are just ordinary human beings with their fair share of strengths and frailties. Just because they have a child who is disabled does not mean they are suddenly endowed with superhuman emotional and physical strength plus the knowledge necessary to raise a visually impaired child with endless patience in a perfect marriage.

During the first 3 years of any child's life, parents and child are learning to live together on a trial-and-error basis. There will probably be more trials and more errors when the child has a disability, but

Figure 6.1. "Fathers are important!" (13 months)

children are tough and parents do learn remarkably fast. There is no absolutely guaranteed right way to bring up a visually impaired child. Whatever methods are comfortable for the parents will be okay for the child. Parents should relax and do the best they can. Nobody could ask them for more than that. Certainly, very real problems cannot be ignored, but the great majority can be resolved with cooperation and a little ingenuity.

WHO CARRIES THE LOAD?

In many young families the mother is expected to function as the emotional mainstay of the family, whether or not she feels able to assume that role. The father may be away at work and she may be responsible for meeting the physical and emotional needs of the children all day, every day. Anyone who has lived with little children knows how exhausting they can be. A father in such a household may come home after a tough day at work and expect a clean house, a good meal, well-behaved children, and an attentive wife. If the stars are

Figure 6.2. Setting the table (2½ years).

favorable, she may just manage to cope with it all, but the emotional price it costs her can be high. Even though many mothers now are working outside the home, in too many families they are still expected to carry the major share of caring for the children and the home. Fortunately, more and more young fathers are realizing that, for the survival of the family, they must share the day-to-day responsibilities involved in the care of young children. They also are finding that by being involved in caring for a child they build a loving, close relationship with that child, which can be very rewarding. Bringing up a handicapped child is too heavy a responsibility for one parent, but two parents working together can share not only the worry and work, but the delight and satisfaction as they see their child grow and flourish.

Figure 6.3. "Let's go, Dad!" (5 years)

After surviving 6 years of caring for a child who was hyperactive, retarded, and blind, with their marriage and themselves remarkably intact, Mr. and Mrs. McKenna were asked how they had managed it. Mrs. McKenna thought for a while and then replied, "Well, Phil helped a lot, and I guess the best thing was we never both felt discouraged on the same day."

WHAT ABOUT THE MARRIAGE?

The very presence of a child with disabilities has an effect on any marriage. If the marriage is a shaky one, the extra work and worry involved in caring for the child will make the situation even more stressful.

Surprising as it may be, in a recent study there were no more marriage breakdowns in 100 families of visually handicapped children than there were in the general population. A number of parents have commented that they believe their mutual concern and involvement in raising a blind child had strengthened their marriages. Together, they had been able to grow and mature and to cope with situations that they never could have managed single-handed. They also discovered how important it is to have someone close for mutual support and comfort on down days and to share the rewards on the good days.

One of the best things parents can do for any child with disabilities is to work at keeping their marriage in good shape. Sometimes there does not seem to be enough time for parents even to talk to each other. They should try to get away together from the children periodically and to treat themselves to something they really enjoy. It is not good enough for the mother to go out one evening alone while the father babysits and the father to go out the next. They can go out together or send the children to their grandparents and stay home.

It is essential for the caregivers of children who are visually impaired to have time for themselves. Time alone will give them the opportunity to recharge emotionally and will help keep them from feeling overwhelmed by the responsibilities of raising a visually handicapped child.

CHILDREN NEED TO GET AWAY TOO

Some parents are too reluctant to leave their children who have disabilities with other people. Mr. and Mrs. Renton felt it was wrong to leave Dianne with a baby-sitter. She was never once apart from at least one parent until she was 6 years old. She slept with her parents and would not go to sleep unless she clutched them both by the hair. Things were further complicated by the fact that Mr. Renton was a shift worker and all three had to change their daily routine when his shift changed. Dianne left home to attend a boarding school for blind children when she was 6. The separation was very hard on her and, despite the fact that she went home weekends, she took a long time to settle down at school.

Parents who are able to leave their very young children alone for short periods find that the children soon learn that, while parents do go off, they also come back. They get used to being separated for short periods. The older they are when parents leave them the first time, the more upset they will be, so parents should begin leaving them alone early. Otherwise, they will create such scenes that the parents will feel too guilty to enjoy themselves. If children reach the stage at which their scenes are so heartbreaking that their parents think going out is not worth it, the parents must realize this behavior will never get better. They must start now!

BABY-SITTERS

Lucky are those parents who have handy grandparents or other relatives able and willing to baby-sit. It is usually easier to trust children to their own grandparents than to a stranger. The best way, however, to get a reliable sitter is through a friend—someone who is known to be reliable and responsible. Sitters are not usually apprehensive about caring for a blind baby, because babies are all more or less alike. To change them, feed them, burp them requires no special skill, whether or not the child can see. Most new sitters, however, are scared to death at the thought of caring for a toddler or an older child who is blind or visually impaired. The solution here is for parents to get sitters when the baby is small and train them as the child grows up.

Good sitters, however, do retire, move away, and get other jobs. If parents cannot find a sitter through friends and relatives, they could try calling the counselor at a local secondary school or the instructor in child care or a family life course or at a nearby school of nursing or preschool education. They should ask the instructor to recommend a reliable student. It is good practice for the students for their careers, and the parents know they are getting someone who is interested in children.

Caregivers can often work out reciprocal baby-sitting with other caregivers ("I look after your children at my house on Tuesdays, and you take mine on Thursdays"). It costs nothing, and the parents may discover that their child is a perfect angel compared to the other child.

SIBLINGS

The reaction of brothers and sisters to a blind child in the family is closely related to the attitudes of the parents toward the child. In the Mitchell family, the two other girls completely ignored the presence of Melanie and she grew up a solitary, lonely girl, with few friends. Mrs. Mitchell, who spent a lot of time with Melanie, made no bones about the fact that she did not want the older girls to be "burdened by looking after Melanie," but later she was resentful that Melanie had no friends. On the other hand, Khalid was right in the middle of four very active brothers and sisters. It never occurred to any of them that Khalid would not climb trees, walk fences, and ride a two-wheeler when the others did, because his parents expected him to do whatever the other children did. From the time he could walk, he had to put away his toys, take his dirty dishes to the sink, and hang up his clothes, just like everybody else in the family. The other children had their share of love and attention so that, on occasion, when Khalid's lack of sight made it necessary for his parents to give him a little extra time, his siblings took it in stride. A brother or sister should be expected to play with their sibling sometimes but also should be free to play with other friends of their own age.

Older brothers and sisters can do a tremendous job of teaching the visually handicapped how to do all kinds of things much more easily than their parents can. Eating is a prime example. Parents

Figure 6.4. Sisters are for helping (7 and 3 years).

always worry about having a well-nourished child, so eating becomes a very serious business to them and to their child. The child tends to react to this anxiety and may not be too excited about eating. A 4-year-old girl wanting to share her potato chips with her blind brother, however, is so convinced he will enjoy them that she has him not only eating in no time but also liking it.

Mrs. Bolan was a conscientious mother who was concerned that 3-year-old Marie consistently refused to try to eat anything on her own. When the counselor suggested to 5-year-old Jason that he share his apple with Marie, he shoved it vigorously into her mouth a couple of times. Marie didn't much care for this so she grabbed the apple from him and ate it, core, seeds, and stem included. The next day Jason and Marie shared a bowl of dry cereal on the back step. It was obvious that Marie had been perfectly capable of feeding herself for some time. Mrs. Bolan gave big brother Jason full credit for the achievement and he was very proud of himself.

Small children quickly discover how to cope with a blind child some time before they truly understand about lack of sight. When 3-year-old Kyle, totally blind, was playing on the floor with his toys around him, little brother Allen, age 11 months, would creep over, grab a toy, and scuttle away to safety without making a sound. Kyle could never figure out where his toys went.

It is not fair to make the sighted brothers and sisters always give up a disputed toy to the child who is disabled. Of course, there will be the usual scraps and disagreements, but the visually impaired child must learn to share and to stand up for himself or herself. The child with little or no vision seldom slaps or kicks other children because the child cannot see to aim, but he or she often becomes adept at defense by pushing and pinching.

As brothers and sisters grow older it is to be expected that there will be times when they are embarrassed about having a child who is different in the family. They will more than likely feel a great need to conform, not to be different from their friends, and having a blind brother or sister is certainly different. It can be a difficult time for everyone as parents find it hard to understand why a formerly loving brother or sister suddenly seems to turn against the blind child. Parents should take a good look to see if they are taking unfair advantage of the brothers and sisters, using them as unpaid baby-sitters or insisting that they always have the blind child tagging along when they go out with friends. Brothers and sisters should be expected to play with the blind child some of the time, but they should also have the freedom to spend time with their friends without their sibling.

Figure 6.5. Roughhousing (5 years).

Parents should talk freely with the child who is ashamed to invite friends over and should acknowledge that it is natural to be uncomfortable and embarrassed by a sibling's blindness. Helping the sighted child figure out ways of coping with the situation is less painful for everyone than making him or her feel guilty and wicked. Remember that just as no parent would deliberately choose to have a child with a disability, no child would choose to have a brother or sister who is disabled. Most adults eventually reach the conclusion that if they cannot change the situation, they might as well learn to live with it, and so do children. But they do not have to like it all the time.

GRANDPARENTS

Grandparents can be a mixed blessing. A blind grandchild brings out the best and the worst in them. They can be a tremendous support and comfort to a young couple if they have a positive attitude toward the blind child. If, however, they believe that blindness is something shameful or that a child who is blind should not be disciplined like other children, they can be a real headache. Understanding grandparents should be welcomed and encouraged to enjoy their blind grandchild. With less understanding grandparents, parents have three choices: (a) avoiding them, which is sometimes impossible; (b) putting up with their hurtful remarks; or (c) sitting down and having a frank talk about how they should act toward the disabled child if they wish to maintain diplomatic relations with the family. This last one is hard to do, but it can work wonders.

It takes a little time for most grandparents to get used to the idea that their grandchild cannot see normally, but once they have done so they can be an important resource. Parents might as well face the fact that grandparents are going to be a little more tenderhearted and indulgent than they are. After all, isn't that what grandparents are for? They will most likely tend to do things for the child that parents insist the child struggle to do alone. They may also let the child get away with behavior that would not be tolerated at home. If the grandparents are unwilling or unable to change after they have received an explanation, the parents may have to give in gracefully and let grandparents and child enjoy each other, while the parents enjoy time off.

The child should know, however, that at home rules are meant to be obeyed and that whining won't change them.

Young Mrs. Holt said very bitterly one day, "It is not that I don't love my mother, but I wish she would not visit so often. I get so confused. Here I am struggling to learn how to be a good mother to my blind baby, and without even knowing it my mother treats me as if I were still her little girl who doesn't know anything. How can I be a daughter and a mother at the same time?" It was pointed out that Mrs. Holt had said her mother was not aware that she was undermining her daughter's self-confidence; Mrs. Holt was asked to try to tell her mother how she felt. When she did so her mother looked shocked and then commented, "You are right. I can see that I am doing exactly what your father's mother used to do to me when you were a baby. I remember how I felt. Thank you for being frank with me. I was never brave enough to tell your grandmother."

IS IT NORMAL TO FEEL THIS WAY?

New parents can be frightened and confused when they discover that, although they love their child very dearly, there are times when they may hate the child and bitterly resent his or her presence. In time they realize that it is perfectly normal to experience these ambivalent feelings toward their child. The closer we are to someone the stronger these feelings can be. Young parents are often shocked at the intensity of their negative feelings and completely overlook the fact that their positive feelings are equally strong. When the child is disabled in any way, this love/hate conflict is intensified, or rather the parents' reaction to their own feelings is intensified. They believe that it is not quite right to be angry at a child who is blind. Each parent may feel differently about this ambivalence and may magnify the other parent's reactions.

Parents may feel wicked when they are only reacting normally. Sometimes, after a particularly bad day, parents may feel like dropping their miserable child down the nearest manhole. Mrs. McKee, the mother of an active daughter who is deaf and blind, very earnestly told a group of parents, "The most important thing I have learned in 6 years of living with Tammy is that you don't have to like your child all the time, but that does not mean you don't love her."

Parents who feel very sorry for their blind children will not want to make them do anything that will make them unhappy. Such parents tend to feel that it must be so awful to be blind that they should "make it up" to the child by making him or her happy. Mrs. Tarbet could not bear to put baby Susan on her stomach on the floor because she always cried. So Susan sat contentedly in her baby seat until she was 18 months old and her grandmother came to visit. The grandmother was appalled at the child's inability to sit or crawl or walk but more so at how skillfully she controlled her mother by her heartbroken sobbing at the slightest provocation. She announced that no granddaughter of hers was going to grow up to be a whining parasite. Susan and her mother both cried quite a bit in the next few weeks, but Susan learned to crawl, walk, and hand-feed herself under the grandmother's firm and no-nonsense approach. She constantly repeated to her daughter the old saying, "You have to be cruel to be kind." Susan's mother learned to overlook Susan's tearful response to any new demands, and, when Susan found that technique no longer worked, she gave it up.

It is normal for parents to want to shield their children from hurtful experiences, but to shield children continually from failure does not help them. They need to learn from experience by trying and failing and trying again until they master the situation. Then they will feel good about themselves. It is hard not to jump up and do it for them instead of waiting and watching them struggle to do it the hard way. Parents who do everything for their blind children take away their incentive to be independent. A pattern of interaction develops that can easily become a habit and can go on unchanged for the next 20 years. If the habit is too strong to change, parents may need the intervention of a third party, like Susan's grandmother, to blast the child out of the rut. Children are remarkably philosophical about changes like this. They fight like mad to maintain the status quo, but if the parents remain adamant the children usually accept the new routine. It is almost as if they feel, "Oh well, you win some and lose some, and we gave it a good try."

There comes a day when you have had enough, as did Mrs. Cross. When her son Jeff was 3 years old she angrily asked, "How long do I have to keep feeding this kid?" The counselor's reply was, "Until you decide to stop." Mrs. Cross decided to stop the following day. She was advised to present the food to Jeff but to busy herself elsewhere—no pleading or coaxing Jeff to eat. Frantic, she telephoned 2 days later and said, "What will I do? He hasn't eaten a bite of solid food, and I have only given him water to drink like you said. I know he will starve to death if I don't feed him!" She was persuaded to hold out for one more day. Sure enough, Mrs. Cross was on the phone the next morning, saying, "Guess what? Jeff ate a whole bowl of cereal and two pieces of toast all by himself. I will never have to feed him again." To prove her point she brought Jeff in for a visit the following week. He sat up at the table and ate a big bowl of chicken noodle soup quickly and neatly.

If parents are too anxious about a visually impaired child's performance the child will react to their anxiety by refusing to learn. Four-year-old Jane was the only child of professional parents. They were a serious, reserved couple who would have had difficulty communicating with any child. Jane's lack of sight was a terrible blow to them, and they determined that if they had to have a blind child, they would have the most brilliant blind child in the country. They played only classical music to her and talked to her like a miniature adult, planning that she would become a musician or a professor. They sent her off to nursery school at $2\frac{1}{2}$. They did not know how to have fun with her, how to help her become a noisy, happy little girl. They spent hours earnestly trying to teach her to talk, but Jane steadfastly refused to utter a word. The more she refused, the harder they tried to teach her. She sat there with a little smile, thoroughly enjoying the attention and their obvious concern. It was almost as if she realized that by not talking she could keep them close to her.

HOW MUCH PRESSURE?

Parents who feel comfortable and confident in knowing just what to expect of a sighted child and when to make appropriate demands may tend to feel uncertain and frustrated when dealing with their visually impaired child. They tend to react emotionally and hesitate to make use of their good common sense and experience. They wait hopefully and patiently for the child to initiate an activity. The months go by and nothing happens. Blind children will seldom let their parents know when they are ready to learn something. Parents have to let them know when it is time to learn a skill and keep sending the message until it is learned. In the early years parents must push and push and push and then push some more to keep the child moving.

Later they can sit on the sidelines and beam with pride. The more they teach the child to function independently in the first 3 or 4 years, the less they will have to do for the child later.

Whether or not to bear down and insist firmly that a child learn a specific skill now or postpone the learning until a later date is the kind of decision that parents of visually impaired children will face daily. When they are calm and relaxed and being very intellectual about it they consider factors like age, stage, readiness, and the time available and make the decision rationally. Parents, however, seldom make decisions this way; who does? A good guideline might be this. If they think the child is ready and they are ready, and if the child's future development depends on learning that basic skill now, then they should get busy on it without any more delay. By basic skills we mean things like sitting, standing, walking, talking, self-feeding, and toilet training. The two areas where parents find it hardest to promote independence are feeding and talking.

It is easy to be critical of parents who feed children until they are four or five, but most people do not realize how hard it is for a mother or father to stop this. This is particularly so if a blind child is the last child. A parent feels good when he or she is needed, so it is easy to be too kind and overindulge a child out of love. It takes even more love to set the child free. Take as your text for the day, "Give him love, limits, and let him grow."

Parents have to be strong minded about insisting that their visually impaired child learn basic skills at the appropriate time, and once they start they must keep on teaching and encouraging the child until he or she masters them. But what about the hundreds of little skills of daily living that the child will have to learn as he or she grows up? This is where the parents can allow a little more leeway.

If after hours of best efforts a child still has not learned to tie shoelaces, the parents may sit back and think a bit. Getting angry at the child for what may seem to be stupidity or pure stubbornness won't help in learning, and parents getting angry at themselves for not being able to teach the child won't do any good either. Is it honestly that important for the child to learn that particular skill today? Will it really matter 10 years from now whether he or she could tie shoelaces at age 5, or not until 6 or even 8? Will his or her life be blighted? If the parents decide to wait a while before teaching it again, it is quite possible they may be able to devise an easier method of doing it.

One mother came up with an easier technique for tying shoelaces. First tie a single knot. Then fold each end in half and tie another single knot with the double strands. Simple, isn't it? Try it with a bathrobe cord or soft rope before moving on to the shoes. If tying shoelaces means still another defeat, then forget about them for a year or so and buy shoes with buckles, elastic inserts, or velcro fastenings. It's a lot easier on everybody.

DISCIPLINE

Mr. Hill looked down at the small blind baby in his arms and told the counselor, "I think I will do okay with this child in everything except discipline, and I am afraid I will find that hard. I can't imagine anyone ever being able to scold or spank a little child who can't see. How could anyone be so cruel?" Three years later that same Mr. Hill was indignantly telling how, despite several warnings, his busy little son had pulled up every last tulip in the garden just before they were to bloom, and how he had applied the hairbrush where it would do the most good. He grinned and said, "Yes, I remember when I swore I would never lay a hand on him, but I can't let him grow up to be a spoiled brat. Anyway, it is different now; I think there are other things more important than the fact that he can't see."

In most families there is a continuing power struggle between a child and the parents. The child wants to have everything his or her way, and parents want the child to learn to be a little bit civilized. Children are adept at finding a parent's most vulnerable point and taking full advantage of it. After all, what could be more exciting to a small child than to get the grown-ups all upset? *To get attention* is the key phrase, and that should suggest the solution: *don't react.*

It isn't any fun for a child to dawdle if nobody pleads with him or her to hurry or finally gets exasperated and dresses the child. Would the world stop turning if the child did miss the preschool bus because of dawdling? How else is the child going to learn that dawdling makes him or her miss the bus, instead of learning that dawdling makes someone else dress him or her? Children need to be forced to take the consequences of their actions. That is the way they will learn to accept responsibility.

Brian's mother looked out the window and saw him busily throwing mud into the swimming pool. She called to him, "Brian, you come right over here. I am going to spank you." Brian walked over to her and with his most winning smile said, "You wouldn't hit a poor little blind boy, would you?" Despite her amusement Mrs. Lunn managed to reply, "You bet I would if he did what you just did." She was surprised that a child that young had already learned he could use his blindness as a lever to get his way with adults, but she was determined that his strategy wasn't going to work with her. An important message to get across to children who have a disability is that they are not entitled to special privileges or special treatment simply because they do not see. We hope they will grow up with the feeling that they are entitled to fair and equal treatment, nothing more.

Misunderstanding

There is one factor that may cause children to appear to be disobedient when they do not intend to be. That is when they have not really understood what their parents want them to do, or not to do. It is easy for parents to forget that since the children cannot see what they are showing them, or pointing to, instructions may not be clear. Parents should take a little extra time to make sure they get their message across to their children loud and clear. "Please put your toys away in the toy box before you listen to 'Sesame Street,' and I mean pick up *every single thing* on this rug and put them over here in this box." If the toys are not put away, the parents should not buy themselves half an hour of peace with "Sesame Street."

Choice

Children usually will react more positively to a choice of activities than they will to an ultimatum. Ultimatums usually end in threats, which put parents in a bad spot if they do not want to carry out their threat. Mrs. Baeza, the mother of four noisy children, used a positive approach. She grew very tired of the children complaining that they did not like what she served for meals, so she tried a novel plan. Every day she had four fillings for the sandwiches, peanut butter and jelly, bologna, hard-boiled eggs, and cheese, all ready when the children came in for lunch. Each child chose the kind of sandwich he or she wanted that day and happily ate it without a word of complaint, whereas if she had served only one kind each day at least three of the children would have whined and complained. Her plan worked so well that she extended it to breakfast by offering a choice of juice and several kinds of cereal instead of rotating them. She said it didn't cost any more and it really paid off in happier mealtimes. The children agreed that having their choice at two out of three meals made up for having to eat what was on their plates for dinner, and the Baeza family was able to avoid the continuous confrontations that so often become a mealtime routine in many families.

Parents should listen to how they ask their children to do something. Do they command them? Do they nag over and over again? Do they say things like "How many times do I have to tell you?" Parents are often very rude to their children, speaking to them in words and tones they would never think of using to a stranger or to a friend. The children who cannot see facial expressions do not get full benefit of the angry faces that often accompany the peremptory voices, but they can and do receive negative messages, and sometimes they do not know why their parents seem so angry.

Courtesy

Parents should try a little common courtesy, asking instead of telling. Of course, along with the courteous request goes the message that they expect the children to do as they ask. They should give a word of thanks if the task is well done. (Most of the time the only word given is one of complaint when the task is not well done.) From their parents' behavior children learn to be kind and courteous. When grown-ups happen to overhear young children playing house it can be a terrible shock to hear the words and tones used by the pretend mother and pretend father to the pretend children. Courtesy helps children maintain their self-respect, and that should be one of the parents' goals.

Limits

Children need a clear definition of what kinds of behavior are acceptable and what kinds are not acceptable. Until parents have made this very clear the poor little kid is playing Russian roulette every time he or she tries something new. If children should not throw food at the table, make it very clear that they can never do it—not just at Sunday breakfast but also at every meal 7 days a week.

Children are very literal, but they also are hopeless optimists, so they will test to see if their parents really meant what they said. Consistency is important or the testing will never cease. If parents weakened on Tuesday, how can the child be sure they won't weaken again on Friday?

Parents are never going to be able to think of all the eventualities that can occur with young children. Mrs. Tompkins carefully put the detergent package on the sink counter and went out to hang some clothes on the line, pausing to chat with a neighbor for a few minutes. When she came in she found the tap running full tilt and mountains of foam cascading out of the sink into a huge drift about 3 feet deep on the floor. She could see the top of a kitchen chair protruding from the foam in front of the sink, and from somewhere near it 3-year-old Bobby piped up, "Gee, Mom, am I having fun doing a washing for you." After that, doing a washing when mother wasn't there was off-limits for Bobby.

Time

Parents can save themselves a good deal of wear and tear if they allow plenty of time for themselves and their children. Hurrying leads to frayed tempers in both children and parents. It takes longer to do some things without good sight, and parents must take this fact into account when organizing the family activities in which they expect their visually impaired child to participate.

Parents should get used to the idea that their children are going to make them angry. They should be able to express their anger, but in such a way that their children do not feel under attack. Children should know their parents are angry at their behavior, not at them. If parents clarify what behavior is acceptable, and where and when, the children will have a better understanding of how they are expected to behave.

Children may often have a good reason to be angry at their parents, too. Parents should help children find acceptable ways of expressing anger, keeping in mind that they have to learn how to do so gradually.

Teaching children to accept responsibility for chores like putting away toys, hanging up clothes, etc., is an endless battle; it taxes patience and takes time, but it's the only way they can learn. Nagging is unproductive since children simply tune it out. A little surprise praise when they do put their toys away, for example, is much more productive.

CONFORMITY—YES OR NO?

The great dilemma facing parents of children with little or no useful vision is to what extent they should insist that their children learn to function in the same way as sighted people do when it is perfectly obvious that the blind child's own method is more efficient for him or her. Parents generally do not approve of children putting their fingers into a cup to play with the milk, yet when a 4-year-old child who is blind puts his or her finger into the glass to check how much milk is left they are apt to smile at the child's ingenuity. Let a 10-year-old blind child do the same thing in a restaurant and people at the neighboring tables are apt to shake their heads in disgust at such behavior. Children with sight are quick to imitate the behavior of people around them, and, with consistent encouragement, they become reasonably well socialized. Children who do not see enough to know what other people are doing and how they are doing it have no motivation to conform. They may continue to function on an infantile level or in their own strange way indefinitely unless parents intercede and insist on more socially acceptable behavior.

Many older children and adolescents who are blind continually stress how important it is to them to be able to do things in the same way as their sighted friends. Their desire to conform with the sighted world becomes much stronger as they grow older and venture further away from home. Lack of good sight is not an excuse for poor table manners in an adult who is blind, but parents tend to forget that their adorable 3-year-old will grow up. It does not seem very important if a blind child continually puts his or her fingers in the food on the plate or touches all the cookies to find the biggest one when he or she is little. How will the child learn the right way if the parents don't teach him or her?

Turning his or her face toward the person or persons he or she is talking to makes little sense to a small blind child, but it is important for social interaction as the child grows older.

Touching is almost taboo in our culture, and the question of when a child who is blind should be allowed to touch is a hard one. If the child cannot touch, how is he or she going to find out about the world? Yet touching at the wrong time and place can get the child in trouble. Mr. Park and his young son Barry were on an escalator when Barry put out his hand at random and felt the fur coat of the woman ahead of him. He stroked it and said, "Oh Dad, feel this lovely soft fur. It's just like Muffy" (their cat). To this the very angry woman growled, "Tell your child to get his filthy hands off my mink coat." Mr. Park felt very angry and retorted, "He did not hurt your coat. He is blind." He felt better and the woman shrank down into the mink coat and walked away, obviously embarrassed. In retelling the incident, Mr. Park was ashamed that he had snarled at the woman who, of course, had no idea that Barry was blind. Mr. Park realized that he was going to have to grow a tough skin so he would not be so easily hurt by thoughtless remarks or questions about Barry. This is painful for parents who tend to be sensitive about their child's eyes, but the wise parent will attempt to be very matter-of-fact in dealing with explanations about their child's blindness. The young child is not at all self-conscious about blindness, and the goal is to keep him or her that way.

Parents should try to take their child into a store or supermarket at a time when it is not busy and when they are not in a hurry; then parents and child can have a great morning checking over all the fruits and vegetables, the soaps, the coffees, and other merchandise that can be identified by touch and smell. At a slack time the cashiers are usually willing to permit a child to be lifted up onto the checkout counter to find out what the cash register is like and what is making all those intriguing noises. It can be very boring for any children to go shopping with their parents and is no less so for children who are visually impaired. The only advantage is that they do not see all the toys and candies on display and, consequently, don't whine as much for treats as their sighted brothers and sisters do.

The parents of a child who is disabled usually feel sensitive about what other people are going to think about their child. If the child insists on lying in the middle of the floor in the doctor's waiting room, the other patients are apt to think he or she is either a weird kid or a spoiled brat. If the child wanders around the room handling everything within reach, the parents will be embarrassed. If, however, the child has been taught to sit properly in a chair and the parents have brought along a small, quiet toy, the visit to the doctor will make the parents very proud of a well-behaved child.

HAVE A LITTLE FUN

The greatest gift parents can give their children is to teach them to enjoy life each day. Unfortunately that is not something they can be taught earnestly and patiently, like tying shoelaces. Rather it is something more like measles—it is catching. Children get it from parents who already have it.

They should start out by sharing something they truly enjoy, like eating ice cream or skating. Of course the child will be reluctant at

Figure 6.6. Waiting for a bite (4½ years).

Figure 6.7. "Which is the front end?" (4 years)

first to try something strange. After parents and children have a little practice in sharing things they enjoy and are having fun together, the child will be less apprehensive about new things.

Next, parents should look around with a child's eye for experiences they think the child might enjoy. Such new experiences as rolling down hills, wading in the lake, feeling all the different kinds of trees on the boulevards, roasting hot dogs, and so on will delight parents as well as children.

Mr. Maravich could be seen regularly with small Joel strolling through a large covered shopping mall after the shops had closed. Joel was absolutely entranced at the echoes bouncing back from the high roof. Mr. Maravich was as pleased as his son when they discovered that if he banged on the trash container then ran over and banged on the barbershop pole, the two notes made a chord that echoed for several seconds. It sounded like a regular symphony when they added a light pole and a wrought iron grill to their orchestra. Forget about your dignity, and share a little fun!

WHAT DO I TELL MY CHILD?

Most parents worry about how they are going to tell their child that he or she is blind or partially sighted and how the child is going to react when they do. A very young child who is visually impaired will not know that he or she is any different from anyone else, but an older child will realize that other people are aware of things he or she doesn't understand. This is a common experience for all children when they listen to adults talking about things that are beyond their comprehension, and visually handicapped children do not seem any more perturbed about it than their brothers and sisters. There are simply more mysteries for them. If a child has never had normal sight then he or she will not be feeling sad about any loss. It is easy for parents to imagine that the child feels as they would if they lost their sight, and children can be affected by how their parents feel about their blindness. If the child's visual disability is never mentioned or is discussed in whispers, the child will get the impression that there is something bad about his or her eyes. The child doesn't know what it is, only that it seems to be terrible and is not to be discussed.

On the other hand if parents can openly use the words *blind* or *partially sighted* in front of the child, he or she will learn to be familiar and comfortable with the terms. Young Carmen came home from kindergarten in tears and told her mother the children were swearing at her. When Mrs. Mouton asked what they had said, Carmen replied that those horrible kids had called her blind, and she knew that was a very bad word. The Mouton family had never spoken about Carmen's eye condition in front of her and had resorted to spelling the word *blind* when they had to mention it.

When a child does ask about his or her lack of sight, a simple explanation that the child's eyes don't work and why they don't usually suffices. Children understand about things that don't work. One 5-year-old told his kindergarten friends that he was blind because he was born too soon and his eyes weren't finished in time.

When 4-year-old Cory started preschool he was asked by another child why he could not see. Cory very nonchalantly replied, "Born too soon; my eyes weren't finished." A year later he was out playing and came in crying. He complained to his father that some of the kids were calling him blind. His father replied, "So what's new? You were blind yesterday, weren't you?" Cory thought a minute and said, "Well, yes I was, wasn't I?" and went off to play. Cory's father said he had felt very angry at the other children and was tempted to go out and yell at them but realized that would only set Cory up for more teasing, and he believed his son must learn to fight his own battles.

HOW DO YOU EXPLAIN WHAT SIGHT IS?

Parents are often at a loss as to how and when they are going to explain to their child who has no useful vision exactly what sight is. The answer is very simple: they can't. The child will never fully understand what sight is, nor can a sighted person ever understand fully what it is like to be blind or partially sighted. The awareness that he or she is different does not really develop until around 5 years of age. As the child grows he or she gradually learns that in some mysterious way other people are aware of things he or she doesn't know about. Yet a 4-year-old blind child will often say, "Here comes the milkman" or "Here comes Grandpa," long before his parents know the car is coming. Because the child has learned to use his hearing more efficiently, the child is able to recognize certain familiar cars in the distance simply by the engine sounds, which are not heard by the parents.

Since the word *see* means to comprehend, be aware of, understand, as well as to observe visually, the visually impaired child will find it confusing and rather silly if the adults try to explain how their seeing is different from his or hers, because the child thinks he or she knows what is going on.

A child of 5 or 6 may start asking questions and testing out what that particular kind of seeing is all about. Marilyn was talking with her mother in the living room one afternoon and suddenly went out into the hall and called, "Can you see me now?" "No." She came back in. "Can you see me now?" "Yes." Out again to the hall. "Can you see me now?" "No." "Gee, Mom, you aren't very smart if you can't see me. I can see that you are sitting on the sofa whether I am in there or out here in the hall."

A 12-year-old told the counselor that he had dreamed about her. When she asked how he knew who it was when he had never seen her, he replied, "Good grief! I have known you since I was a baby. Why wouldn't I know you?" Blind teenagers are frequently interested in discussing with sighted friends the difference between seeing with eyes and seeing with the other senses but admit they don't really understand the difference.

WHAT ABOUT TELLING OTHER PEOPLE?

The question of whom parents should tell about their child's visual impairment has no simple answer. Each family will work out its own solution according to the circumstances each time. However, the simplest guideline is to tell those people who will be seeing the child more or less regularly so that they will be able to respond to the child in ways he or she will understand. For instance, if the parents are going to be taking the child to the supermarket each week, it would be nice if the cashier knows the child by name, rather than just smiling at him or her or even ignoring the child. The mail carrier and the milkman are daily visitors the child will want to greet. Of course, friends and relatives will be aware of the eye condition from the time the child is a baby, but any new ones should be told. Other new people like Sunday school teachers and day-care or playground supervisors will need to know that the child cannot see or how much the child sees and how they should behave to be comfortable with the child. The child's condition should be made clear to all these people whether the child is blind or partially sighted.

There is no question that many people do have real prejudices and misconceptions about blindness and partial sight, but fortunately the situation is changing for the better. Parents of a visually handicapped child can do something about changing the attitudes of sighted people. The most effective way to help this change is for them to provide an opportunity for people to get to know their child personally. Prejudice and misconceptions are often based on fear and ignorance. Some people have very strange ideas about blindness, because they have never actually known a person who could not see.

Adults in the immediate neighborhood will be interested in watching a blind child grow up. At first they will be a little uncertain about how to act, but they will get used to the idea that although the child does not see normally he or she is still one of the neighborhood kids, and in time they will accept him or her as such. Through knowing one child they will probably feel differently toward other visually handicapped people. The children in the neighborhood will be able to grow up without prejudice toward blind people if they play with a visually impaired child before they have acquired their parents' prejudices. Other children will be openly curious about a child's lack of sight but not embarrassed about it. Nor is the child going to be particularly concerned. The Barry family moved to a new neighborhood and Mrs. Barry, spying two little girls across the street, asked them over to meet their blind daughter, Betty, age 4. Betty was busy swinging on her new swing when her mother said, "This is Betty. She is blind, and that means she sees with her fingers instead of with her eyes." Betty immediately piped up, "You're wrong, Mother. I see with my ears too. Would you kids like to have a turn on my swing?"

Both children and adults may seem to ask a lot of stupid questions, but they are asked not out of malice or idle curiosity but out of a real interest. A little public education will pay off later and will help parents cope.

If parents want their child who is blind or partially sighted to participate in community programs as he or she grows older, they should start their campaign early, and there is no better place to start than in their own neighborhood. By facilitating their child's friendship with the small children living nearby through making their yard the best place to play, by volunteering at Sunday school, and by getting involved in the local cooperative preschool, they will lay a good foundation for the future. If they take their child along so that all kinds of children and their parents get used to the idea that a visually impaired child is just a child who doesn't see normally but who can function well in a group of sighted children, the job is almost done. Once other parents are convinced that a child who is blind can cope alongside theirs, they should be willing advocates for the blind child in the community.

Chapter 7

Challenges Facing Parents and Some Solutions

♦ ♦ ♦ ♦ ♦ ♦

Some days parents feel they have had it up to here with the children and they can't stand the sight of them for another minute. That is the time for them to say to the children, "I am tired and cross and need some time for myself so I will feel better." They can send the children to the basement, the backyard, their room, or to a neighbor and tell everyone they need peace and quiet, or, as Carlos told his father when he came home from work, "Don't bother Mommy; she is having very peace and quiet."

ENOUGH IS ENOUGH

Parents should not feel cruel or guilty about needing time for themselves to recharge their emotional batteries. It is good for children to learn that parents have rights and needs of their own. If they learn to play quietly alone for short periods when they are little, it will be much easier to cut the apron strings as they grow older. At a conference for parents of deafblind children, Mrs. Yeo related that when she got thoroughly fed up with the demands of her 8-year-old child, who would not let her have a minute's peace, she would flee to her bedroom. But the child would kick and scream and pound on the door until she finally came out. The child was cooperative and well behaved at school, and his mother and father could not understand why he was so demanding with them. The other parents pointed out that his kicking and screaming paid off at home because he always got his own way if he persisted long enough. Bill was smart enough to have learned that kicking and screaming in school resulted in immediate isolation with no staff reaction, so he no longer bothered to try it. At the conference the following year, Mrs. Yeo reported that there had been an unbelievable improvement in her son and both parents were less stressed.

A number of parents and professionals seem to believe that if any problems arise in the family of a visually impaired child, they are naturally caused by the child's blindness. Certainly if a marriage is already strained or there are already problems with other children in the family, the added responsibility of caring for a child who is blind will not help the situation. It is wrong to conclude that the presence of a blind child automatically causes family problems. In fact, as stated in Chapter 6, a research project carried out by the authors found that divorce and separation are no more common in the families of children who are visually impaired than they are in the families of sighted children.

Sometimes, a professional who focuses solely on the child, rather than on the child and his or her family, will automatically assume that if the parent is not following instructions to the letter or questions the merit of the instructions, the parent has a real problem and should see a psychiatrist or a social worker. Professionals should consider how they themselves might react to such a suggestion. Might they not find it disconcerting to say the least?

Parents are going to meet professionals in several disciplines who may not be particularly knowledgeable about or comfortable with blindness. They may react as if it were the greatest tragedy that could befall a human being, or they may deny that it should have any effect at all. If they seem interested in learning more about children who are blind, the parents could refer them to an agency that serves such children and suggest that they read a textbook on blind children such as those mentioned in the list of supplemental sources in the back of this book.

If the parents believe that a psychiatrist or social worker would be helpful to them, they can ask their doctor to refer them to one that would be compatible with them. Parents should express any disagreements regarding the professional's assessment directly to him or her, and they should also ask for an explanation of vague generalizations like "overprotective" and "not having accepted the child, the blindness, or the problem." Parents should be aware that such vague statements may reflect the professional's own preconceptions about blindness, and they should ask the professional to please be more specific. Certainly there are professionals who make too much or too little of a child's visual impairment, and parents should always seek clarification of the statements of professionals. Parents should always use their own judgment about whether a professional can be helpful to them.

WHEN YOU FEEL LIKE BLOWING YOUR TOP

There will be bad days as well as good days, as there are in the life of any family. If parents feel they are having more than their fair share of bad days there are some things that can help lighten the load.

Don't Bottle Up Your Feelings

Someone to talk to about those things that worry or frighten parents is a necessity. A close friend, social worker, public health nurse, family doctor, or another parent are all possibilities. Someone who is not too close to the parents personally should be able to help them look at their situation more objectively, and in talking about their situation the parents may get a new perspective.

Develop a Sense of Humor

Parents of visually handicapped children can learn to laugh instead of cry about some of the weird things that happen. For example, Mrs. Jorgensen phoned her social worker late one Sunday night in an obvious panic. She said, "An awful thing has happened and I don't know whether to call the pediatrician, the ophthalmologist, or you." Eventually she calmed down enough to blurt out: "Elizabeth has swallowed her artificial eye. What will we do?" The social worker laughed so hard she could not answer, and Mrs. Jorgensen said indignantly, "It is not funny. Tell me what to do." She was told that there was nothing to do but wait for a couple of days. Then she too started to laugh and said, "You know, it really is funny; just wait until she grows up and we threaten to tell her boyfriends about this! Won't she be mad?"

Support Groups for Parents of Children Who Are Visually Impaired

Parents should seek out and join a group of parents of children who are visually impaired. Even if they have to travel a considerable distance to attend the meetings, the majority of parents find the association with other parents rewarding. They will find that other parents have not only managed to survive but are actually enjoying themselves. Mutual discussion of problems can lead to solutions that could not have been achieved by one family alone. When parents are feeling good about themselves and their child, each family can pass on the favor by taking under their wing the parents of a younger visually handicapped child.

Parents of visually handicapped children do not get together to grieve or commiserate with one another. Their meetings are very much like a PTA meeting, a diverse group of people who share a common interest and want to do something constructive about it. An organization of parents of visually impaired children can mobilize their creative and constructive energies to develop new programs and new facilities and to provide transcribing and transportation services, scholarships, and other resources that will benefit many children. Through involvement in such activities many parents have discovered new and unusual talents within themselves and have found greater personal fulfillment and satisfaction.

Social workers or counselors, any local agency for the blind, and the special education department of a local school system can help parents locate parent groups. In Canada the majority of such groups are associated with the Canadian National Institute for the Blind

(CNIB). In the United States there are state and national organizations of parents.

Parent–Tot Groups

In many communities there are parent–tot groups sponsored by community centers, churches, YWCA or YMCA, family service agencies, and other organizations. The groups are primarily designed to provide a convenient and friendly place for lonely parents to go with their young children to have some fun, to learn about child rearing, and to make some friends. Caregivers who previously were working and now are staying home to care for their children frequently feel isolated and miss the companionship of their former co-workers. Activities in these parent–tot groups may be based on water play in a warm-water pool, on exercises, or on dance activities. All involve both the parents and the children. In some programs parents will work with their own child; in others they will take on someone else's child. It is surprising how good one's own child can look after struggling with someone else's.

In all such programs there is time allotted for the parents to get together without the children for coffee, conversation, and a chance to get to know each other. Sometimes a speaker will discuss some aspect of parenting with the group, to be followed by discussion. It can be surprising and also reassuring to the parents of visually impaired children to discover that the parents of sighted children often are coping with the same doubts and problems that are worrying them and to realize that kids are kids whether they can see or not.

Some public health well-baby clinics operate a drop-in for coffee two or three times a week for new mothers and fathers. These coffee parties are strictly informal and are designed to help new parents meet and make new friends. Lasting friendships often develop from such groups, and the parents go on to baby-sitting for each other as well as social activities.

The centers provide an opportunity for both parents and children to enjoy the company of people their own age and to acquire new skills. Each parent can learn more effective parenting skills from observing how the other parents handle their children, noting what works well and what should be avoided. A parent–child center can sometimes serve as a substitute for the extended family when the family is living far from all relatives.

TO WORK OR NOT TO WORK

More and more mothers are returning to work after having a baby. Some are obliged to work out of financial necessity, others have skills that are needed by the community, and others want to work for their own personal fulfillment. Whatever the reason, choosing the right time to return to work poses a painful dilemma.

Six months of maternity leave is now part of some employer–employee working agreements. This period enables the mother to give the baby a good start and provides time for the child to get to know and bond with the mother. If by then it is possible for the mother to return to her work or her studies part-time, she will still be able to spend enough time with the baby. Job sharing with another person who also wants to work part-time is one increasingly popular solution.

Separation from the mother is difficult for any child in the first few years of life and particularly from 6 to 18 months, when the child is forming emotional bonds with the caregiver. The separation is even more difficult for the visually impaired child, who has a more difficult task in learning to recognize and love his or her parents through other senses. The love of a child for the parent is the foundation for that child's learning, because of the desire to please the parent.

Sometimes when both parents work they are able to juggle the work schedules so that one parent is always available to care for the baby, but it takes split-second timing and a deep commitment from both parents.

CHOICES FOR ALTERNATE CARE

Fortunate are the families who have grandparents, other relatives, or a close neighbor who is concerned about the baby and is willing and happy to care for the child while the parents work. The young baby who is blind needs lots of cuddling, coaxing, and encouraging if he or she is to overcome the limitations imposed by lack of sight. Members of the family are much more apt to be emotionally involved and much more able to respond with praise and enthusiasm at the infant's first smile, first steps, first words, etc., than is a strange caregiver. This emotional involvement helps the child to feel loved, contributes to that child's sense of personal security, and is the beginning of the development of the child's lifelong pride in achievement.

When both parents must work and there is no relative or close friend to come to the rescue, the family has to make other arrangements for the child's care. That care should not be simple babysitting. The best solution is to find a warm, intelligent person who has experience caring for babies and loves doing it. It would be a godsend if he or she had even limited experience with a visually impaired child.

It is preferable for the babies to be cared for in their own homes so that they will not be uprooted from their familiar surroundings. When the children begin to crawl and then to walk it will be less confusing if there is only one house to map.

The second choice would be care by such a warm, caring person in his or her home. This arrangement means more pressure on the baby and the parents, including the need to deliver and pick up the baby morning and night. Ideally the caregiver should have no more than two children under 18 months in his or her care, or three if they are between 18 and 36 months. Otherwise the caregiver will not have enough time to spend on cuddling the baby and teaching him or her all those things he or she would not be able to learn if left alone too much.

A gradual start with several get-acquainted visits will give the child a chance to get to know the caregiver and to feel safe with him or her.

A caregiver should be given any information the parents have acquired about the special needs of children who are visually impaired and special ways of meeting those needs. It is a good plan to check the quality of care by dropping in unexpectedly to ascertain if the children are being left alone to entertain themselves and are just sitting or lying there doing nothing. When parents notice any small accomplishment by the child they should make it a point to compliment the caregiver so that he or she feels his or her efforts are appreciated. Parents know only too well how much time and effort it takes to teach their blind child a new skill. Parents and caregiver should agree on what the child should learn next and the methods and words to be used to avoid confusing the child.

Day-care centers with many children and several caregivers are not suitable for very young blind children, who need a good deal of individual attention if they are to develop to their potentials.

Regardless of the type of child care available, it is important for the parents to spend quality time with the child each day before or after work, no matter how tired or rushed they feel. A little loving and a little play time will let the child know that he or she is loved and that the parents like to be with their child whenever they can.

THE SINGLE PARENT

It cannot be presumed that every child who is visually impaired will be blessed with two loving parents, and these days a good many of them are being raised by one parent. Most often it is by the mother but occasionally by the father. The single parent may be widowed, divorced, separated, deserted, or unmarried. How each parent meets the situation will depend to a great extent on what support he or she can draw from family or community. Mrs. Andrews was widowed when her daughter was a few months old. She was fortunate to have parents who could help her care for Doreen and who encouraged her to return to her former work as a nurse. Mr. Coghlan was deserted by his wife, who left him with 2-year-old Marney, a partially sighted child. With no family nearby and determined to keep his child, Mr. Coghlan worked on night shift until Marney was old enough to attend nursery school in the morning. Then he arranged with a neighbor to care for the child until he returned from work at dinnertime. He found a trustworthy baby-sitter and tried to give himself one night off each week to go bowling with his friends. Mrs. Chiang, divorced from her husband, had three children, one of whom was totally blind. She decided that it was most important to her and the children that she be a full-time mother for a few years until the children were all in school, and she is managing to keep the home going on her child support payments plus public assistance. She hopes to be able to work when the children are no longer so dependent on her.

An increasing number of unmarried teenagers are deciding to keep their babies instead of placing them for adoption. Providing adequate care for an infant who is blind and possibly has other disabilities is a heavier burden than some have anticipated. The easiest solution is when the teenager's parents accept the baby as part of their family and help the young parent so that he or she can return to school or work to support the child. This is a difficult arrangement for the teenager, who has to combine the roles of child and parent, but is usually easiest for him or her and the baby until the teenager is able to establish a home for himself or herself and the child.

In some larger cities school boards have made provisions for young single mothers to return to school by providing a day-care facility in one of the secondary schools. The young mothers are expected to spend part of each day with their children to learn parenting skills. Because of the number of different caregivers such a facility is not suitable for a blind child under age 3, and if at all possible other arrangements with a single caregiver should be made to provide for stability.

Unfortunately, many of the babies born to very young mothers have other problems in addition to their impaired vision, including neurological and other physical or mental impairment, irritability, and failure to thrive. Some of these children spend months in the intensive care nurseries and on discharge tend to be very difficult to look after.

Those teenage mothers who are living on their own or with a friend find it difficult to care for the baby and to have much of a life for themselves. Jane, who has partial sight and mild cerebral palsy, was born to a 17-year-old girl who was living with her boyfriend. He did not want to have anything to do with a disabled child and disappeared. In 2 years Jane and her mother have moved three times and have had a series of different roommates, none of whom were very interested in Jane. The child has recently been admitted to a hospital because of delayed development. There is no question that this mother loves Jane and wants her home, but she does not understand the child's special needs. She is inconsistent in her use of community resources, and it is doubtful that she will be able to provide for Jane's needs adequately.

If there is no family help available, the single parent should seek the help of a public health nurse or a social worker to find out the kinds of resources the community might offer. Day care, nursery schools, infant stimulation programs, and part-time foster care may all provide at least a temporary solution. Single parents, whether working or not, may be so busy attempting to fill the roles of both mother and father that they tend to ignore their own needs. They need time for themselves, time to see friends and to participate in at least some social and recreational activities or to take a night class—anything enjoyable at least once a week. Caring for a child with a disability day in and day out without a break can result in a parent becoming exhausted, depressed, and discouraged. If it gets too bad the parent may tend to blame the child for depriving him or her of a more normal life. If the parent will also consider his or her own needs as well as those of the child, they can have a very happy life together— hard, but happy and satisfying.

WHAT IF YOU CAN'T COPE?

There are some instances where, despite their best efforts, parents are faced with the painful fact that they simply cannot cope with the heavy responsibility of raising a child who is severely disabled. They believe that keeping the child will be bad for the child as well as the family. One of the parents may suffer from continuing poor health, either mental or physical, which makes it impossible to give the child needed care; the child may require extensive therapy that the parents are unable to carry out themselves; the parents may be unable to transport the child as often as needed to receive medical treatment or therapy; or, rarely, neither parent may want the child. Social workers at the local child welfare office or at medical centers should be able to provide information and help to arrange for additional help in the home or temporary or long-term placement for the child, whichever seems to be in the best interest of the child and the family.

Chapter 8

Children with Multiple Disabilities

◆ ◆ ◆ ◆ ◆ ◆

In recent years the use of new medical and technological developments in the intensive care nurseries has resulted in the survival of more infants who are born premature or seriously ill. Unfortunately, after their long struggle to survive some of these infants are left with a variety of physical and mental disabilities.

The child born with one or more disabilities is in double jeopardy. The child's entire life will be affected not only by the real limitations imposed by the disability but also by the reactions of the family to those disabilities. How much the child will be able to achieve depends to a considerable extent on how the parents perceive him or her and what they expect. When a child has multiple disabilities, the problems that face the parents are compounded many times. It is often difficult for them to obtain a definitive diagnosis of the nature and extent of the damage, information on the availability of treatment, the prognosis (both immediate and long term), and information about the daily care of the child. It is essential for the parents to know exactly what they have to deal with; otherwise, they will feel as if they are traveling in unknown country without a road map.

Before a final diagnosis is made, there will be numerous medical appointments with all kinds of specialists, often spread over several months and many miles. Each professional tends to specialize in one area, such as ears, or eyes, or seizures, or the heart. Few of them are trained or knowledgeable about all disabilities and multiply disabled children do not fall into any one specialist's particular area of expertise. For example, the ophthalmologist is not trained to make a diagnosis of mental retardation, and yet when confronted with a blind child who is obviously not functioning normally for his or her age the doctor may tell the parents that the child is retarded.

Some years ago in a Canadian city, the parent counselor at an agency for the blind received a very moving phone call. A young woman said, "I have a baby. She is blind. She has a heart condition. She has seizures. She has a bowel problem. I have had to take her by bus to an eye specialist, a heart specialist, a brain specialist, and a bowel specialist. I have been traveling from one office to another all over the city and each specialist seemed to be interested in one piece of my baby. I felt so desperate that I finally phoned the telephone operator and told her my story. Then I asked if there wasn't somebody in this whole city who cares about me and my baby. She told me to phone you. Now what are you going to do about it?"

The counselor arranged a home visit that same day and found the mother to be a 19-year-old Danish girl who had recently moved to Canada with her husband. The young husband had been totally overwhelmed by the thought of raising a severely disabled child and had just taken off, leaving enough money in the bank for a couple of months. Reassuring Monika of her continued interest and support, the counselor arranged to have baby Marieka seen at a diagnostic clinic at a nearby children's hospital. She arranged with the director of the clinic for the baby to be seen by the necessary specialists at the clinic. All reports were to be funneled through the director (a pediatrician) to Monika, with the director coordinating any treatment required.

It was determined that little could be done for the baby, who would require a great deal of care. Monika wanted to keep the baby but realized it would be very difficult if not impossible to support herself. After a couple of months and numerous phone calls to Denmark, Monika decided to return to Denmark to her parents' home. Her mother had agreed to help look after Marieka, and Monika hoped to train as a nurse.

If at all possible the parents of a child with more than one disability should press for an early diagnostic assessment at a multidisciplinary clinic. These facilities are usually associated with large hospitals or

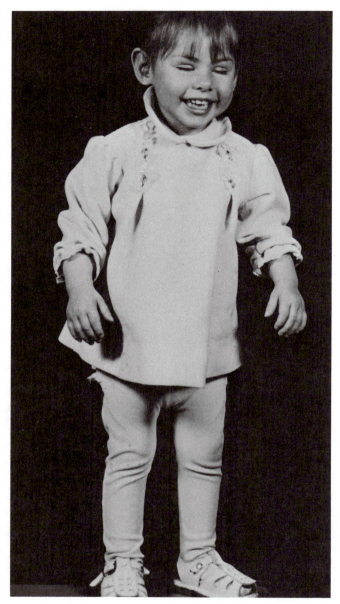

Figure 8.1. "Look, I'm standing alone!" (blind and microcephalic, 16 months)

medical schools. In such a setting the various specialists can examine the child, pool their information, and discuss their combined findings and recommendations with the parents. Both parents should be present for any discussion about the diagnosis, whether at a clinic or at the individual specialists' offices, so that they both will have the opportunity to contribute observations and opinions and to ask questions rather than receiving the information secondhand from the other parent. When the two parents are fully informed, they are in a much better position to work out jointly plans for the care and treatment of the child who is disabled. The responsibility for daily care of the disabled child, transportation to treatment centers, plus running the house and caring for other children should be shared between the parents.

When parents do not go to a multidisciplinary clinic, they may run into the problem of how to cope with what may seem to be conflicting advice and opinions given them by professionals. If the disagreement is about the diagnosis itself, the parents might be well advised to seek consultation with a recognized expert in that particular field to clarify the situation. If the conflicting advice is concerned with therapy for two different disabilities, for example, blindness and cerebral palsy, then parents should trust their own judgment to select from each program those parts that make sense to them. In other words, they should feel free to brew up a unique blend to meet the complicated needs of their child in his or her particular situation.

It sometimes appears as if an enthusiastic therapist zeroing in on one particular damaged part tends to forget that sometimes, because of the presence of additional disabilities, there are other demands on parents' time, that there may be travel difficulties, and so on. The therapist may tend to feel that the parents are uncooperative, whereas in reality they are doing their best but cannot possibly fulfill all the demands on their time and energy. Instead of feeling guilty about not being able to drive a blind child with cerebral palsy 40 miles five times a week for therapy or for not having taught a deafblind child to sign for toilet in one week because the other kids had the measles, the parents should inform the therapist of the difficulties in trying to carry out the prescribed program and should try to work out a mutually agreeable compromise. Sometimes parents are reluctant to request changes for fear of offending the therapist; but in all fairness, how can the therapist know about the difficulties if the parents do not discuss them and seek his or her cooperation in resolving

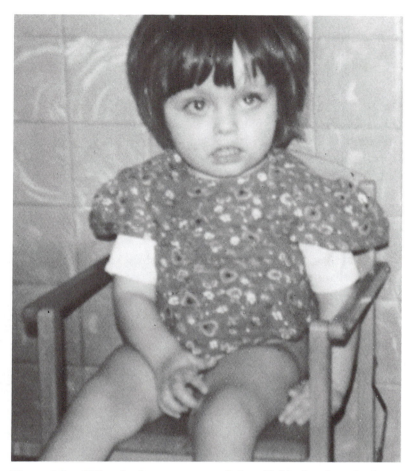

Figure 8.2. "What do they want me to do here?" (blind with multiple disabilities, 2 years)

them? It is far better to explain the situation and try to reach a mutually satisfactory compromise than to smolder with resentment at what may seem to be unreasonable demands. If this happens, the whole exercise can become a disaster for everyone, and the positive effects of the therapy can be neutralized if the child is aware that the parents are angry about the therapy. The child may not understand what is going on but can feel the undercurrents.

The child with more than one major disability, such as blindness, mental retardation, cerebral palsy, or deafness, presents a tremendous challenge to both the family and all the concerned professionals. Until a few years ago it was assumed that such children had no capacity to learn, and parents frequently were advised to "put the child away" into an institution rather than to try to care for him or her at home. A few stubborn and concerned parents and professionals have shown that many children with severe disabilities can make a good deal of progress if their needs are adequately met. There is still much to be learned about the management of babies and children with multiple disabilities, but more and more people are becoming interested and getting involved and more and better services are available today than in the past.

In almost every community there are agencies and organizations concerned with different disabilities and medical conditions that offer a variety of services. Parents of blind children who have other disabilities should make a point of approaching such an agency to learn about the disability and any services that might be helpful to them and their child.

Sandy, a bright and friendly child who is totally blind, attended preschool at the Cerebral Palsy Association. Sandy, who had to use a walker because of her cerebral palsy, also received physiotherapy treatments twice a week. The medical director, Dr. Pinkerton, was quite charmed by her sunny disposition. He would greet her in the hall each morning, "Good morning, Sandy. It's Dr. Pinkerton." After about a week, Sandy, recognizing the sound of the doctor's footsteps one morning, sang out, "Good morning, Dr. Pinkerton. It's Sandy."

Each child is so different that there can be no blanket prescription for management for any one group of children. Individual programs will have to evolve for each child based on the profound conviction that the child is capable of growing and learning. Existing information should be tried and tested. If unsuitable it should be discarded, and a continuing search should be made for experiences through which the child can learn about himself or herself and the surrounding world. The question that seems of most concern to parents is how much their child can develop and learn and at what cost in effort and time. No one really knows the answer.

How much the child will learn and whether or not he or she can become independent will depend on the number and severity of disabilities, the child's personality and motivation, the kind of family, the opportunities for learning, and the availability of facilities.

There is no doubt that there are a few multiply disabled children who have almost no capacity to learn because of severe brain damage, but certainly these children are in the minority. Most children with multiple disabilities are capable of learning. How much and how fast, however, is difficult to forecast.

Parents who seem to be most successful approach the task with determination and optimism tempered with reality, as did Mr. and Mrs. Tyler. They brought 3-month-old Samantha from a small mining town into the city for a complete diagnosis because she obviously had multiple disabilities. They were told that she was totally blind and microcephalic (had a small head) and that she would be severely retarded. The mother was referred to the counselor by the neurologist "for support, as the child obviously has little future." Although the mother expressed some doubt about how the doctor could be so sure the child was retarded, she was realistic in acknowledging that Samantha was blind and had a small head. The social worker,

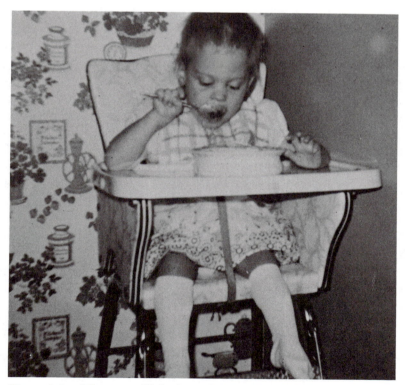

Figure 8.3. "This is good!" (hydrocephalic and blind, $2\frac{1}{2}$ years)

impressed with the mother's warmth and strength, agreed that while the baby probably could learn something, no one knew what her potential was. She suggested to Mrs. Tyler that for 2 years she work very hard with her daughter, providing maximum teaching and encouragement. At the end of that time if Samantha was capable of learning she would have been given maximum opportunity to learn without losing any time. If she was not capable of learning, Mrs. Tyler would at least be comforted by knowing that she had done her best and that no one could have done more for the child. Mrs. Tyler agreed and returned with the baby to their isolated home in the north. Occasional postcards said Samantha was doing well. Ten months went by and the parent counselor was astounded to have Mrs. Tyler arrive unannounced at her office, with Samantha walking along beside her. Surprise followed surprise as Samantha demonstrated some of the things she could do. The child was functioning within normal limits in every way. She could walk, was finger feeding, could find her hair, eyes, nose, and feet, and could put blocks in a pail, clap her hands, say two or three words, and even turn a somersault.

When Mrs. Tyler was asked how she had accomplished such amazing results, she replied, obviously very pleased and proud, "Well, I just decided no child of mine was going to be that dumb if I could help it, so I spent hours and hours teaching her. Now I am convinced that she's just as smart as my other children." The next year Mrs. Tyler was determined that Samantha have the opportunity to attend nursery school and, undaunted by the lack of such a facility in her small town, she rounded up the parents of a few other disabled children and some interested citizens. By the time Samantha was 3 years old the nursery school was in business as a community project, with Mrs. Tyler as president and Mr. Tyler in charge of the committee to make the furniture and toys.

One of the neighbors turned out to be an experienced nursery school teacher who was happy to work a few hours each day. Two years later, when Mr. Tyler's employment resulted in a transfer to another town, the Tyler family left behind a legacy of a community-operated nursery school for all of the disabled children in the town. Samantha, at age 5, was enrolled in the regular public school kindergarten and functioned within normal limits.

The original neurologist was so impressed with Samantha's progress that she made a videotape to teach medical students how wrong they could be in underestimating a child's potential and how to acknowledge the power of a determined parent.

Certainly, we know that most microcephalic children (in fact, 93%) are mentally retarded and can't all turn out like Samantha, but what if her mother hadn't given her a chance? It would be cruel to imply that all families of children with several disabilities can expect to "make a miracle" as the Tyler family did with their daughter. But until a child is given a chance to learn, how will anyone know how far or how fast he or she can go? Each child deserves that chance—and so do the parents.

It would not be possible to discuss the many and varied disabilities that a child who is blind might have. We will limit our comments to a few that are most common and trust that parents of children with multiple disabilities will make use of the suggestions offered throughout the book as well as in this chapter and adapt them to their own particular situations.

CEREBRAL PALSY

Cerebral palsy is a motor disability due to brain damage before, during, or shortly after birth. It may be minimal or severe. The body and limbs of these children may be stiff, limp, tremulous, or unsteady and are always poorly coordinated; the limbs may show involuntary movements. All of these effects may be present in different mixtures. Cerebral palsy is not a progressive disorder and not an illness. Because children with cerebral palsy tend to have multiple disabilities, a multidisciplinary approach to the diagnosis and treatment is important. Physical and occupational therapy and orthopedic surgery are particularly helpful in their treatment. Neurosurgery also can be beneficial in reducing stiffness. In most major medical centers cerebral palsy clinics exist where all these services are provided and coordinated. Each child must be handled individually. After a child has been diagnosed as having cerebral palsy, the parents should read about the condition and should ask a public health nurse or doctor for suggestions about books and also agencies offering services such as therapy and preschool facilities for children with cerebral palsy.

The child with little or no sight and impaired motor function often gives the impression of being unresponsive and unaware and may be mistakenly diagnosed as grossly retarded. Sandy and Robbie, both premature babies, totally blind with severe impairment of their legs and less in their arms and hands, grew up in very different homes. Sandy, a twin, was one of a farm family of 10 children. Her mother was so busy raising children, chickens, and raspberries that she had little extra time to work with her multiply disabled daughter. Sandy quickly found her way all around the farmyard on her small, calloused knees. When she was 18 months old her parents were told that she should be committed to an institution for the retarded. (Nowadays, institutionalization is only rarely recommended.) The parents refused and continued to keep her at home, driving 40 miles each week for physiotherapy to the clinic where she charmed the staff with her cheery "Good morning." Sandy soon learned to eat her meals quickly and without fussing, otherwise one of her hungry brothers would do it for her. At 6 she was able to walk with crutches and was enrolled in a school for the blind, where she stayed for 10 years. She moved on to regular high school and to college, where she recently graduated with a Bachelor of Fine Arts (Music) degree. She hopes to teach music and have her own small apartment.

Robbie was the first child of a young city couple. They had just become used to the idea that their baby was blind when the cerebral palsy was diagnosed. Mr. Anderson, an avid skier and ardent sportsman who had been planning how he was going to teach his blind son to enjoy sports, was naturally very disappointed and depressed. Mrs. Anderson, a quiet, thoughtful woman, in talking about her husband's reaction said, "Don't worry, he'll get over it and find other things to do with Robbie. Anyway, he can ski with our next child." Sixteen years later the Anderson family, father, mother, and two younger boys (both good at sports), attended Robbie's graduation from the local high school. They were tremendously proud when Robbie was awarded the scholarship as outstanding all-round student in both scholastic and student activities and received a standing ovation. How did Mr. and Mrs. Anderson feel after their years and years of hard work, driving Robbie to therapy, doing home exercises, taking an active part in the PTA at the school for the blind during the 8 years Robbie attended it, supervising homework, learning Braille and doing some transcribing, helping Robbie take part in local youth activities, and listening to the rock band practice in the basement? The parents said that, although they had been thrilled and moved at the

Figure 8.4. "Hi, Dad!" (cerebral palsied and blind, 4 years)

graduation ceremony, their high point had come the month before when they were given copies of the letters written by the school staff recommending Robbie for the scholarship. As they sat in their living room and read letter after letter stating what a delightful boy he was, what a good student, and how much he had contributed to the whole school through his enthusiasm and happy personality, they looked at each other, a little tearfully, and both said together, "Did you ever think it would turn out like this?"

Both Robbie and Sandy were fortunate in having little impairment in the use of their arms and hands and thus were able to attend first a school for the blind and then public school. Some of the children who are more severely damaged will not be able to accomplish as much. Yet 4-year-old Tricia, who was totally blind at birth and so spastic she could not move her arms and legs, was given a very poor

Figure 8.5. The birthday girl (spina bifida and blind, 4 years).

prognosis by the professionals, but her mother insisted she should have a chance. After much hard work by both her parents and several physiotherapists, the child now attends a nursery school for children with disabilities. She can eat sandwiches and cookies, get herself up to sit unsupported, kneel, and pull herself erect. Although she initially had been diagnosed as totally blind, she can see bright colors and moving objects and likes to roll a ball to her little brother and her father. At this stage no one knows how much farther she can go, but she is certainly a happy child and a real joy to her family.

DEAFBLIND

The term *deafblind* is commonly used to describe those children who have both defective hearing and defective sight. It is a misleading term since it implies the children have no hearing and no sight, whereas we include in this category children who may have some hearing and some sight, some hearing and no sight, some sight and no hearing.

By far the great majority of children who have impaired hearing and sight are so-called rubella babies; their mothers were exposed to the rubella virus early in their pregnancies and the developing baby was affected. Some of the children also suffer damage to the heart, skeleton, or brain, in addition to the eyes and ears. In most instances the eye defect is diagnosed first and usually involves one or more operations for removal of the cataracts, followed by numerous trips for the fitting of contact lenses or glasses. Then follow the suspicion and later confirmation that the child is deaf or hard of hearing. Sophisticated electrical tests are now available to diagnose deafness early, and most physicians are eager to rule out hearing loss in infants with cataracts. Next comes the fitting of the hearing aid and the campaign to get the baby used to wearing a hearing aid plus glasses or contacts. Parents are constantly amazed at how one small child can lose his or her lens, disconnect the hearing aid, or break the glasses so often and at such inconvenient times. It is very easy to become so involved in the efficient use and maintenance of all the apparatus that one forgets that the small child attached to them has very special needs that will tax the ingenuity of his or her parents.

We know that the deafblind child growing up in a world that he or she sees and hears poorly, if at all, is living in a world far different from the one that a normal child experiences. The child can be as

Figure 8.6. Signing for juice (deaf and partially sighted, 5 years).

isolated as a hermit unless people deliberately set out to establish communication with him or her. Of course the first message to be sent is "I love you," by the same cuddling, holding, and togetherness that were suggested for the child who has only a visual impairment. The deafblind baby is more apt to resist physical contact, and extra efforts may be required to help the child learn to enjoy it.

Four-month-old Didier was quite content to lie on his back beside a lamp on the living room floor, seemingly oblivious to the family life swirling around him. When anyone attempted to hold and cuddle him he resisted strenuously by stiffening his whole body, almost shooting out of their arms. Since she knew it was extremely important that he be close enough to see a human face and to hear a voice (if he had any residual hearing), Mrs. Johnson found that he would sit on her lap without struggling if she bounced him up and down on her knee and vigorously patted him on the back while she talked to him. This was obviously more pleasurable than just lying on his back, and from that beginning Mrs. Johnson has taught Didier to enjoy being played with. At 10 months he is wriggling his way across the room to her, is searching for and locating toys strewn in his path, and sits unsupported. His mother talks to him a great deal and is making use of gestures and simple signals to establish beginning communication skills. Since Didier is still too young to tell exactly how much he sees and hears, he is being exposed to both speech and signing at every opportunity. His mother signs for milk and says, "Milk," before she feeds him. She also taps the side of his leg before changing him and makes sure to put his hand in the bathwater to warn him before she puts him in the tub.

When the deafblind child does not have any communication skills it makes for an almost intolerable situation for the whole family. The child gets frustrated at the family's inability to receive messages. The parents feel upset at their inability to explain things to the child and about not knowing what is troubling the angry or weeping child. Establishing some kind of communication early is absolutely imperative if the child is to have any kind of chance in life. Parents should talk in simple, short phrases, using the same ones each time, and should talk with the child facing them at very close range so that the child can, if partially sighted, see their faces and get some clues as to whether the parents are sad, happy, or angry and can hear them if there is any residual hearing. When signing for words like *toilet, bath, cookie,* and *jump,* parents should make the sign very close to the child's face. When the child is about 2 years old, the parents should take his or her hands and show the signs one at a time. *Cookie* is a good one to start. After it is mastered, move on to the signs for *drink, toilet,* and so on. Parents should always speak the word as they sign and as the child signs. Agencies for the deaf will likely be able to provide picture guides to the more commonly used signs. A list of books that may prove helpful can be found in the list of supplemental sources in the back of this book.

Ruth was a rubella baby, the child of a teenager, and was placed in a foster home shortly after birth. The foster mother was asked to provide custodial care for Ruth, who had been diagnosed as deaf, blind, and retarded, until she could be admitted to an institution. The foster mother did exactly that, and at one year Ruth could not sit or stand, was unresponsive, and spent her time lying on her back propped in a baby seat flicking her fingers back and forth in front of her eyes for entertainment. When Ruth was 13 months old, the foster mother died suddenly and Ruth was placed with a new foster mother who had had previous experience with multiply disabled children and who simply could not bear to see a child left lying idle. Ruth was a long, lean, limp child who objected strenuously to being disturbed. Undaunted by the screaming rages, the passive resistance, and the apparent lack of intelligence or motivation, the foster mother and father were determined that Ruth could and would learn to enjoy life. They have been successful, almost beyond their fondest hopes. Ruth at $4\frac{1}{2}$ is a pretty little girl with a real zest for life. She is attending a kindergarten for deaf children (despite her minimal sight) and participates in all the activities with some extra help from a teacher's aide. She pays attention and understands most simple instructions given by signing and speaking simultaneously and is now able to make her wants known. At snack time she peers carefully at the variety of drinks available on the table and quite spontaneously signs, "Chocolate milk, please." Ruth puts on her glasses as soon as she awakens, and if one of her hearing aid molds falls out or is too loose and whistling she will call attention to it. She has found out that life is more interesting if all her appliances are in good working order and seems to feel she will miss something unless she is tuned in.

Phuong is a very bright little girl who is profoundly deaf but has usable vision. She has grown up in a large extended family (grandparents and uncles and aunts). They all love her dearly, have taken a special interest in her, and were a great support to her young parents.

She has been signing and apparently doing some speechreading (lip-reading) since she was very young and doesn't seem to miss very much of what is going on. Her two younger hearing sisters both started to sign as soon as they learned to talk, without anyone teaching them to do it. They were obviously convinced that everyone communicated by mouth and hands together. All three play happily with the other children in the neighborhood, with the little sisters being very protective about traffic and rough play. Phuong's family spent a great deal of time and energy in helping her to learn when she was very small, but now that she is a self-sufficient 6-year-old they no longer need to single her out for special attention, and they treat her in very much the same way they do her sisters.

Deafblind children are often exhausting to live with since they are dependent on their families for both entertainment and exercise. Any play equipment that involves strenuous activity—trampolines, spring horse, jungle gym, slide with ladder—will help tire out the children. Other members of the family, as well as baby-sitters and friends who have frequent contact with the deafblind children, should learn how to communicate with them and should try to include them in as much group activity as possible. It is surprising how quickly young brothers and sisters accommodate to an older sibling's limitations and learn to put toys into his or her hand, or touch him or her and communicate by simple gestures to get their messages across.

Parents should make arrangements to have some regular respite from the demanding and frustrating job of caring for a deafblind child. They need to get completely away for a short while each week and should try to arrange for a longer period to recharge their batteries every few months.

MENTAL RETARDATION

The usual definition of mental retardation is an intelligence quotient (IQ) of 70 or less. The IQ range from 50 to 70 is often referred to as *educable mental retardation* and those in the 30 to 50 range are called *trainable*. Trainable implies that these children are less likely to learn school subjects. The public image of a person with mental retardation as a person who is helpless or who cannot develop self-care skills and who learns nothing, is an inaccurate one. It is especially important for parents to know that many mentally retarded persons can, with special assistance, become productive members of society.

For many years it was commonly believed that blindness in a child would automatically be accompanied by mental retardation. Although this attitude is slowly changing, some new parents are still being mistakenly told that their blind child will be retarded. Despite good intellectual potential, a child with visual impairment whose parents have not had access to special help may exhibit the delayed development that can lead to such a conclusion. Such a child may be nonverbal, have poor coordination, be late in walking and in other motor development, be unable to chew solid food, or be lacking in play skills. To the uninformed observer such behavior is indistinguishable from that of a child with severe mental retardation.

It is difficult to evaluate whether such a child is truly mentally retarded or simply developmentally delayed for a number of reasons, not the least of which is the traditional attitude toward blindness. An effective evaluation of a child who is visually impaired should rightly be carried out over a considerable period of time and should consider factors such as whether there is actual brain damage and its cause and extent, the duration of hospitalizations, whether the child has been deprived of learning experiences and opportunities by parents who unwittingly do too much or too little, the expectations they have, and the actual limitations on normal development imposed by the child's sensory deficit or deficits.

Mr. and Mrs. Regan attempted to enroll their 5-year-old, Barry, in a kindergarten and were shattered when told it did not accept retarded children. They then applied to a school for blind children in another city and were given a similar answer but also were referred to a parent counselor. Barry was dragged in by his parents by the hands. He protested at entering a strange building by screaming and trying to lie on the floor. Obviously used to such behavior, the parents smiled shamefacedly and eventually managed to coax him in. They tried to settle him down by showing him all the toys available, which he sniffed, tasted, shook, and then threw over his shoulder. In walking, Barry exhibited the typical gait of the underdeveloped blind child: stiff knees, toes turned out, his feet slapping the floor at each step to produce an echo, and his hands flapping aimlessly. His parents reported that he refused to go to bed at night until 11 p.m. and woke them three or four times each night to demand food, which was given to him. His upper four front teeth had all rotted to the roots from going to bed with a bottle of juice every night. Both parents changed their voices when talking to Barry, using a sickeningly sweet tone that seemed to send the message, "You aren't going to do what I ask, are you, poor baby?"

For the previous 2 years Barry had been spending 5 hours each weekday at a day-care center. It appeared he was allowed to do anything he wanted to keep him happy but had gained little or nothing from the experience, except to be taken for a walk each day. There was no question that these parents loved Barry very much and, having done their best to keep him happy, were shocked and frightened at being told he was mentally retarded. When it was suggested that they were reinforcing his undesirable behavior by giving him what he wanted on a peace-at-any-price basis, they agreed it might be a possibility.

Barry screamed to interrupt the conversation, and it was suggested to the mother that she put her hand over his mouth and say "no" firmly. Instead she said, "Barry, you know mother can't hear you when you scream like that." Barry looked very pleased and continued to scream at intervals for the balance of the visit. It was suggested that he be put to bed earlier so the parents could have some time to themselves and that he not be fed during the night, but the parents replied that they did not mind having him up in the evenings and if they did not feed him he would come into their bed.

While the parents expressed regret that they had not been able to find out how to care for their blind child earlier and that they now realized they would have to teach him rather than waiting for him to learn on his own, it is doubtful if they are going to be able to change their attitude toward, and their handling of, the child without a good deal of ongoing support. If they do not change their expectations and handling, Barry may continue to function far below his age level, despite much greater potential.

In contrast to Barry's parents, Ann's parents were fully informed of the fact that their child had a considerable amount of brain damage because of a large cyst in her head. Everyone agreed that her potential would be very limited, but Mr. and Mrs. Weiss felt that they would like to give her the best possible chance to learn to do as much as possible. Despite several hospitalizations as a result of seizures, Ann has made considerable progress. Each small gain is the occasion for great rejoicing. At 3 she can partially feed herself, performs when placed on the toilet, can sit unsupported, and much to everyone's surprise has demonstrated that she can stand erect if her hands are held. She spends 2 afternoons a week at a center for children with mental retardation.

While Ann's gains have been slow and very limited when compared with those of a normal blind child, her parents take great satisfaction from the fact that she has been able to make some gains simply because they have given her that opportunity, and they feel good about themselves. When Ann is a little older and can spend more time at a center, Mrs. Weiss wants to go back to school for training so that she can work with children who have disabilities, because she has found she has a natural aptitude for it and also enjoys it. She feels that if she had not had Ann she never would have discovered that she finds such a career fulfilling.

Bobby Hanley was a severely damaged baby. He had a malformed brain and skull that caused him to be totally blind and severely retarded and to have frequent seizures. Because of his limitations Bobby was not able to make any gains from the loving and intelligent care of his parents. At 18 months he weighed 8 lbs and was totally unresponsive, and the seizures were almost continuous, requiring constant monitoring. When his little brother was born Mr. and Mrs. Hanley placed Bobby in an extended-care hospital nearby, where they still visit him regularly. They were not able to consider placement, as recommended by their doctor, right after he was born, but after 18 months they were able to make the decision without feeling guilty that they were no longer able to give him the care he needed.

Barry, Ann, and Bobby are all children functioning at a retarded level, Barry because of his environment and the other two because of actual brain deficits. There is a wide range of functioning in blind children, and their development is frequently uneven. They may be good in one area, poor in another, and average in still another. Until it is determined that the child is definitely unable to learn any more, he or she should have a chance at further training and education. The difficult thing is to determine just when ability to make progress has leveled off and the child has reached what appears to be peak performance.

Parents of children who are blind and retarded are faced with the problem of finding a solution to their need for some long-range care. In many areas group homes for young adults with disabilities are being established. Competent houseparents provide board and room and supervision for six to eight adolescents with various disabilities who have cerebral palsy, sometimes in conjunction with a sheltered workshop. Most of these facilities were set up as a result of parent action, and they are proving to be a viable solution to what seemed heretofore an insoluble problem. For persons with more severe disabilities, the large government-run hospital facilities gradually are being replaced by local extended-care facilities, often attached to local general hospitals. Information about group home facilities can be obtained from local associations for the mentally retarded and other groups interested in children with disabilities.

EPILEPSY

Epilepsy is another name for recurrent seizures. It is an uncontrolled electrical storm that may involve a part or all of the brain. Depending on what area is affected by this disturbance, the pattern of seizures varies. Some children stare into space or freeze momentarily; others suddenly fall to the ground and have a convulsion. Epilepsy is more common in children with visual impairment because in many cases the difficulties that caused the eye problems also affected the brain. Anticonvulsant treatment in the majority of children can stop the seizures or significantly diminish their frequency. Fortunately, many children eventually outgrow their predisposition to epilepsy and eventually do not require treatment. A thorough medical investigation is most important. The treatment of epilepsy is more than just handing out medicine. This disorder affects the person's total life, and the more the parents know about this medical disorder the better. A number of comprehensive books on epilepsy are available.

LEARNING DIFFICULTIES

Learning is a complex physiological task. Because during learning children rely on much of their brain, even subtle malfunctions here and there may disturb their receptive and expressive language, auditory perception, short-term and long-term memory, fine motor coordination, and many other necessary skills. The best way to manage a visually impaired child with a learning disability is to obtain a careful psychoeducational evaluation that pinpoints strengths and weaknesses. Psychologists must have experience with testing students who are visually impaired and must clearly understand how the type of visual impairment affects the child's learning, otherwise they often underestimate or overestimate the child's abilities. Again, this type of evaluation is best done in a multidisciplinary clinic where a number of professionals can freely exchange their impressions. Then an appropriate remedial teaching curriculum can be designed to fit each child's needs. A thorough evaluation, good teachers, and a suitable class are the keys to successful remedial teaching.

HYPERACTIVITY

Hyperactivity has been a popular and overused term applied to many sighted and some visually impaired children, especially in North America. The official term, however, is now *Attention Deficit Disorder*, to focus on the basic problem of attention, concentration, and distractibility. These children may or may not have a truly abnormally high activity level, low frustration tolerance, poor impulse control, or learning disabilities. Diagnoses and management are not simple in visually impaired children, and misinformation, confusion, and fad treatments abound in this field.

OTHER DISABILITIES

There are many other disabling conditions associated with blindness, such as hydrocephalus, spina bifida, congenital heart disease, diabetes, and others, each of which brings its own unique problems in management in addition to the limitations of impaired vision. A list of suggested readings on specific disability can be found in the back of this book.

HOSPITALIZATION

The multiply disabled child may spend a good part of his or her first year in a hospital for one reason or another. It is certainly essential for a child to be in the hospital for diagnostic procedures or for treatment, but any lengthy hospitalization may interfere with a child's development. A child will miss the one-to-one relationship with family members and the familiar sounds and smells. He or she can become disoriented and withdrawn and fail to develop. Parents frequently report that their blind child did not make any progress while in the hospital and actually lost ground, a development that is most distressing and discouraging to them. If at all possible the parents should spend much time with the hospitalized child. Familiar toys, food, and activities can help to minimize the traumatic effects. Hospitals often use hand or arm restraints to keep a child from pulling off dressings. If the child is visually handicapped some other solution should be found. Since a blind child cannot see when not permitted to use his or her hands, the child is literally "out of touch," a frightening experience.

PARENTAL ATTITUDES

It is tremendously difficult for the parents of a blind child with other disabilities to cope with all the complex problems confronting them. It is easy to be overwhelmed by feelings of inadequacy and bewilderment, and these result in a tendency to provide too much security and safety for the child. Do not worry about doing the wrong thing; it is much better to do *something* than never to take a chance and just let the child sit there with no hope. Children are remarkably tough, and if the parents' intentions are good the method doesn't matter that much. If one way doesn't work, they should try another and send the message that they expect the child to learn.

GUARDIANS AND WILLS

Parents of a child who is severely disabled and blind, who will probably not be capable of independent living, may worry about the child's future should something happen to them. Most parents of normal children designate a friend or relative to become guardian in case of their death, but any such guardianship will be self-limiting as the children will in time grow up and become able to manage their own affairs. When a child is severely disabled, the choice of guardian becomes more difficult and will require a good deal more consideration. Consultation with the staff of agencies serving the child who is disabled should provide possible solutions to this problem as well as information about government financial assistance available to persons with disabilities who require it for their maintenance.

PLACEMENT OF OLDER CHILDREN WITH MULTIPLE DISABILITIES

By the time a child with multiple disabilities reaches the middle or late teens the parents may feel burned out. They are exhausted from the years of effort invested in their child and may begin to wonder if there is no end to their heavy burden. Marriages can be wearing thin and siblings becoming more and more resentful of their disabled brother or sister. One family decided to explore other sources of care when their 15-year-old sighted daughter threatened to run away from home because she found it so difficult to live with her 17-year-old brother who was retarded, deaf, and blind. He pestered her friends if they came over, destroyed her belongings, and took a major part of their parents' time and concern. The parents reluctantly decided that for everyone's sake his placement outside the home was the only viable solution for the family as a whole. He now visits every weekend and apparently is happy in a small institution.

Parents can gradually become aware that despite their best efforts their multiply disabled child is no longer making much, if any, progress. When they reach this stage it is easier for them to investigate other alternatives to see whether their child would be just as happy and well cared for outside the home.

Parents who find it difficult to accept placement in a state or, in Canada, provincial institution may find it much easier to consider a group home. These group homes are fairly new and are a welcome alternative to the old, large institutions. Some group homes are operated by health or welfare or education departments and accommodate a mixture of 6 to 12 youths who are disabled (e.g., paraplegic, blind, retarded, cerebral palsied) in a large home with a housekeeper and staff. The skills of independent living are taught according to the youth's ability to learn. Some other group homes are established by the parents of children with a particular disability. Mr. and Mrs. O'Brian, whose daughter Brenda is blind and autistic, were active in an association for autistic children and were involved in the setting up and operation of a group home for 12 young adults who were autistic. Brenda has lived in this setting for 2 years, and she and her family have both benefited. The parents were able to take their first holiday alone in 19 years, and the two younger teenagers now feel free to invite their friends over. Brenda comes home every other weekend.

Chapter 9

Play and Playthings

♦ ♦ ♦ ♦ ♦ ♦

WHAT IS PLAY?

The dictionary defines *play* as "to sport or frolic; to take part in a game; to amuse oneself; to imitate." A child playing engages in an activity for its own sake and because the child finds it pleasurable. Through play a child can learn to use and enjoy his or her body and to develop physical skills—to run and jump and climb, to push and pull and lift, to use his or her hands with dexterity and sensitivity. The child can gain increasing mastery over the environment by learning to open doors, ride tricycles, hammer pegs, dig holes. He or she can learn that the companionship of other children will enhance the enjoyment of many activities. The child can learn to persevere and improvise, to cope with failure as well as success. Finally, through play the child can develop a capacity to enjoy life each day—to be silly and clown around, to laugh and giggle, and to feel happy about himself or herself and the world.

HOW DOES IMPAIRED VISION AFFECT PLAY?

It comes as a surprise to some people that children without useful vision will not spontaneously learn to play. If left alone the only play activities children who are blind will learn are those that involve their bodily sensations, such as rocking, flicking the fingers, and pressing the eyes (see section on mannerisms in Chapter 5). A number of factors may be involved. Babies who are visually impaired tend to be inactive, with little drive to move around and explore their unseen environment. They may be unaware of the toys nearby and so lack the opportunity to manipulate them. They are not able to observe how toys are played with by others, nor are they aware that playing with a toy is enjoyed by others. Hence, they have little motivation to play and make no attempt to initiate play with parents or other children. Because lack of opportunity results in lack of practice, the blind child's hand dexterity and coordination may be poorly developed, making it difficult to hold and use a toy. The child is frustrated by this failure, as are the parents.

There is a natural tendency to keep the child happy by giving him or her only old familiar toys with which the child plays in the same stereotyped way. The child does not learn from this type of play; rather it becomes like a pacifier that enables the child to tune out, becoming almost unaware of his or her surroundings. Even if the child wanted to play with something else he or she is incapable of glancing around the room to see what else is available; instead, the child who is blind is dependent on those around to bring things to his or her attention, to encourage interest in playing with them, and to show him or her how to find them again.

The physiotherapist at a center for children with disabilities had strapped Sonia into a standing position during therapy for cerebral palsy. She automatically handed Sonia her favorite string of wooden beads, which the child swished aimlessly back and forth on the table. When the beads were replaced by a stack of small foil plates, Sonia fingered all the plates, smelled them, bit them, bent one in half, straightened it out a few times, banged two plates together, then stacked them all into one pile, intrigued with the way they fit together. The physiotherapist was astonished at the child's capacity for improvising so many ways of enjoying the plates and promised to introduce her to new playthings regularly.

A child who does not see has to learn about cause and effect by experimenting more than do sighted children who can observe the actions of others. For instance, shake a rattle—hear a noise is a fairly obvious sequence to the sighted baby. If a child who is blind accidentally touches the rattle with his or her foot and it makes a noise, he or

Figure 9.1. Kicking a football (5 years).

Figure 9.2. Playground fun (5 years).

she may kick it again and again to hear the noise. Not until someone shows the child how to hold it in his or her hand and move it does the child know there are two ways of making that noise.

It is so easy to get hung up on the "right way" of playing with a toy and insisting that the child use it that the child is prevented from learning to play creatively and constructively. It is a fine line to walk between no help, too rigid help, or too much help. The child can be shown one way to play with a toy but also encouraged to invent different ways. Parents may find it difficult to keep things light if they are convinced the child would have more fun playing the right way. They must convince the child that they are having so much fun digging in the sand that the child will be unable to resist learning this substitute for banging a shovel on a rock. After a child digs a few holes, the parents might add a little variety by having the child drop rocks into the holes and cover them up, then dig them up again.

WHO TEACHES PLAY?

When parents are feeling worried about their own "qualifications" for raising a child with a disability (or any child for that matter), it is next to impossible for them to teach a child how to play. They are just too grim and earnest about the whole operation. Mrs. Lebkowski cried out in desperation one day, "Jeffrey is going to learn to ride this tricycle if I have to kill him." Jeffrey hadn't the slightest desire to ride on that tricycle. It had a narrow uncomfortable seat, he couldn't touch the ground, the darn thing moved, and his mother kept yelling, "Pedal with your feet." Who calls that fun?

It is much easier on everyone if the blind child learns some play skills from other children rather than from the parents. Six-year-old girls who like to organize everybody and everything in sight make excellent teachers. Parents without any other young children could try to borrow some from a neighbor and give them the job of teaching their visually impaired child how to roll and catch a ball, wind the music box, or use the new paddling pool. Other children have no doubts about the visually impaired child's ability to learn; they just expect the child to learn and send him or her good, positive messages. Sometimes the deep concern and anxiety felt by parents can interfere with their teaching play in a lighthearted way. They may send the child confusing messages: "I want you to learn but I am not sure you can" or "This is fun but I don't think you will like it." Other parents want to share their pleasure in a favorite sport or activity with their child, which can be a happy experience for both.

Mr. Matte, a young father interested in soccer, knew that his blind son could never enjoy it, so he decided that he and Fernando would both learn to skate on the pond near their home. Mr. Matte had never learned to skate in his native Portugal, but, equipped with new skates, they set out. Mr. Matte laced on Fernando's skates first and held him up until he got the idea of shuffling his feet along on the ice. Then Mr. Matte put on his own skates and stood up, only to fall flat on his face or his back time after time. No matter how hard he tried he could not stand up without falling. Meanwhile Fernando shuffled his way to the far end of the pond, and poor Mr. Matte, laughing uproariously, had to crawl the length of the pond, turn Fernando around, and follow him back down the pond still on his hands and knees.

As mentioned earlier the parent–tot groups can help mothers and fathers find new ways of playing with their children and having fun with them.

SHOULD THE CHILD WHO IS BLIND PLAY ALONE?

Children need to learn to play alone for short periods of time. It is not fair to a child to be taught to expect that there will always be someone there to entertain him or her every single minute. This can happen, particularly if parents have been told that children who are visually impaired should be constantly stimulated. How exhausting for everyone! No parent should be expected to play with a child all day. The blind child will need some extra help to learn to play independently but should learn. When the child becomes bored, the parents can suggest two or three things to do, offer a change of activity or surroundings, or even spend a few minutes getting the child interested in a new toy. The child will know the parents are nearby and interested in what he or she is doing. Canned goods make good toys to play with while an adult washes dishes, or grown-ups' shoes can be put on while the bedroom is being cleaned. Learning to help make

Figure 9.3.   "Here I come on my new bike." (3 years)

beds, wash floors, or put away groceries can be a learning experience for the child that will be useful later on. Incidentally, there is nothing like a small, wet rag for scrubbing floors, doors, and refrigerators to keep a child happily busy.

WHAT ABOUT PLAYMATES?

If there are other children in the family the problem of playmates seldom arises, but if the visually impaired child is the first child or an only child he or she will need some assistance in making friends. The simplest way to find playmates is to use childbait in the back yard—nice, interesting playthings—and the children will just appear. They will come at first to play on the slide, climb the jungle rope, paddle in the pool, and roll the barrels and the inner tubes, but in time friendships will develop. The backyard may become a neigh-

Figure 9.4.   The strongman (5 years).

borhood hangout, but the confusion will pay off in playmates for the child.

Children are not particularly kindhearted. They will not give a child any special privileges because it is his or her yard or toys, or because the child does not see. They will treat the child as an equal. Mrs. Bert learned the hard way when she scolded the neighborhood children for taking toys away from 3-year-old Sarah. The children stopped coming over to play in her yard, and Sarah was left to play alone. In telling about it, Mrs. Bert said that she recalled that at the time Sarah did not particularly mind when the visiting children wanted to play with her toys since she was so pleased to have them visiting. It was Mrs. Bert's own resentment that made her drive them away, and it took her several weeks to lure the children back again.

Any time there are children around there will be spats and near disasters, but that is part of growing up. Parents will have to become

Figure 9.5. "I'm up, you're down!" (5 years)

accustomed to the fact that when their child who is blind goes to play at a neighbor's house there may not be the strict supervision they take for granted. Yvette, age 4 and totally blind, came home from playing across the lane at her best friend Susan's house. Her mother was highly indignant when she saw that Yvette's bangs had been clipped off at the roots. She was marching across the lane ready to do battle when she met Susan's mother coming the other way, equally ready for a fight. Yvette not only had cut Susan's bangs but had hacked hair off all over her head. The child was practically scalped. Five years later Yvette and Susan are still the best of friends.

TOY STORAGE

If toys are kept in the same place the child will learn where to look for them. A large toy box, preferably one with wheels or casters, makes it easy to keep toys accessible and is also good for pushing around and riding in. Visually handicapped children should be taught to put their toys back in the box or on the shelf at the end of playtime. Habits of neatness instilled early will make it easier for them to find things all their lives.

WHAT ABOUT SPECIAL TOYS?

There is no need for special toys for the child with little or no sight. The appeal of a toy is not visual but in what he or she can do with it and in knowing the other children are enjoying it. For example, dolls have little appeal to the majority of children who are blind because they do not see that dolls look like little people, but a blind child who plays with children who love dolls becomes interested too. Furry or fuzzy toys, which are so attractive to adults, seem to frighten most visually handicapped children and they do not like to touch them.

Figure 9.6. "It tickles my tummy when it buzzes." (3 years)

They prefer toys that they can use actively, rather than those that perform for them. Isn't this what we want to encourage—to be a doer not a sideline-sitter? Toys that have an interesting feel, taste, or smell can often be found around the house. An old leather belt complete with buckle, or a brand new bathtub plug on a chain, both meet these criteria.

Many educational toys are very expensive when purchased in the stores, but an ingenious parent can improvise excellent substitutes from material around the house. Nesting cups can be made from four cans: a large one like a tomato can, one from canned corn, one from soup, and one from baby food. Save all the small bottles and jars with lids that can be used for matching, screwing, unscrewing, pouring, and filling. Real stove bolts and nuts are less expensive than the toy ones, and while at the hardware store parents can look around for other interesting objects that might be fun to play with.

An old spring mattress for jumping or a rope ladder for climbing will keep active children happy for hours. A 5-ft. folding stepladder was the favorite Christmas present for a 5-year-old boy. He spent hours exploring all the high places like the tops of doors both inside and out. Large cartons encourage children to invent their own ways of playing with them.

The following suggestions for play activities may prove helpful when parents run out of ideas for amusing their blind child on a rainy day.

Suggested Indoor Playthings For Very Young Children Who Are Visually Impaired

- Buy two or three cheap saucepans with lids that will fit one inside the other and keep them in a low, accessible cupboard or drawer.

- Save plastic jars and bottles with screw tops. Raisins can be hidden inside of some for a surprise now and then.

- Inexpensive nesting toys can be made from four different sized cans, such as baby food, soup, vegetables, and jam cans.

- Millwork ends make great building blocks after a little sanding to get rid of the slivers. They often can be obtained free from lumberyards or door or furniture factories.

Figure 9.7. At the beach (5 years).

- Large pegboards teach a child to find the hole and put the peg into it. Perforated ceiling tiles and golf tees make acceptable substitutes. Small mallets or hammers may be used with large pegs and a board with large holes to accommodate dowels for pegs.

- A collection of spools and large beads can be used to teach stringing. Thread the spools first onto a knitting needle. Later use a shoelace with the end of the lace stiffened by dipping in nail polish.

- A piece of soft wood, some nails with large heads, and a hammer will delight any would-be carpenter.

- Simple puzzles with just a few pieces, preferably of wood.

- Silly Putty and Play-Doh—add a few drops of perfume so it smells nice. Do not use Plasticene, as it coats the fingers with grease. Most visually impaired children refuse to use it and do not like the smell.

- Shape balls, with a number of different shaped holes and corresponding blocks, are too complicated until the children are older. They can be used if all but two holes are covered with tape and just the square and the round blocks are used.

Other blocks can be added one at a time. Homemade shape boxes can be made from shoe boxes and wooden blocks.

- Large cartons are a source of great delight for the 6-month-old, who can sit in one for support, and for the older toddler, who can climb in and out, use it for a pretend car, boat, or house, and hide in it.

- Balloons filled with air and also water can be fun once the children get over being scared when they pop.

- A cassette player can be used in many ways. Children can clap and march to the music, and they can sing along to familiar children's songs. As they get older they can listen to stories. They can accompany the music by playing homemade instruments.

Children's toys are very expensive, and the bright colors and current fads have little charm or interest for children who cannot see them or have not been sold on them by television ads. Simple homemade articles will usually have far more appeal than an expensive, bought toy.

Suggested Outdoor Play Activities For Young Children Who Are Visually Impaired

- A dishpan or baby bathtub with sudsy water and some tins, cups, old teapots, and a squirt bottle. These also can be used while sitting in the big bathtub indoors.

- A small wooden box for sitting on, stepping up and down, and finally learning to jump off—very scary as the child is jumping into nothing.

- A sandbox with shovel and pails.

- A bucket of water and an old paint roller and brush to paint the back door, the house, and the fence.

- An open-ended old beer barrel to crawl through and roll in.

- A running line of wire stretched across an open space between two trees, a fence, or a post, at waist height for the child. A small ring is threaded on the wire and a 6-in. strap or loop of rope is tied to the ring. Stoppers are placed 3 ft from each end of the wire to stop the ring from going right to the end. The child holds onto the strap and runs. The running line enables an energetic child to run freely without holding someone's hand and to go as fast as desired. The line should be placed where there is no danger of anyone accidentally walking into it.

- A rope ladder hung from a tree branch and a cargo net can both encourage children to climb and use their large muscles.

- An old spring-filled mattress covered in plastic to keep it dry can be a safe substitute for a trampoline.

- A wooden beam, 4" by 4", set firmly in the ground can serve as a walking beam to help the child learn vertical balance and to improve gait. Many children who are blind walk with their feet too far apart, making them appear to waddle. Walking the beam will help them to walk more normally. All children, sighted or blind, enjoy the challenge of walking curbs, fence tops, etc., as they like the element of danger in it.

- Two or three inner tubes (ones from trucks are the most fun) that are well washed and have the valves tied down with tape can be used in all kinds of imaginative ways by any small children.

- The usual swing and slide set, a tree house or a play house, plus the junkyard equipment mentioned above will not enhance the look of the backyard, but it will provide a child who is visually impaired a place to have fun and develop muscles. However, it also can serve another valuable function, and that is to attract other small children in the neighborhood to come and play with the equipment and in time to become friends with the child who is blind.

Toys and Playthings

The following list of toys has been collected over many years of observing small, visually impaired children at play and of admiring the ingenuity of their parents for finding them.

Infants

A small, light basket or box filled with shiny metal jar lids; spools on a string; a bracelet; a string of beads; a small metal cup; buttons on elastic; little bells tied together; squeaky toys; a small chain; a rubber stopper; a bunch of keys or measuring spoons; and mobiles and cradle gyms.

Toddlers

A Slinky; party noisemakers; flashlight; leather belt; old vacuum hose; empty boxes; foam ball; foil pie plates; clothespins and box; push toys; rubber tubing; riding toys; beach balls; spring horse; plastic pool; bath toys; simple stacking toys; friction cars; rocking chair; and simple, talking electronic toys that respond to a push button.

Preschoolers

Nesting cans; beanbags; screw tops and plastic jars; jack-in-the-box; talking toys; small radio; tape or record player; construction toys with large, simple parts; toy phones; large nuts and bolts; tricycle; doll carriage and dolls; books; hammer and nails and board; finger paints; scissors for cutting; Play-Doh or Silly Putty; toy dishes; brooms; and some simple electronic toys.

Chapter 10

Preschool and Kindergarten*

◆ ◆ ◆ ◆ ◆ ◆

WHY SEND A CHILD TO PRESCHOOL?

Parents send children who are blind or partially sighted to preschools and kindergartens for the same reasons they send their children who are sighted: they expect them to learn and grow from the experience. Children will learn how to be away from their parents, to accept the authority of the teacher, to share the teacher's time and attention, to play and work with other children, to wait their turn, to sit quietly for short periods, and to listen and concentrate on one thing at a time. They will learn new skills that prepare them for school and experience the fun and satisfaction of being part of a group. Last but not least, school provides parents with a badly needed respite from the constant demands of a young child.

READINESS FOR PRESCHOOL

About 6 months before parents expect to enroll their child who is visually impaired in a preschool, they should check out their child's

---

*Parents may wish to share the contents of this chapter with their child's preschool or kindergarten teachers. It also may be used as a guide for teaching a child at home some of the skills he or she will need at preschool or kindergarten.

readiness so that they can be realistic about the placement. They will most likely be surprised at the blanks they will find in the child's knowledge and skills in areas that sighted children would have picked up on their own without parental input, like little Emily who asked her mother where her house went when she was not in it.

The following checklist is simply a guide of desirable, but not necessarily essential, information and skills the child should have mastered in order to adjust more comfortably to preschool.

- ☐ Can separate from parents without being upset.
- ☐ Can hand-feed and use a cup.
- ☐ Can ask for and use the toilet with minimal help.
- ☐ Can follow simple instructions like stand up, sit down, come here, be quiet.
- ☐ Can go up and down stairs.
- ☐ Can run, jump, clap hands, stamp feet, etc.
- ☐ Knows body parts—head, eyes, nose, ears, mouth, shoulders, elbows, fingers, knees, toes, etc.
- ☐ Knows left and right, up and down, back and front.
- ☐ Can sit quietly and listen to a short story or record for a few minutes.

CHOOSING A PRESCHOOL

Choosing the right preschool is serious business to the parents of children who are visually impaired. Very naturally they may feel anxious about their child's first venture into the outside world. Some parents have found it less stressful if they did a little research the 6 months or so before they hoped to enroll their child in a preschool by determining what preschools were available in their area. Friends, neighbors, preschool counselors, community centers, and agencies for the blind are all possible sources of information about the number and quality of such schools. Parents then can arrange to visit the ones that have been recommended and make an informed choice as to which one will best meet their child's needs.

First impressions are important. If the teacher is friendly and warm, relates well to the children, and responds with interest to the possible admission of a child who is blind, that is a good sign. So, of course, is the cleanliness and orderliness of the facility. The noisy chaos of some preschools would overwhelm any child without sight. The nonprofit preschools, parent co-ops, and those run by parent groups seem to be preferable to the ones operated for profit.

It is recommended that a child who is visually impaired be placed in a small group, not more than 8 or 10 children, with the same teacher at all times so the child can get to know the other children and bond with the teacher. Groups of 24 children cared for by three or four teachers are too confusing.

It is hard for parents to choose what is best for their child over what would be most desirable or convenient or inexpensive for themselves in assessing whether their child is ready for preschool. Such a decision is easier if made with the help of a social worker, preschool visitor, or other professional who is familiar with the child and the resources available in the community for children who are visually impaired. Sometimes the decision is made that the child is not ready at present but would be in 6 months if everyone cooperates in the get-ready process.

In other instances where the child who is visually impaired has additional disabilities like cerebral palsy, spina bifida, or deafness, the family may be associated already with specialized agencies for ongoing treatment. Agencies such as Child Development Centers and the Cerebral Palsy Association often operate excellent preschools, and children who are visually impaired have been enrolled in them for many years most successfully.

During the 1960s and 1970s when large numbers of children who were visually impaired were enrolled in regular preschool for the first time, they were the first children with a severe disability to be integrated. On the whole they did very well, possibly because it was the "in thing" to have a child who was blind in the local preschool, and the teachers were considered "progressive" by their peers. The children with visual impairments who were enrolled in local preschools were at first only the brightest and most promising students, and there was usually only one such child in any one preschool. Few if any children with other disabilities were accepted in those decades, and a teacher would have only one child with special needs. Thus most teachers coped well and found the experience a positive one.

The passage of legislation in the 1970s and 1980s in the United States, Canada, and Great Britain, dealing with the rights of all disabled children, has resulted in the enrollment of many children with other disabilities in the preschools, and the position of the child who is visually impaired as favorite child has changed to that of just one more special needs child. Many preschool teachers feel frustrated about not having enough time and the lack of sufficient back-up help to do a good job.

These and other factors have caused an increasing number of parents of children who are visually impaired to investigate with renewed interest the preschools operated solely to meet the unique needs of children who are blind or partially sighted. Some of these preschools are operated in or serve as outreach programs by state schools for the blind or by state or local agencies concerned about what they believe to be inadequate preschool programs for small children who are visually impaired. They usually are staffed by teachers who have special training and experience with children who are blind.

REGULAR OR SPECIAL PRESCHOOL?

Families may wonder whether it is better to send their children with visual impairments to neighborhood preschools or to special preschools for children who are visually impaired. The integration of children who are blind into regular preschools and kindergartens has been carried out successfully in many areas for more than 30 years. Attendance at a neighborhood preschool provides children who are blind not only with the opportunity to learn the same new skills and independence as the other children but also with some additional advantages. As they work and play with the sighted children they gradually learn that, though they can do many of the things the other children do, there are some things that are impossible, like seeing the pictures in the book the teacher is reading to the class or recognizing colors.

They find out about being different at a time when it is least damaging to them. Their difference may have been explained to them (some people see with their eyes and some with their fingers) but they really do not understand it and are not too concerned about it. After all, they have been living with sighted people since birth.

Sometimes parents ask if their child who is blind would not be happier and safer in a special preschool for visually handicapped children in the care of specially trained teachers. Admittedly, such programs are probably easier on those parents who tend to worry about everything and who find it very hard to let their children take some of the risks involved in learning to be independent. On the other hand, a visually handicapped child who cannot go to the neighborhood preschool with siblings and friends and who has to go to a "special" preschool may become convinced that he or she is not equal, cannot fit in, and is not welcome. Some parents fear that their child who is blind will feel inferior in a sighted class if the other children can do things quicker and better. The reverse seems to be true. Children who are blind learn gradually that, while they are different from other children in one way, they can be just like them in many other ways.

When 5-year-old Judy returned from kindergarten one day and asked her mother what it meant to "color inside the lines," her mother was upset and anticipated all sorts of dramatic repercussions like "Why am I blind?" "I wish I could see like the other kids," etc. The mother carefully explained that there were marks on the paper that were visible only to the children who saw with their eyes, and the children who saw with their fingers could not feel them. Judy astonished her mother by replying, "Oh, is that all? I thought it was something important" and ran off to play.

A child who is blind may be ready for various preschool activities earlier or later than the suggested ages depending on degree of maturity, the amount of vision, other disabilities, and the presence of other children to engage the child's interest. Parents and some professionals tend to want to rush the child who is visually impaired into a group experience without seriously considering the child's readiness for group play. A child with good partial sight may be ready for group experiences at the same age as siblings or friends. In most regions the trend is to enroll children in groups at the age of 3, but the child with little or no vision is seldom ready socially or emotionally at 3, although perhaps he or she may be ready intellectually. Such a child has had much less experience with the world and has a much more difficult time in getting to know and communicate with other children until age 4 or even 5. Frequently the child with visual impairments

Figure 10.1. Painting a fine day (3 years). (Courtesy the Vancouver *Province*)

who has been placed with a group of sighted children who are a year or so younger seems to fit in better. The age differential tends to even things up for the blind child who may not have some of the same skills as the sighted children but who may be a little smarter.

ATTITUDES OF THE TEACHER

The attitude of the teacher toward the visually handicapped child is the single most important factor in determining whether or not the preschool experience will be a positive one. The teacher's reaction to blindness is clearly a very personal thing and is related to experience and needs. Fortunate indeed is the teacher who, as a child, either went to school or played with children who were blind. Such a teacher will have long since discovered that a child who is blind is just a child who cannot see and will have little difficulty in accepting the child into the classroom.

Teachers who have had no previous experience with a child who is blind will frequently panic at the very thought of having one in the class. It is comforting to realize that the child's parents did not have any experience in handling blind children either, but that they and the child have all survived in good shape. Children who are blind adapt surprisingly well to the sighted world, and their parents are usually more than willing to pass on to the teacher some of the useful techniques they have learned through trial and error.

Until a teacher actually meets the blind child who is to be in the class, it is only natural to feel apprehensive about all manner of things that might or might not occur in the future. That is what happened to Mrs. Panton when she learned at the end of the school term that a boy who was blind would be in her kindergarten class in the fall. She expressed her great concern to the school nurse, who phoned the agency for the blind and asked the counselor if it could be arranged for Mrs. Panton to visit another kindergarten where a blind child was already in attendance. When the counselor learned that Mrs. Panton had never met Kelly, the child in question (who just happened to live across the street from the school), she arranged to take him and his mother over to the school the next morning. Kelly, a bright, competent little boy, was waiting at the gate to make this long-awaited visit to his new school. When the counselor introduced him to Mrs. Panton he said, "Hi, are you the new teacher? What are you going to show me today?" Mrs. Panton very gingerly suggested he might like to touch her pet guinea pig. Before she could say much more Kelly felt the guinea pig all over and said, "It's soft like our cat, but where is its tail? Why does it snuffle like that? What does it eat? Can I pick it up?" After holding the guinea pig for a minute he put it down and said, "I'll just look around to see what else you have to play with and find out where things are." He checked over the toy shelves and then began to amuse himself on the big slide. Mrs. Panton kept shaking her head and finally said, "You know, I did not sleep a wink last night and I have had an upset stomach for a week worrying about having

Kelly in my class. Now I can't understand why I was so scared. He is one of the most delightful children I have ever met and he is certainly ready for kindergarten."

Mrs. Panton was able to ask straightforward questions about what Kelly could and could not do, what special precautions would be necessary, and how she could help him remain as independent as he seemed to be. She was assured that Kelly was one of the brightest and most competent blind children in the district and that he had been blessed with excellent parents. Before the visit was over, she brought in two other teachers to meet Kelly and his mother, and she really seemed proud that he was going to be in her class. After the new term was underway, a phone call brought the report that neither she nor Kelly was having any special problems and he was fitting in well with the other children. Mrs. Panton is an experienced kindergarten teacher who, much to her own surprise, reacted with real panic at the thought of a blind child in her class. Parents should not be upset if a teacher or principal reacts this way when they make inquiries about enrolling their visually handicapped child; they should realize that it is a whole new idea that takes a little getting used to. A child who is partially sighted is not quite so threatening because people tend to think of him or her as an ordinary child who happens to have poor sight.

Until teacher training colleges include some experience with children who are visually impaired in their education courses, teachers are going to be reluctant to take on the challenge of such children without some kind of support. They will be concerned that the child who is visually impaired will make unfair demands on their time or that the parents of other children might feel their children won't get their fair share of teaching. Also, the whole issue of blindness is a great mystery to them. If the visually impaired child is well prepared and ready for kindergarten, he or she will fit into routine activities very quickly with a minimum of extra help. The little extra help that may be needed occasionally can usually be provided by the other children under the teacher's direction until the child who is blind is able to manage independently. Parents can offer to provide an extra pair of hands from time to time, preferably helping with children other than their own.

Feeling sorry for the "poor little blind child" does not do the child any good; in fact, it may encourage the child to become manipulative. The child does not feel sad or sorry or deprived because he or she has

Figure 10.2.   Learning shapes and sizes (5 years).

lost sight that was never there to lose. Sympathy or pity should not blind adults to the child's needs. The child needs to be accepted as a worthwhile person, with the right not only to learn but also to receive loud and clear from the teacher the message that learning is expected, even if some tasks are harder to do without good sight or have to be learned through different techniques. The child who is blind can learn to take pride in developing independence just as sighted children do. Blindness is a very real social handicap, and so it is doubly important that the child who is blind learn early to be a cooperative, pleasant person.

It will take a little time for the preschool teacher to get to know just what to expect of the visually handicapped child. It takes time to become acquainted with the sighted children in the classroom. The teacher may frequently underestimate the blind child's ability to do a given task out of pity and a desire to spare the child the experience of failure. If, however, the child is allowed to do only familiar things and never has a chance to try new experiences, he or she would be better off at home. Conversely, a teacher may overestimate the child's capabilities and believe that blindness is not a handicap, resulting in a student who is discouraged by repeated failures and the teacher's lack of understanding of the limitations imposed by the disability. The great majority of teachers discover that their fears are groundless and that they actually enjoy the challenge of having the child who is blind in their group. They find that when they try out new teaching techniques developed for the child who is blind the whole class benefits, and they continue to use them after the child has moved on to another class. Teachers report that they learn to look at the world in a different way, becoming much more aware of all the different shapes, sizes, textures, and smells that abound in a classroom. One teacher commented that having a child who was blind in her class made the class expeditions much more fun. All the children had a great time, feeling the smooth leaves and the spiky needles, tasting gum off the evergreen bark, scuffling in the fallen leaves, listening to the humming of the telephone poles, and feeling the force of the rainwater running in the gutters.

The relaxed and comfortable attitude of the teacher toward the child who is visually impaired will be adopted by the children in the classroom. If the teacher accepts the child as a fully participating member, so will they. Of course, there will be bad days when a teacher will get discouraged about a child's slow progress and feel she or he is just not getting through to the child. This is the time to recruit help from the other children. For example, an elderly preschool teacher was reluctant to accept her first pupil who was totally blind, giving as her excuse the fact that he would not be able to go to the bathroom by himself. The counselor asked another 4-year-old to take Marcus to the bathroom and followed with the teacher. The sighted boy carefully placed Marcus at one side of the toilet, placed himself on the opposite end and, loud and clear, said, "Unzip! Ready! Aim! Fire!" Marcus got the message loud and clear—and so did the teacher. Marcus was accepted.

EFFECT ON OTHER CHILDREN

Teachers are often surprised that preschool children do not have the same feelings about blindness as adults; young children have not yet learned about prejudice. They are openly curious about any differences like skin color, leg braces, missing limbs, and blindness. They show no hesitation in asking very direct questions about the new and different child about whom they want to know everything, including how the child got that way. When Jerry was brought to the kindergarten by the parent counselor on his first day, she was concerned to find that the teacher had not been able to bring herself to tell the class that a child who was blind would be coming. Before the counselor could introduce Jerry to the children, a little boy came bounding up and said, "Say, lady, can't that kid see? Are his eyes broken?" Of course, all the children immediately gathered around while the counselor explained, "Yes, his eyes are broken. No, they can't be fixed. No, his sister did not drop him on his head when he was little." After this exchange, the little boy nodded very wisely and said, "Okay, Jerry, come with me and I will show you where the sandbox is." And off they all went. The child who is blind becomes a bit of a nine days' wonder, with the other children rushing to be helpful for the first few days. This situation usually rights itself when that child insists on doing things himself or herself, or when the teacher notices that he or she is receiving too much help and is not getting a chance to learn to cope alone.

It is not uncommon to notice the sighted children attempting to walk around with their eyes closed to find out what it is like not to see. A smart teacher will use such occasions to help the children understand that keeping pathways clear and putting things away in the same place makes it easier for the kids who don't see well. It also will help the children to be a little more tolerant when their blind friend accidentally walks over their tower of blocks.

The presence of a child who is blind or partially sighted in the class can provide an excellent opportunity to discuss with the children how they are all different. Some are tall, some are short, some have long hair, some have curly hair, some can run fast, some can sing well, some can see, and some can't. Children enjoy this kind of discussion and come up with some remarkably astute observations about individual differences.

Preschool teachers frequently have to provide reassurance to the parents of the other children that the presence of a visually handicapped child is not going to deprive other children of their fair share of attention, that their children will actually benefit from the opportunity to learn that there are people with disabilities in their world, and, in a few cases, teachers actually have to convince them that blindness is not catching. Mrs. Smith, the mother of a sighted child, asked to speak for a few minutes at a parents' meeting of her cooperative preschool. She said that after the first week of preschool she had asked her young son about his new friends at school. When he said his best friend was Maureen, who was blind, the mother was upset and told him most emphatically that he was not to play with Maureen. The boy did not mention her again until he and his mother were planning his sixth birthday party. He insisted on inviting Maureen, who came to the party with the other children. Mrs. Smith was astonished to discover that Maureen was an attractive, bright little girl who most efficiently helped her organize the games at the party and even admonished her young host for gulping his milk so loudly. Mrs. Smith said it had been disturbing to her to realize how prejudiced she was, and she suggested that the other parents examine their attitudes to find out if they, too, might learn about tolerance from their 5-year-olds.

THINGS TEACHERS WANT TO KNOW

No special skills are required for working with a visually handicapped child at the preschool level (that is, before the child learns to read), just the same skills that make preschool a positive experience for the other children: love, discipline, and the opportunity to learn.

We have been emphasizing that the child who is blind is first of all a child. While not exactly like a sighted child, each child who is blind is also different from other visually handicapped children. In other words, each is unique. The child who is blind may be confident, noisy, and aggressive or shy, dreamy, and withdrawn. He or she may have been pampered and kept so safe that taking chances is frightening; or the child may have been encouraged to be free and independent, to expect the normal bumps and bruises of growing up.

What About the Child's Sight?

Obviously, sight is the area where the child will be most special. The child may see nothing at all or may even have two artificial eyes (incidentally, a great status symbol to the other children). He or she may be aware of light and shadows, an awareness that is useful in orienting because it tells where the windows are. The child may see fairly well at a few inches but not be able to see the teacher's face or what is happening across the room. Medical reports and terminology provide very little practical information to the teacher, who will want to know just how much, if anything, this particular child sees in order to teach him or her. Parents can give very useful information to the teacher about the child's visual efficiency, and the teacher can observe the child's functioning and draw some reasonable conclusions, although a child who seems very competent at moving around may fool the teacher. The sensible solution to discovering just how much a child who is partially sighted can see in any particular situation is to ask the child. Who would know better? The teacher will want to know if the child can see the picture in the storybook or the actions for a singing game or the snail someone brings to show-and-tell from a few feet away or a few inches away, or if the child needs to see with his or her fingers.

Children who are partially sighted can be very good at bluffing, pretending that they see the same as everyone else does. This bluffing is natural since they do not have any idea just what the other people see when they look at a given object. For instance, a tree may look like a blob on the end of a stick to a child with poor distance vision, but since the child knows trees have leaves he or she will probably imagine seeing the leaves on a tree. A teacher should persevere when questioning a child. Told by a child that he or she can see the blackboard, the teacher may find on further questioning that the child cannot see the writing on it.

Teachers and parents are often worried about straining the eyes of a child who is visually impaired. Except in extremely rare instances, the partially sighted child cannot harm sight by using it. In fact, the more he or she uses it the more visual efficiency increases.

Children with partial sight may need to be close to the books they are looking at or the picture they are drawing. Each child will determine the distance for best functioning. Some children see best with papers right at the end of their noses.

Since it is physically tiring to bend over a table to see a book up very close, a child who is visually impaired will be more comfortable lying on the floor or with a book propped upright on the table. Similarly, drawing and painting are much more pleasurable if the child stands at an easel or if a large pad of newspaper is tacked to the wall. Then the child can get as close as needed.

Mannerisms or Blindisms

Teachers may wonder if blind children press their eyes because they hurt. This habit is almost universal with young children who have little or no vision and, as we mentioned in Chapter 5, seems to serve the same function as thumb sucking. They press their eyes when they are bored, tired, fearful, or shy and also when listening intently or just sitting daydreaming. Distracting the child by offering some other more enjoyable activity is the simplest way to help him or her stop. Nagging or scolding usually results in increased eye pressing. Since there seems to be evidence that prolonged eye pressing can result in very deep-set eyes with dark circles, the teacher should try to help the child break the habit. A small toy to handle during rest or story time can be very comforting to children at a time when they would otherwise tend to press their eyes or rock.

Visually handicapped children also may indulge in repetitive physical behavior, like rocking, flicking their fingers in front of their eyes, and head flapping, rolling, or banging. They find all these and other similar activities stimulating and satisfying. It is obvious that a child who is unable to watch people, animals, cars, or television or to look around to see a toy nearby waiting to be played with can't sit in a vacuum. Such a child will use his or her own body as a plaything. As the child learns how to play with toys and other objects and also how to find them, he or she will be able to replace the rocking, banging, and other physical mannerisms by activities that are both more satisfying to the child and more acceptable to adults.

Communication

Any teacher of young children is aware of the tremendous amount of visual communication that is going on in the classroom, the smiles and frowns that let children know how the teacher feels. The teacher, in turn, responds not only to the children's facial expressions but also to their body language. Young children frequently seek reassurance by glancing up to see if the teacher is still there caring for them.

The child who is visually impaired may not be able to see the teacher's face and, if he or she has no vision, may not even be sure a silent teacher is there. For this reason, the newly enrolled child who is blind may call out the teacher's name every few moments at first. A simple "Yes, Jimmy, I am helping Susie right now. You go on with your puzzle and I'll see it later" will let the child know that all is well and that teachers do other things for other children during the course of a normal day. This situation may be different from that at home, where the parents may be able to give the child their sole attention. Teachers should always make their presence known and should identify themselves, if they are strangers, until the child recognizes them by voice alone. They should let the child know they have entered or left a room by uttering a word or two. A greeting by name, a pat on the head or shoulder, or a hug can replace the teacher's smile or look of approval. A frown is easily translated into a change of tone in the teacher's voice.

It is almost impossible to tell how a child who is visually impaired feels from observing his or her facial expressions. Such a child may look sad when listening intently or worried when playing. The child is unaware of what his or her face is doing. If the child has not yet learned that it is polite to turn toward the speaker, this practice may not make much sense, since the child can hear just as well turned away from the teacher. Children who are blind, however, are continually having to learn to conform with the way sighted people behave, although it may be hard and awkward for them at first.

Teachers should not exclude the words *look* and *see* from conversation. The children use these words themselves when they want to know about something or to show it to another. "Let me see" means "Let me touch it, peer at it with residual vision, smell it, and find out all about it." In conversation the teacher should treat the visually handicapped child like the other children as far as possible. The child is used to being blind; blindness is a part of him or her. It should be mentioned without apology whenever necessary. The quickest way for the teacher to find out if the child understands instructions is to ask if he or she understands or needs any help. The child should be addressed by name when spoken to so he or she will know the teacher expects attention and response by words or action. The child does not know when the teacher is looking at him or her when asking a question unless specifically told so.

Orientation

The child who is visually impaired will need an opportunity to become acquainted with a new place. Once familiar with it, he or she will be able to move around alone. Most of the time being independent is especially important; the teacher should see how much the child can do alone before offering any help. Most children who are blind are able to walk toward a person speaking to them or to a steady sound like a record player or a loudly ticking clock. They should be allowed to take the odd bump from an out-of-place chair without everyone getting unduly upset, but it is helpful if the other children learn to keep the pathways reasonably clear. Instructions like "Bring it here" or "Put it over there" are meaningless to a child who is blind. Be specific or indicate the location by tapping; "Put the box on my desk" makes more sense. For the first few days a friend can help the child learn where the toilet is, where the basin and paper towels are kept, and where the play corner is. Pushing or dragging the child will not teach him or her to find his or her own way.

Assigning the first coat hook in the row to the child who is blind will make it a lot easier for him or her. Wire coat hangers are an abomination to a child who cannot see; it is hard enough to find the neck of the coat and get it to stick on the metal hook without having to fiddle around with a wire contraption.

The child's chair should be readily accessible—the one by the playhouse door, or by the radiator, or at the end of the table—and easy to find. At first, the child may need someone to stand by the chair and call his or her name until the child can go directly to the chair. As the child gradually becomes familiar with the location of the equipment in the classroom and in the playground, he or she will be forming a mental map of it and, eventually, will move around quite independently. In unfamiliar territory, of course, the child will have to take someone's hand. Half-open doors can result in bumped heads; it is much safer to have them shut or fully open.

Since visually handicapped children are more dependent on verbal instructions for moving around, it is important that they learn the meaning of *right* and *left* as early as possible. They also have to know what words like *nearer, farther, over, under,* and *beside* mean so they will understand verbal directions and gain more awareness of their environment. If told, "The ball is by your left foot," the child who is blind can find it more easily. Expressions used in defining location, like *on top of, underneath, beside, inside, in front,* and *behind,* cannot just be picked up by the blind child; physical experience is needed before the child can comprehend their meaning. As Yvonne was playing with her ball, it rolled under the rocking chair. When told it was "under your chair," she found it readily. When told it was "under the TV," she felt around on the top and the front of the TV. Obviously "under your chair" was a specific and familiar place while "under the TV" had no meaning for her and she could not find the ball.

It sounds difficult and complicated, yet blind children of 4 and 5 do learn to move freely and confidently around their classrooms in a remarkably short time. Things should be left where the child has placed them; a child who is blind finds things by remembering where he or she left them. If it is necessary to make any changes in the placement of furniture or equipment, the child should be informed.

Participation

The experienced preschool teacher makes daily use of children's desires to conform, to do the same things in the same way as the other children. The new child watches the other children take off their coats, hang them up, and sit down in their chairs and very quickly catches on that this is the way the children at this school are expected to behave. Unfortunately, this easy way of learning by observation and imitation cannot be used by the child who is visually impaired unless he or she is told exactly what the other children are doing, where they are doing it, and how. Somebody will have to show the what, where, and how, whether it be washing hands or finger painting. Sighted children are usually very anxious that the child who is visually impaired do everything in the right way, whether the child wants to or not. Few teachers would seriously consider asking a child who was totally blind to serve the juice at snack time, yet Barry's classmates insisted that he have a turn. As Barry made his way with his pitcher of juice behind the children seated around the table, each child turned in his or her chair, put a glass under the spout, and said,

"Pour now! Stop! Next!" Barry beamed with pride, and so did all the other children.

Games where all the children are blindfolded allow the visually handicapped child to compete on more even terms and also help the sighted children understand that it is harder to do some things without good sight. All the blindfolded children should try to identify a child by his or her voice or by feeling him or her or to seek and find a specific toy, like a music box or a ticking clock (really a blind version of hide-the-thimble). Other games that involve hearing and touch can be invented using tapes of voices or familiar sounds such as doors closing, refrigerators humming, sirens, animal sounds, kettles boiling, and so on. Identifying hidden objects in a box or bag without looking (called "feelies") is a popular game, as is identifying common objects by their smell, like popcorn, grass, chocolate, bread, and shoes. Such activities are fun for all the children and help them to learn to use and enjoy all their senses.

Snack Time

Children who are blind tend to be picky eaters, and it may take a fair while before they can enjoy snack time. Since they have never been able to observe firsthand the pleasure other children have from eating, they are, as a rule, conservative eaters who will accept only a very limited diet, namely, those foods to which they are accustomed.

As they become aware that fruit, cookies, and carrot sticks are considered treats by the other children, their reluctance to try new foods will gradually lessen. A casual approach by the teacher will work much better than an expression of concern or any pressure on the child to eat.

Story Time

For generations, people with good vision have been trying to provide illustrations in books for the blind without any real success. A raised three-dimensional image (even one with textures) does not convey the same message to a child who is visually impaired as a printed two-dimensional picture does to a sighted child. The child who can see will look at a picture of a dog and recognize it as a dog. To the child who is blind, a dog is a warm, furry thing with a tail that can whack, a wet tongue that can lick, toenails that can clatter on the floor, a mouth that can make huffing noises or loud barks, and fur that smells awful when it is wet. How does an illustrator convey that?

When the teacher is reading to the class from a book in which pictures form an integral part of the story, then it will be necessary to describe to the class (so the child who is blind can understand) exactly what is happening in the pictures. If the pictures are only there to enhance the book visually, there is no reason to mention them. The child who is totally blind will never really understand about pictures. The child with residual vision will want to look at the pictures and should be encouraged to sit near the reader and look at close range. Simple pictures, uncluttered by detail and printed in strong colors, are easiest for such a child to see. For the child with no useful vision, wallpaper sample books are nice for practice in turning pages. They are also heavy and big and look very important.

When children with sight get bored listening to a story, they can entertain themselves by looking around the room, at the pictures on the wall, or out of the windows or by watching the pet hamsters in the cage; the child with impaired vision has no such choice of alternative entertainment. When a story becomes boring, such a child will start to wiggle and pester the other children, but, if permitted to hold and play quietly with a small "twiddle toy" like an elastic band, a string of beads, or a small car (anything that can be manipulated), the child will be less distracting to the other children, who will readily accept the explanation that since he or she cannot look around as they can, it is okay for the child to look with his or her fingers as long as he or she sits quietly and does not disturb them.

Field Trips

Visually handicapped children enjoy making a visit to the local fire station, bakery, or park if there is the opportunity for participation and a chance to try on the firefighter's hat, to feel the hose, or to slide down the pole in the firefighter's arms. If there are going to be sudden loud noises, like sirens or air hoses, a warning and explanation will avoid scaring the child. If the child has little or no vision, he or she will be happier holding the hand of a familiar adult who can explain what is happening and help the child explore safely.

Motor Activities

When teaching an action song or a singing game—or for that matter, any physical skill—the teacher should demonstrate the movement by moving the blind child as a model (something like a marionette) rather than using his or her own body; everyone will then learn at the same time. If the teacher says, "Reach up and pretend you are touching the sky," the child who is blind will not have a clue of what to do; but if the teacher positions the child's body, the child will know what to do the next time he or she hears the instructions.

Since vertical balance is harder to learn without the use of sight, extra practice is needed to master skills such as jumping, hopping, and beam walking, all of which help the child who is blind learn to handle his or her body more easily.

Visually handicapped children seldom run freely, probably because they are not sure of what is ahead of them. However, they can learn to enjoy running down a hill toward a familiar voice or running with a friendly hand clasped in theirs. Climbing ladders, ropes, and jungle gyms can be lots of fun, and children who are blind have no fear of heights. One 6-year-old boy who was partially sighted could scoot up a rope to the ceiling of the big school gym and was greatly admired by the whole class. Throwing, rolling, and catching skills are easier to learn with big beach balls, cushions, or beanbags and lots of "get ready, here it comes" warnings. The usual playground equipment of slides, swings, teeter-totters, large cartons, crawling tunnels, trampolines, roller skates, and tricycles all can be mastered and enjoyed.

Because the visually handicapped child cannot observe the other children having fun, he or she will be reluctant to try any new experience or equipment. If the teacher gently and firmly insists that the child try it a few times, the child will learn that it will not hurt and in due time will come to like it. Vigorous physical exercise at school is, in any case, doubly important for children who are visually impaired. It not only helps to improve their posture and muscle tone but shows them ways to blow off steam physically, which makes them easier for others to live with.

We all recognize how important it is that young, visually handicapped children learn to use their hands skillfully. A child who is going to be a braille reader will have to be able to distinguish the number and arrangement of very small dots by first grade. A child with limited vision will need to use his or her hands to supplement the limited information available visually, so practice in learning to use the fingers skillfully is essential.

It is not unusual for visually handicapped children to arrive at nursery school or kindergarten with little or no idea of how to use their hands and with a reluctance to touch anything strange at first; they may, indeed, seem to be terrified at the idea. Perhaps we can understand how they feel if we think of our reaction at being asked to reach into a bag and encountering a piece of wet, raw liver, a bristly brush, or something furry, or our reluctance to pat a huge barking dog that bounds up and jumps on us while his fond owner assures us he is as gentle as a kitten. Hand and finger muscles of visually handicapped children are often underdeveloped and the hands may seem like mitts with no independent finger activity. One teacher described a child who was blind as having "cloth hands."

Introduction of new toys, tools, and activities to blind children will often require a little extra time so they can get used to the idea and make up their minds that, since the other children are enjoying

Figure 10.3. "This piece goes here . . . ." (4½ years)

it, they might be missing out on something and will want at least to give it a try.

Many children who are visually impaired have a real aversion to handling sticky or greasy materials. One father suggested it might be that any coating on the fingertips impaired their sensitivity and likened it to how much he disliked looking through dirty glasses. For this reason, homemade modeling clay and dough made from flour and salt are preferred to commercial preparations, which are greasy and have a strong odor.

"Cutting, coloring, pasting—where does it get you?" was the comment of a small sighted boy after a hard morning at preschool. It is more than obvious that a visually handicapped child might share the same reaction unless these activities can be made more satisfying. Of course, the beauty of the finished masterpiece will not be apparent to a child who cannot see it. It is equally unsatisfactory for the child if the teacher pastes the features on his or her jack-o'-lantern because the child knows he or she did not do it. In this instance, a little ingenuity involving minimal time and effort can solve the problem: the teacher could mark the spot where the jack-o'-lantern's eyes go with small pasted stars or rough spots scratched on the paper that can be found by small fingers.

An Easy Way to Teach Cutting

Use of scissors comes with difficulty for a child who cannot see what is happening and who does not really understand what is supposed to happen. The following technique has been used successfully by a number of teachers:

1. The teacher makes a biting sound with his or her teeth while the child feels the teacher's cheek.

2. The teacher asks the child to bite.

3. The child gently bites his or her own finger.

4. The teacher holds the scissors, pointing them away from the child, and asks the child to listen to the scissors bite.

5. The child feels the scissors bite.

6. The child holds the scissors at right angles to his or her own body with the thumb in the top handle and two fingers in the bottom handle hole.

7. The teacher asks the child to make the scissors bite; the child will bite with his or her teeth at the same time, which helps get the idea of the movement required.

8. Strips of crisp paper, 1″ wide (colored pages from magazines or catalogs are good), and an aluminum foil pie plate are then produced.

9. The child holds the scissors while the teacher puts the paper into the scissors and the child makes the scissors bite it. The child hears the piece fall into the foil plate.

10. After several strips are cut in this manner, the child should feed the strip of paper into the scissors' mouth for it to bite.

A use must be found for these bits of cut paper. Various possibilities include threading them on a string for a necklace, a mobile, or for tree decorating; pasting them on a sheet of colored paper to make a pretty picture to take home; or pasting them on a jar or can for a present for parents. All the children in the class will enjoy this type of handiwork. After the visually handicapped child is adept at one-bite cutting, move on to two-bite strips and eventually to cutting a sheet of paper in half. If the child has no sight, it is almost—but not quite—impossible to cut around patterns. A few children will be able to master it. However, the partially sighted child usually can learn to follow clear black lines on simple patterns.

Pasting

Like all young children, children who are visually impaired are interested in the taste and smell of paste. If it does not smell nice to them, they will not be enthusiastic pasters. If the paste is put in a tin or jar, it is easier for the blind child to find than when it is just on a piece of paper that could get brushed aside and lost.

Coloring

Few visually handicapped children have used a pencil or crayon before attending nursery school, so they may need to be shown how to
hold one and what to do with it. Children with partial sight will be
able to see that they are making marks on the paper; just how clearly
they see only they know. It is usually too difficult for them to see the
lines to color any mimeographed or duplicated pictures; these are
simply too pale. Sometimes, if the pictures are outlined with a black
marking pencil they may become more visible. For children with no
useful vision, a piece of mesh or screening placed under the paper
when using a wax crayon produces a picture that can be felt. Finger
painting means getting fingers sticky and wet and is not particularly
satisfying, and yet most children who are blind will go along with it
because the other children enjoy it. Poster painting with a long brush
and an old shirt for a paint smock is more satisfying for the dressing up
than the actual art. Children with partial sight can get very close to
their work if they are standing at an easel. While they may occasionally get paint on their noses, they are painting in the same way as the
other kids.

People who are blind frequently are asked if they can recognize
color by touch. The answer is no, but they use color words in their
conversation because everyone else does. One girl, on being asked if
she had a favorite color, replied it was pink and explained it was
because she received more compliments when she wore pink dresses
than when she wore dresses of any other color. Small children who
are blind will talk about the colors of paint they are using and will
want to choose purple today and green tomorrow because the other
children can choose the colors they use. The counselor was teaching
Timmy how to hold and use a crayon just before he was to enter
nursery school. He colored away very industriously and then asked,
"What color am I using?" The counselor replied, "Blue. What are you
making?" and Timmy replied, "I am making a fine day."

Drawing

Drawing is no fun and has little purpose for a child with no useful
vision. But partially sighted children should be encouraged to draw to
help them develop eye–hand coordination. Children who need to be

very close to the paper to see what they are drawing should be permitted to lie on the floor or stand and use a big sheet of paper fastened to the wall. In these ways, they can get up close without having to hunch over a table, with the resulting neck and back fatigue. Black marker pens provide good contrast and make it easier for them to see what they are drawing or printing.

Reading Readiness

Any good reading readiness program is designed to do a number of things: first, to arouse in the child an interest in books and the desire to learn to read; second, to help the child get physically acquainted with books, to find out about covers, pages, tops, bottoms, how to hold a book, how to turn a page, and how to read from left to right; third, to help the child to learn to discriminate between shapes, sizes, differences, and similarities so that he or she will be ready to recognize letters and words.

Children who are blind and those with too little sight to see pictures have seldom had much experience with books before they get to nursery school or kindergarten. Those with enough residual vision to see pictures (perhaps only with their noses right down on the page) are usually familiar with books and how to use them.

Concepts

Children who cannot see must learn to use their fingers to give them information. They can learn about differences and similarities and to follow instructions by sorting or matching buttons, nuts, cereals, spools, cards, etc. Muffin tins, egg cartons, and trays with edges help to keep work material in a safe place where it won't get accidentally brushed off the table. Gummed paper shapes of different sizes can be pasted on cardboard by the teacher and used for matching and arranging in order.

Thumbtacks pushed into cardboard in different patterns or with different sizes of tacks may be used to "find which one is different from all the rest." Sandpaper and rough wallpaper make a change from gummed paper if they are used for pasting on shapes.

Some teachers have made intriguing books for blind children by stitching or stapling actual articles onto either cloth or cardboard pages. They have used safety pins, combs, keys, golf tees, pegs, and small plastic toys to make a workbook. One delightful one was called "What Do I Use in the Morning?" and contained a small piece of terry toweling, a toothbrush, a comb, and other similar articles. Another was made by an ingenious mother at a cooperative preschool to teach numbers and counting. These books are always enjoyed by all the children in the group.

Braille or Print?

The child who can see a print letter $\frac{1}{4}''$ high, even though he or she must hold it very close, should be able to learn print letters along with the other children. The belief that if one makes the letter bigger the child can see it better is not necessarily true, for the child may see just a fragment of it. The most practical size is in the $\frac{1}{2}''$ to $1''$ range. Chalk writing on the blackboard is very hard to see, and the child may need to be within 3 or 4 ft. before realizing what is there. The way to discover where and what the child sees best is to ask. Remember the child will not hurt his or her residual sight by using it but will learn to use it more efficiently.

The child who has no useful vision should not be encouraged to learn print letters by means of blocks, cutouts, or textured letters, since this learning will only be confusing when he or she begins to learn braille in school. It is best to avoid teaching braille at the kindergarten level; use the time and effort to teach the child to use his or her fingers deftly and with sensitivity.

SOCIAL INTERACTION

Impaired vision does interfere with the normal social interaction of young children in a new setting. Children who are blind cannot see where the other children are or what they are doing. They do not know if the other children would welcome or reject them because they are not receiving any visual messages; nor, for that matter, do they send any. Aggressive blind children may simply barge in, but

Figure 10.4. Kindergarten Christmas party (5 years).

others may need some help from the teacher to get to know the other children. It is confusing to children who are visually impaired to learn to identify a number of new people just by their voices at the same time. It is much easier for everyone if the teacher assigns the great honor of being "friend for the day" to confident and outgoing sighted children. After a week or so of assigned friends, one or two natural friendships develop and help is spontaneously given where needed. The friends usually tend to be too helpful at first but are soon set right by the blind child's own wish to be independent.

Teachers are sometimes concerned about what seems to them to be excessive passivity in a child who is visually impaired. The child cannot look around the room and see what the other children are doing or look over all the toys and decide to play train. The child will learn to be more independent if the teacher will announce that Jim, Alberto, and Billy are playing with the cars; that Simone and Keith are building a sand house; and that there are some building blocks on the table, thus letting the child decide what to do. Choices rather than directions help children grow. At first the teacher may need to enlist the help of some of the children in teaching the blind child how to play with specific toys or equipment and to find out that it can be fun.

Sometimes there is very little opportunity for fun in the life of a

Figure 10.5. "How high is up?" (5 years)

child who is blind. People are so anxious for the child to learn skills and to do things right that life tends to be too earnest. Children who are blind need to learn from the other children how to be silly and giggle about things grown-ups don't understand.

Suggested Goals for Preschoolers

Leave home without being unduly upset at parting from parent.

Be in a structured group of other children—nursery school or Sunday school.

Dress and undress. Button front and side buttons.

Wash face and hands unassisted and dry them.

Ask to go to the toilet and be able to take care of himself or herself at the toilet.

Dress oneself (except tying strings).

Travel in the immediate neighborhood unattended without crossing streets.

Run simple errands indoors or for a next-door neighbor.

Jump with both feet from a low box or from a bottom step.

Skip or hop on one foot.

Use roller skates, tricycle, wagon.

Be familiar with the type of clothes he or she wears.

Know which room he or she is in at home and what activities take place in each room.

Name the furniture in the rooms of the home.

Name dishes and silverware used at the table.

Put pegs in large pegboard without help, using both hands.

Use snap-on blocks (they help to train hands and fingers).

String buttons, beads, or popcorn.

Cut and paste.

Tell the difference in sizes, for example, whether shoes are big or small.

Tell the difference between top and bottom, above and below, left and right, and so on.

Use simple musical instruments such as bell, drum, harmonica.

Be interested in projects that carry over from day to day.

Ask questions about the meanings of words and how things work.

Finish work that has been started.

Use pronouns—I, me, you—appropriately.

Know some number concepts, for example, that three stones, three boys, three jumps, all mean three.

Learn to follow a regular routine, for example, take off coat, hang it up, take off boots, and put on slippers when arriving at school.

Sing songs.

Recite nursery rhymes.

Listen attentively to a simple story that has repetition and familiar characters.

Dramatize songs and stories.

Tell a short story accurately.

Chapter 11

School Age Issues

◆ ◆ ◆ ◆ ◆ ◆

CURRENT TRENDS IN EDUCATION AFFECTING STUDENTS WHO ARE VISUALLY IMPAIRED

There is growing concern among parents and educators of children who are visually impaired about the adequacy of the education being provided in the public schools for children who are blind or partially sighted. Depending on the country in which these children reside the system is variously known as inclusion, mainstreaming, or integration. A brief review of the drastic changes that have occurred in just the last 30 years and the reasons why they have occurred will help to clarify the present situation and will provide useful information when decisions must be made for these children's schooling.

These changes have occurred in the United States, Canada, and Great Britain at slightly different times and speeds, but the general reactions to the results of these changes are remarkably similar at the present time.

Prior to the 1960s almost all children who were blind or partially sighted were educated in residential schools for the blind from age 5 or 6 until the completion of secondary school, or until they quit school in their late teens. The general premise at the time was that only "experts" could adequately train and teach such children, and most

209

parents were considered incapable. In England many preschoolers were enrolled in residential Sunshine Homes for the Blind. The schools for the blind operated for the most part in isolation, with little or no interaction with the public schools. Upon graduation many of the graduates were ill-prepared for life in the sighted world. Many lacked social skills and were considered unemployable and remained dependent on family members who had become almost strangers to them. There were small numbers of bright, strong students who were able to go on to postsecondary education and successful careers.

By the late 1950s the number of children who were visually impaired decreased steadily as the causes of blindness (primarily infections) were discovered and eradicated, and the enrollment in the residential schools dropped dramatically.

During those same years, hospitals began to modernize their nurseries, with oxygen piped into the incubators for the very small premature babies. Unfortunately many of these small infants who survived had little or no sight due to what was then called retrolental fibroplasia but is now called retinopathy of prematurity. Within a short span of years there were literally hundreds of children who were visually impaired requiring an education, and the residential schools were unable to accommodate them all. Coincidentally a drop in the public school population made accommodation available in the public schools. The residential schools responded by moving senior secondary students out to the public schools, thus making room for the beginners.

The large number of infants who were visually impaired made plausible the development of new services designed to provide counseling and information for the parents of these children. The availability of these services resulted in a generation of visually impaired 6-year-olds who were much more mature and ready for school than previous generations, and parents who were both knowledgeable and outspoken. They wanted their children to live at home and to be educated in their local schools, not to have to send them miles away from home to live in residential schools for the blind. These parents lobbied strenuously both governments and local school boards, with the result that a number of school boards, particularly in western parts of both the United States and Canada, set up programs in some of the larger centers for children who were visually impaired to be educated close to their homes. The movement gradually spread across both countries and to Great Britain a little later.

Help came from another source. During the early 1970s there was great concern about civil rights, including the rights of people who were disabled, which of course included the visually impaired. Segregation became a dirty word, and local and senior governments began to react to the pressure to admit children with disabilities to the public school system. Legislation was passed in all three countries regarding the integration of children with disabilities into the local schools.

The legislation in the United States was the most far-reaching when in 1975 the federal government enacted Public Law 94-142 (Education for All Handicapped Children Act), to take effect in 1977. This act mandated free and appropriate education for all children with disabilities in the least restrictive environment. This meant that every child had the right to be educated in the regular classroom if at all possible with the use of supplementary aids and services where required.

This law has been amended and is now known as IDEA, or the Individuals with Disabilities Education Act. It places greater emphasis on what it calls *inclusion* (formerly known as integration or mainstreaming) and provides for a continuum of educational services. An Individualized Education Plan is to be prepared for each child who is disabled, including each child who is visually impaired, from preschoolers to those ready to leave secondary school. These students are entitled to transition planning to facilitate their move on to post-secondary education, trade training, skills of daily living centers, group homes, etc., as are students changing schools.

The inclusion of students who are visually impaired in the regular classroom has been accepted in varying degrees by most developed countries, and with varying degrees of success. The degree of success appears to be closely related to the adequacy of the special support services provided to these students.

Successful education of a child who is visually impaired in a public school requires the full support of the family, local school officials, and a classroom teacher who welcomes the presence of a child who is blind in the class. It requires that the teacher either has special training in the education of the visually impaired or will receive regular help from a specially trained itinerant teacher and that all Braille, large-type, or taped lesson material and texts used by the class be available, as well as any devices needed to ensure the student can keep pace with classmates.

WHAT WENT WRONG?

There was widespread acceptance and enthusiasm as more and more children with visual impairments were enrolled in their local public schools and great optimism for the future of these students. By the 1990s a whole generation of students who were blind or partially sighted had passed through the system, and many parents, students, and concerned educators were questioning just how adequately the special needs of these children were being met.

It is probable that most of the problems that have arisen are due to the fact that visual impairment is a low-incidence disability. That means that there are relatively few children who are blind and they are scattered over wide areas, making it difficult and expensive to make adequate provisions for their education. Consequently, many students who are blind or partially sighted get short shrift when it comes to the hiring of specially trained teachers for them. There is a trend toward the hiring of generalists for all disabled students, and unfortunately they lack the specific skills needed for the students who are visually impaired.

There is a chronic shortage of itinerant teachers of the visually impaired, and those who are employed are often unable to allot sufficient time to each student as their teaching load is too heavy. Sometimes the special braille or large-print texts are not available at the time the student needs them, and specialized equipment is obsolete or in short supply.

In some school districts where there were only one or two students who were visually impaired the districts were not prepared to hire a qualified itinerant teacher and the students and the classroom teachers were left to struggle on their own. The inclusion of children with other disabilities in the regular classroom also means that the teacher has less time to spend meeting the special needs of the students with visual impairments.

Unfortunately the result has been that many students who are visually impaired have graduated from secondary school as social and educational illiterates. Funding cuts not only are affecting the hiring of adequate numbers of qualified itinerant teachers but also have resulted in the closing down of some training programs for such teachers.

Classroom teachers, unprepared academically and emotionally, feel overwhelmed by the special needs students that are being placed in their classrooms and are growing more and more frustrated at their inability to meet their students' needs because of large classes, insufficient time, and insufficient help in special skills instruction. Budget cuts have resulted in the loss of teaching assistants and aides as well as the qualified itinerant teachers.

Despite the problems mentioned above there are still some school districts offering excellent services to their visually impaired students, and whose graduates are well prepared to live and compete in the sighted world. In the 1960s and 1970s the controversy between those favoring residential schools and those favoring integration was hot and heavy. Neither side seemed willing to listen or to compromise, each being convinced there was only one right viewpoint—theirs. But in the last 10 years positions have softened, most likely because both groups were genuinely concerned about the needs of children with visual impairments. The residential schools did not die out as many had predicted but have continued to function. In the more rural regions where visually impaired children cannot be served locally, the children attend the residential school. The schools are recognizing that it is essential to maintain close ties with family and neighborhood and whenever possible arrange for frequent home visits for the child who is blind and family weekends at the school. Residential schools for the blind are interacting more with their local communities and sharing facilities like swimming pools with them.

Children who have other disabilities in addition to their visual one, or who have developmental delays, are now being enrolled in some residential schools. Others are offering outreach services to preschool children who are visually impaired through home visiting and preschools operating in different centers by staff who are experienced in working with children who are blind or partially sighted.

A number of residential schools serve as resource centers for their state or geographical region in all three countries. They supply the special texts and other aids and equipment needed by students who are visually impaired in the public schools and also in some instances provide the trained itinerant teachers.

Some schools are offering short-term courses for those visually impaired children in the public school who need remedial work or special instruction by qualified teachers in such subjects as braille, mathematics, orientation and mobility, daily living skills, etc. These courses can last from 2 weeks to 10 months.

Summer camps arranged by some residential schools provide the opportunity for students who are blind or partially sighted to meet and get to know other students like themselves and to discover that other children are facing the same problems at school and at home. The students really enjoy such camps.

This growing cooperation between the residential schools and the public schools is actually being encouraged by legislation in some regions, like the Canadian Maritime Provinces. They set up a Special Educational Authority to coordinate the educational services to visually impaired children, with 719 integrated into the public schools, 35 at the school for the blind, and 101 preschoolers. The school serves as the resource center, providing educational assessment and planning, vocational assessment and career training, short-term placements, access to and production of material in braille, large print and tape, a professional library, a toy library, loans of electronic equipment, and special materials. Consultation services are provided by a variety of specialists, including orientation and mobility instructors, physiotherapists, psychologists, speech therapists, medical staff, and teachers of the visually impaired. As in other regions where a cooperative approach is being used, the old antipathy between residential school and public school personnel has been replaced by goodwill and shared interest in providing a well-rounded education for the students with visual impairment in the region.

History shows us that when a big social change occurs the pendulum usually swings as far as possible from the old ways. Then when the new way does not work out as well as expected the pendulum swings partway back to encompass some of the old ways and settle there. This would appear to be what is happening in the field of education of the visually impaired. People are beginning to discover that the new way—integration, mainstreaming, inclusion—is not the perfect solution, and they are beginning to swing back a little and incorporate some of the values and methods from the past.

As professionals deeply concerned and involved with children who are visually impaired for many years, we have watched with interest the changes occurring in their education over the years. As the first students who were blind began to move out from the residential schools to the public schools, we felt hope, followed by excitement, enthusiasm, and satisfaction, which gradually was replaced by disappointment and disillusionment. The wonderful dream that if children who were blind were educated just like sighted children they would turn out just like sighted children did not come true. It can't come true, because they *are different*—they cannot see—and they have different and specific educational needs that must be met if they are to receive a fair and equal comprehensive education.

WHAT IS A COMPREHENSIVE EDUCATIONAL PROGRAM FOR VISUALLY IMPAIRED?

Any curriculum designed to enable students who are visually impaired to function well in the sighted world must take into account that those students will require not only special supplementary instruction in the regular academic subjects but also special instruction in subjects specifically related to their lack of vision. The public school classroom teacher has neither the training nor the time to provide such instruction, which should be provided by qualified instructors.

A comprehensive educational program for students who are visually impaired will encompass instruction in academic subjects, orientation and mobility training, daily living skills, social behavior skills, and career planning. Parents of young children need not be concerned about the career training at present but certainly will want it to be available in the future.

Academic Subjects

The ability to read and write braille is as essential for a student who is blind as the ability to use a pen or pencil to make notes is for a sighted student. Although there are now electronic aids that can read print and speak the words and many texts are available on tape for older students, students who are blind will make use of braille all their lives, perhaps not as extensively as in the past before computers, etc., but it is still an essential skill. Students who are blind require braille copies of the prescribed texts, plus a braille writer to write the lessons.

Students with partial sight will require large-print texts, special paper and pencils, magnifiers, and book rests, as well as some material used by the students who are blind.

Older students will require special materials like embossed maps, math equipment, tape recorders, computers, electronic aids, etc., to be made available, plus any special instruction in their use. The special equipment and special instruction permit the students who are visually impaired to participate in classroom activities, rather than just sitting there trying to make sense out of what they hear, and sometimes simply tuning out.

Orientation and Mobility Training

"Orientation is how you know where you are, and mobility is how you get there from here" was a 10-year-old's definition. To adults, orientation is the ability to identify one's location in relation to one's environment, or in other words, one's place in space. Mobility is the ability to move safely and effectively from one place to another. Instruction in the basic concepts that enable students who are visually impaired to understand their immediate environment and familiarity with the skills necessary to move about safely and independently should be an integral part of their education. In the primary grades such training might involve teaching students how to find their seat, the teacher's desk, the coatroom, the bathroom, the school hallway, and the door. Then gradually the student should be able to find other parts of the school, both indoors and outdoors. Over a period of years students who are blind will be taught to use the long cane as a mobility aid. Both blind and partially sighted students can be expected in time to travel to and from school by themselves if they have received adequate instruction, are sufficiently mature, and have the will to do it.

Life Skills Instruction

Life skills, also known as skills of daily living, include all those things children need to be able to do independently and efficiently without sight, in a manner appropriate for their age level. For first graders these could include such skills as taking off and hanging up outdoor clothing, taking care of toilet and washing needs, the correct handling of educational material, etc. For older students it can include instruction in grooming, personal cleanliness, handling of money, making a purchase, and household skills like cooking, cleaning, and budgeting.

There is a wide discrepancy in the amount of instruction in life skills required by students who are visually impaired. Some families are able to work very hard and help their children develop these skills at home. Their first graders arrive at school ready to learn to read and write and do other academic subjects. Other children whose families for one reason or another were not able to teach their children to do things for themselves arrive at school functioning at a 2- or 3-year level and will need a lot of help before they are ready to participate in the school activities.

Social Skills Instruction

In Chapter 4 the effects visual impairment can have on an infant or toddler's ability to recognize and interact with other people were discussed in detail. Also mentioned was how much more difficult it is for children who cannot see to observe and copy the actions of others when it comes to everyday activities as well as social activities. "It's hard to know how to behave and to talk to the other kids so they will not think you are weird" was how a 12-year-old girl who is blind described her predicament in a local school. Like all children she wanted to conform but was unsure how to do it. For a first grader, some help is needed in learning to share and take turns, to say please and thank you, how to play simple games, and how to approach other children.

For older students it could include assistance in learning some social skills like dancing, chess, computer games, skating, how to dress like the others, how to invite a potential friend over or to a show, etc.

Again, as in life skills instruction, the family that takes the time and effort at home to teach their child who is visually impaired things such as good table manners, conversation with friends and visitors, proper behavior when eating out, and how to play simple table games and that allows the child to have other children over to play can help send a self-confident, friendly child off to first grade.

Career Planning and Training

During the first home visit by a counselor, the parents of a 3-week-old baby who was blind asked many questions about blind people, but the second question the young father asked was "Do they ever get jobs?" He seemed very relieved to learn about the employment opportunities that are open for competent, well-educated young adults who are blind. Although their visually impaired child may be very young, parents do want to know that their children will have access to the kind of education that will prepare them for productive and satisfying employment suitable to their intellectual and physical abilities.

Such an educational program should include vocational counseling and assessment, career options, and planning and assistance with the transition from secondary school to job training and placement, with the necessary support services. Students who have the ability should be encouraged to go as far as possible academically, as postsecondary education will enhance their employability, if they also are able to fit into the sighted world.

Students also should have access to new technological developments and instruction in the use of those that will enhance their employability and independence.

TYPES OF EDUCATIONAL PROGRAMS

The parents of children who are blind or partially sighted are naturally concerned about the kind and quality of education available for their children. They search for answers to questions about school almost from the time they learn their child cannot see.

There are a number of factors that parents should take into account when planning for the education of their visually impaired child. The first is whether their child has sufficient residual vision to read print. The second is whether the child has any other disabilities that may require special treatment or training facilities. The third is what educational programs are available to the child in both local and residential facilities. The selection of the appropriate school should not be left to the last minute. It should be determined well in advance through consultation with knowledgeable people who are familiar with and can discuss the alternatives with the parents. In choosing a program parents should keep in mind that the school they choose now should be one that meets the needs of their child at this time, and not 1 or 3 or 5 years in the future. In most areas it is not too difficult to transfer from one program to another for short or longer periods to meet specific educational and social needs of that child.

Public Schools

As mentioned in the last chapter, the enrollment of students who are visually impaired in the regular classroom in local public schools is called mainstreaming, integration, or inclusion, depending on the country where the child lives. The usual classroom teacher has had no special training in how to teach children with impaired vision, and many have not even met one before one is enrolled in his or her class. In most instances an itinerant teacher with the necessary special training travels from school to school in the district to provide the individual students with any necessary specialized instruction. The itinerant teacher consults regularly with the classroom teacher about current lessons and any problems that may have arisen. The preparation and procurement of all lesson materials and necessary books and equipment for the student who is visually impaired is the responsibility of the itinerant teacher, as is instruction in life skills, orientation and mobility, etc.

These special educational services supplied by or through an itinerant teacher are commonly called support or back-up services, and the quality and quantity of these services are the key factors in determining the adequacy of the education the child with a visual impairment will receive in the local public school. There are no firm rules about how much time an itinerant teacher should spend with each student, as there are many variables, such as age, intelligence, amount of vision, attitude and competency of classroom teacher, etc.

Before making the decision to enroll their child in the local school, the parents should inquire about the amount of special instruction that would be available to their child and the qualifications of the special instructor. Some school districts make a practice of simply hiring teacher's aides, who perhaps have training in child care but have none at all in the education of children who are visually impaired. In some instances they simply baby-sit the special needs children. In communities where there are only one or two students who are visually impaired, the school boards may be unable or unwilling to hire a trained itinerant teacher, as there is no provision in their budget for one and the money is needed elsewhere.

If there are shortcomings in the educational program offered by the local school to a child who is visually impaired, parents also should take into account if it is important for their child to live at home and go to school in the neighborhood, and how much that contributes to the child's well-being and potential growth. They also should consider if they themselves might be able to provide some of the extra help their child needs if the child were to live at home.

Residential Schools

Residential schools in the United States, Canada, and Great Britain still provide an education for 20% to 30% of the visually impaired students according to where they live. Some students come from rural areas where there are no itinerant services for them; others have one or more additional disabilities that make it more difficult for them to manage in a regular classroom. Some are there because their parents prefer to send their children to boarding school, as is common in England. And some are attending for short terms to have remedial instruction in specific skills or subjects, which they have not received in the local schools.

The teachers and other instructors in the residential schools are trained and experienced in all facets of the education of children who are visually impaired. As discussed in the previous chapter there have been extensive changes in the philosophy and the operation of many of the residential schools designed to maintain and strengthen family ties. If parents are considering enrolling their blind child in a residential school, they should visit the school, meet the staff who will be instructing their child, check out the facilities and the opportunities there for association with sighted children, and ask about the frequency of home visits during the term.

Which School?

It will be obvious to the parents of a child who is blind when considering where to send their child to school that there are positive and negative aspects to enrollment in either a public school or a residential school. If possible they should talk to the parents of other students who are blind regarding how they feel about the quality of education being provided for their children at a particular school. Factors such as the attitude of the classroom teacher, the adequacy of itinerant or back-up services, the maturity and intelligence of the child, and whether or not the family wants the child to live at home will all affect the decision.

Those parents who live in areas where there is no back-up service for the special educational needs of their child will have to base their decision on the readiness of their child to leave home to attend the residential school. In some instances they may decide to have the child attend the local school or kindergarten for another year until he or she is more mature.

The decision about placement of blind children who have one or more other disabilities should be based on the quality of the total educational program being offered at the different facilities, rather than on the "civil rights" of the child.

MODES OF COMMUNICATION

Braille

Braille is a special reading code written in the form of raised dots that has been used by people who are blind for some time. By using one or more dots in a basic six-dot cell, it is possible to write all the letters of the alphabet as well as numbers and musical notation. Because braille reading tends to be slow, many abbreviations and contractions are introduced to reduce the reading time involved. A good braille reader can read at approximately the speed of normal conversation, which is considerably slower than sight-reading the same material. Braille may be written by using a braillewriter, which is a form of typewriter with six keys, or by using a slate and stylus.

Should the Student Learn Braille or Print?

Years ago when most students with visual impairments were educated in special schools, they were all taught braille, though some had

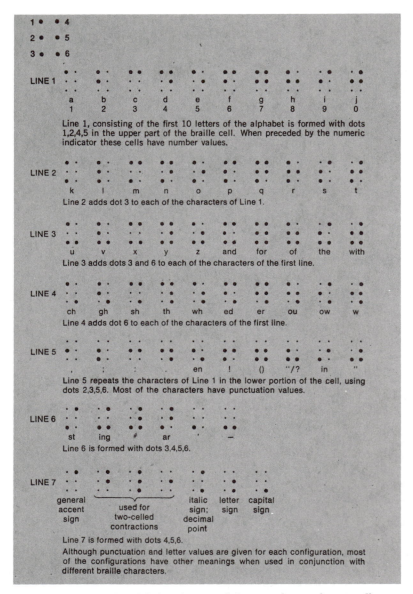

Figure 11.1. Braille alphabet (reprinted from *Understanding Braille*, published by the American Foundation for the Blind, Inc., 1969; reprinted by permission).

enough vision to read print. Then, as it does, the pendulum swung the other way and teaching print to children who had any vision at all received great emphasis. Currently the trend seems to favor the teaching of print to children who are able to see print of any size and braille to those who cannot. There is a much greater emphasis on the training of children to use their low vision more efficiently. The more the children practice using what sight they have, the more efficient they become. Parents can help by encouraging their preschool children who have any sight to look at books and pictures. Some children with minimal vision are being taught to read both braille and print. They do their schoolwork in braille but are able to read signs, etc. The decision about whether the individual student is to use braille or print should not be made lightly. The interdisciplinary assessment team, the parents, the preschool worker, and the kindergarten teacher should share their information with the resource room or itinerant teacher who will do the actual teaching, and a joint decision can be made, with the teacher having the final say.

Parents can perform a simple test at home to give them a good idea of whether their child should be reading braille or print. Unfortunately, this test will work only for about two thirds of the visually impaired children. If the child seems to have useful vision he or she should be asked to pick out the letters *o* and *l* from several pages in a primer; if he or she can do so at any distance it is quite likely that he or she will learn print. Those who have no useful vision will, of course, be braille students. Children in between those with useful vision and those without will require a professional to decide which medium they will use to read.

Should Parents Learn Braille?

Classes are available for parents of braille students in some school districts. Other parents take a braille transcriber's course at a local agency for the blind. Some of those parents have volunteered hundreds of hours transcribing school texts into braille for the visually impaired children of their community. Parents do not need to aspire to become speedy and fluent readers of braille. They should learn enough to keep ahead of their children for the first few years of school. After that they will be left far behind, but the children will no

Figure 11.2. Braillewriter.

longer need their assistance. Sighted persons read braille with their eyes, which is easier and faster than learning it by touch.

Other Educational Devices

Taped books are used for reading supplementary texts and also for pleasure reading by braille students. The tapes are much less bulky to store than braille books. Once a student has become sufficiently profi-

Figure 11.3. Braille slate and abacus.

cient in braille to make and read notes, there are a number of electronic devices that are able to translate print into braille or the spoken word. Senior students find them very useful and timesaving. There are also typewriters that will tell the student if there is a spelling error and also will read aloud the typed material. Such devices are still expensive, but the prices are dropping gradually and new aids are coming on the market.

The abacus, the traditional oriental device for mathematical computation, is used by some braille students, but the new calculators that can speak most likely will replace them.

There are numerous other aids and appliances useful to students who are blind, such as raised maps, measuring devices, games and puzzles, etc.

FOCUS ON TEACHERS

How Do Teachers Feel About Students Who Are Blind?

As discussed in the preceding chapter, the most important factor in the successful integration of students who are blind into public schools is the attitude of the classroom teacher. Parents should discuss with the principal their desire to enroll their visually impaired child in the school and ask for cooperation in placing the child in the classroom of an understanding teacher. The teacher also should be informed about the availability of any back-up consultant services and special materials like braille and taped books and should be assured that the parents are prepared to do extra reading and taping for the child if the material is not available elsewhere. It is important that the teacher accept the student who is visually impaired as an equal to the other children in the class and that the child be given the same rights and responsibilities as the others. If the teacher feels positively toward the child, the children in the classroom will also.

Communication Between Parents and Teachers

Teachers employed in schools for the blind will be familiar with the special needs of their students and how to interact with them, but parents may wish to share the following suggestions with public school teachers faced with their first blind student. Parents may find suggestions for ways they could help their child at home with schoolwork.

1. Parents can be exceptionally helpful (if asked) in providing answers to the many "how can," "what if," and "should I" questions that naturally arise when a teacher enrolls her or his first student who is blind.

2. Many of the suggestions given in Chapter 10 for nursery school and kindergarten are applicable to grade school.

3. As mentioned in that chapter, the young student who is blind will not be embarrassed by his or her lack of sight and is usually quite comfortable about answering questions about it or discussing ways and means to function in the classroom.

4. The teacher should address the student by name and inform him or her of the presence and identity of any visitors to the room.

Figure 11.4. Braille map.

5. The teacher should speak aloud when writing on the blackboard and should develop the habit of describing verbally any pictures or charts used for illustration.

6. Because braille reading and writing are slower than print work, the teacher should either allow extra time for tests and assignments or reduce the quantity of work.

7. The young braille writer will need time to practice on the braillewriter and also with the slate and stylus.

Figure 11.5. Reading braille.

Figure 11.6. Reading print with an Optacon.

8. Typewriting instruction should be given as soon as the child's hands are big enough to reach the keys. It is most helpful to the teacher if the child who is blind can type assignments so that they will be easier to read, and typing is faster than writing in braille.

9. The student should learn to use a tape recorder for practicing language skills and for taping some assignments.

10. The student who is blind may need some help from the teacher initially to make friends and to become involved in playground activities.

11. Students who are blind should be included in physical education because they tend to be inactive. Participation in gym, skating, and swimming should be encouraged.

PROGRAMS FOR PARTIALLY SIGHTED STUDENTS

A generation ago many school districts organized "sight-saving" classes for partially sighted students on the assumption that excessive use of sight or eye strain would further damage the vision. Most of the instruction was given orally and large-print texts were used. The whole concept of sight saving has been discarded because it has been shown that, in most cases, the visual efficiency of partially sighted children actually can be improved if they use their eyes. The more they read, the more efficiently they learn to use their little bits of vision.

With the disappearance of sight-saving classes, students who are partially sighted no longer need to be segregated and usually are enrolled in regular classes. It is very easy for a partially sighted child to remain undetected, particularly if his or her eyes look normal. For this reason it is important that parents ensure that the teacher is informed at the beginning of the school year about the child's partial sight and that the teacher be made aware of the child's special needs. The average classroom teacher will not be familiar with the problems that confront the visually impaired child and will want information about how the child can best function in the classroom. If the school district has made provision for an itinerant teacher's service to the visually impaired, then the classroom teacher can seek assistance from her or him.

Because children with partial sight may use their little bit of vision very skillfully, they may require less instruction from their parents about how to do things than do children with no useful vision. Many of them seem so competent when they enter school that everyone assumes they will do well. Unfortunately many of them do not do well because of the limitations imposed by their particular kind of partial sight. It is impossible for a school to ignore a student who is totally blind, and instruction in braille and the necessary books and tapes are supplied. But it is too easy to assume that the partially sighted student who walks around confidently will cope with academic work without any special assistance.

In our search for new information for this edition of *Can't Your Child See?* we talked to the majority of the children mentioned in the first edition published in 1977. We were surprised to find that most of the young adults or senior students with partial sight (including some of the brightest preschoolers) had found their school years, particularly secondary school, to be exhausting, discouraging, and frustrating. Only a small number with quite useful vision were interested in going on to college to equip themselves for a professional career. The others stated firmly that it was not worth the price they would have to pay physically and emotionally. They chose instead to settle for jobs that were far below their intellectual capability.

SUGGESTIONS AND INFORMATION FOR TEACHERS AND PARENTS OF PRIMARY STUDENTS WITH PARTIAL SIGHT

1. Parents should request that a special sheet be attached to their child's permanent school record that should come to each new teacher's attention, advising that teacher that the student has partial sight and requires certain specific help to function most efficiently in the classroom. Any new information about how and where the student functions best should be noted on that sheet for the next teacher.

2. The teacher and the parents will have to work closely to ensure that the student can experience success.

3. Some students find that glare is one of the most difficult problems they have to cope with since it cuts down their vision.

4. Glasses cannot give normal vision to these children but some special aids can help.

5. The teacher should make sure that the student is seated where he or she can function best. This seating may have to be ascertained by trial and error and discussion with the student.

6. The child may have to move to within a few feet of the blackboard to see the writing on it. This is preferable to having the child walk up for a look from a front seat, since the child may forget the information while walking back and it takes too much time. Some children use a

Figure 11.7. Partially sighted student using monocular.

monocular, which is half a binocular, to see the blackboard once they have learned to read.

7. If the child cannot see the blackboard at any distance the teacher may provide a clear copy of the material to use at the desk.

8. Partially sighted students in the elementary grades can usually manage to use the regular textbooks. They obtain the necessary magnification simply by holding the book closer to their eyes. For example, when a student brings a book from a spot 16″ from the eyes to one 8″ from the eyes, the size of the print is doubled; and if he or she places it 4″ from the eyes the print looks four times as big as at 16″. Some students read effectively at a distance of only 2 or 3″ from their eyes. As the student grows into the teens this built-in magnification grows less and he or she may have to use outside magnification in the form of low-vision aids.

9. A very black pencil or a black nylon-tip pen should be used for printing, and the pale blue lines in the exercise book should be darkened if the child cannot see them. This can be done by parents.

10. Care should be taken that the child is taught the correct direction of strokes when learning to write letters, since he or she cannot see how the teacher does it on the board.

11. Duplicated material is difficult to see if it is in pale blue or purple or even a poor copy in black ink. If no clear copy is available parents should be willing to darken the lines.

12. If it is necessary for the child to get close to the book for reading or writing, propping the book up on an easel will lessen the neck and back fatigue that can plague children who tend to crouch over their desks in order to see.

13. Children with partial sight may have extra problems with number concepts since they have had less experience in looking at groups of objects. Extra experience to learn about numbers should be provided.

Figure 11.8. Use of easel reduces fatigue.

14. Some partially sighted children will require encouragement to participate in sports and physical education. They need the opportunity to improve their coordination, and they also need the exercise since they tend to be inactive. Games that involve a moving ball are difficult for them, but they can be involved as scorekeeper, equipment manager, or in some support role.

15. The teacher who finds that the partially sighted student is not able to finish the tests in the allotted time can either extend the time allowed or reduce the number of items in the test and prorate the marks accordingly. The latter method is more fair since a student may become too tired

to think if the test time is extended. Other than allowing for the time factor the teacher should use the same standards in grading for these students as for the rest of the class.

16. A student with less than normal vision is usually tired at the end of the school day because of the extra pressure. Since poor vision is a less efficient tool than full sight, the student must work harder to keep up. Long hours spent copying notes will leave the student with no time to play and relax. If it takes the visually impaired student longer to do arithmetic problems, the teacher might consider assigning him or her only one half or two thirds. If there is research reading a fully sighted partner could read to the student and thus save time. The teacher could talk to the parents and they could arrive at a reasonable amount of time that the student could be expected to spend on homework.

Figure 11.9. Closed circuit TV as a reading aid.

Acceptance

Children with impaired vision attending public schools will be teased by some of their classmates. Most 7- or 8-year-olds have absorbed some of the prejudices and attitudes of their parents and friends, and any child who is different is automatically teased. Parents of children with impaired vision should help those children grow a tough skin so they will not be hurt by the teasing. It is common for a mother or father to express their hurt feelings or indignation when someone comments about their child's vision in the presence of that child. If they can conceal their feelings and shrug off the incident with comments such as "Oh, they don't know what they are talking about" or "Don't pay any attention to them, they don't know what a nice boy you really are," it will help to play down the insult.

After Mary and her mother had been playacting how she would respond to teasing with an appropriate retort she remarked, "Oh mother, I can hardly wait until those kids are mean to me so I can tell them to get lost." Tina, on the other hand, was a most confident 10-year-old and needed no coaching. When asked if she were ever

Figure 11.10. Biking with a friend.

teased she replied, "Sure, but it doesn't bother me. Last week a boy asked me why my eyes wiggled all the time and I just asked him why he couldn't wiggle his."

Appearance

Conformity is most important to school-age children, and those who don't conform stand out. To dress as the other children dress is important even if the visually impaired child cannot see enough to know which brand of shoes is in style and which hopelessly out. This is where the observant parent can help the child to be less different.

The maintenance of good grooming and posture (the cause of much parental nagging in most families) is doubly important for the child who cannot look in the mirror. Children who are visually impaired miss out on the daily feedback other children get from seeing themselves reflected in mirrors and store windows.

Social Skills and Parental Participation

Children who are visually impaired are not able to learn social skills by observation and imitation as other children do. Their parents can help them fit in at school in this regard. They may need help in getting to know some of the other children and learning how to play with them. By inviting schoolmates one at a time over to play after school, for lunch on Saturday, or to go on a picnic or swimming, parents can provide an easy social situation for their child. Such events should be arranged frequently; parents should not wait for their child to be asked back. All his or her life the child is going to have to go more than halfway to have a good social life and he or she might as well start young.

Driving children to Brownies, Cub Scouts, and music and dancing lessons goes on much longer for the parents of visually impaired children, but the skills the child learns in such activities can serve well in the future. Later the child can go skating or to judo class with a friend.

Meeting Other Children Who Are Visually Impaired

Children attending residential schools for the blind used to be encouraged to attend summer activities for sighted children so they could be acquainted with both groups of children. Now with most visually impaired children attending public school there is a new emphasis on summer camps to enable a child who is visually impaired to meet other children who have little or no sight and to discover how they are coping with the same problems. Such camps are also geared to teaching some of the special skills of daily living with little or no sight, skills that are usually not taught in the public school setting. Some residential schools offer short summer courses or day camps for children with impaired vision who attend local public schools.

A student may feel he or she is a real oddball if he or she is the only student who is visually impaired in a class or even in the whole school. It is important for such students to have the opportunity to meet and get to know other children who are blind or partially sighted and to share experiences with them. Students who attended one 2-week camp said meeting others who were coping with the same problems was very reassuring to them and gave them more confidence in their ability to cope.

Is It Worth It?

When exhaustion sets in and parents wonder if they are going to survive this rigorous child-raising experience, they should regularly remind themselves that time invested now will pay off many times in the future. They will be able to sit back with pride as their independent and competent offspring makes his or her way in the world. With the support of an interested family a child who is visually impaired should be able to go as far in school as intellectual potential allows. The child will have to work harder to achieve his or her goals, but it can be done. Financial help is usually available for university or vocational training, and no student who is visually impaired should have to drop out because of lack of funds.

Chapter 12

What About
the Future?

◆ ◆ ◆ ◆ ◆ ◆

Parents will have found some of the answers to their questions about the present and the immediate future in the preceding chapters, but being only human they will be wondering what the future holds for them and their visually impaired child.

No one is sure what the future will bring, but a look at what has happened in the past 20 years may provide some clues as to the direction in which we are moving. There is no doubt that the greatest single obstacle with which blind people and their families must contend, and the one over which they have least control, is the attitude of the sighted public. Certainly a considerable change has occurred in society's attitude toward most minority groups; and the blind do make up a minority group in the mind of the public, in whom the traditional feelings of pity and rejection have been mixed with feelings of awe and mystery based on many strange and unfounded beliefs about the blind. It is natural to feel impatient at how slowly social changes take place, but the rate of change seems to be accelerating as more and more people who are blind or partially sighted are being integrated into the community, providing both groups with the opportunity to work and play together and to break down barriers.

We have seen the development of greater interest by the medical profession in the causes and prevention of blindness in children.

239

More doctors have become directly involved in diagnosis, treatment, and research, which has led to a better understanding of a number of eye conditions and a marked decrease in some of them. A vaccine for rubella is now preventing pregnant women from contracting the disease with the subsequent risk of giving birth to a baby with disabilities. Since the major cause of infant blindness in western countries is now genetic, it is reassuring that genetic research has resulted in more information being available to parents of disabled children seeking genetic counseling or to those parents fearing such an eventuality.

There is, however, a most regrettable change occurring in the population of children with visual impairments. With technological advances in the care of very small premature infants, more of these babies are surviving, some with a birth weight of less than one pound. Unfortunately, despite their long and valiant struggle to survive, many of these infants have multiple disabilities, including blindness, mental retardation, cerebral palsy, seizures, etc. As a consequence the percentage of visually impaired children with additional disabilities is steadily increasing.

With society's growing concern for its disabled members, more and better services for visually impaired children are being provided and should continue to improve. Better diagnostic and treatment facilities should permit parents to consult with professionals who are knowledgeable about the special needs of children who are blind or partially sighted and their families. The importance of early intervention to the future of the child and entire family is now being recognized, and the parents should look for an improvement and expansion of counseling services.

Professionals are changing their traditional attitudes toward parents and gradually are recognizing the importance of the role of the parents, of how much parents can contribute to diagnostic assessments, treatment programs, and long- and short-term planning for their child. In short there is a growing trend to consider parents as cotherapists, something that was unheard of in the past and is long overdue.

Children with impaired vision have been attending community preschools in many areas for over 30 years. It has proved a valuable experience for both blind and sighted children, as the latter learned to accept visually impaired children as equals before they were infected by the prejudices of their parents. It is hoped that this will continue.

Figure 12.1. Skiing on the mountain (12 years). (Courtesy *North Shore Times*)

The inclusion of all disabled children into the public school system that now is occurring or slated to occur can put additional strain on the already strained support services devoted to the visually impaired students in those schools.

Some governments are finally being convinced that it is more economical to educate and train people with disabilities to be self-sufficient than to support them on welfare all their lives. Funds are being made available for early intervention programs for visually impaired children, for the extension and upgrading of facilities in the residential schools to include more people with multiple disabilities, and for the development of good support programs to facilitate the mainstreaming of visually impaired students in the public school system. A recent change in government policies is causing considerable concern among parents and professionals in the United States and Canada. With federal, state, and provincial governments all preaching fiscal restraint in their budget planning, severe cutbacks in the funding of special education are beginning to take place and are expected to continue. Unless this trend is reversed, the quality and quantity of services available for visually impaired children will suffer seriously.

Financial assistance to cover the cost of vocational or professional training should be available to enable those visually impaired young people who are capable of benefiting from such training to become self-supporting members of the community. A wider choice of vocations is steadily opening up as individuals who are blind prove they can succeed in previously untried occupations. New facilities are slowly being developed to provide varying degrees of independent living for those blind adolescents and young adults who are not capable of managing on their own. These consist of supervised light-housekeeping apartments, group homes, and small boarding or nursing home units, which will enable the parents of multiply handicapped children to plan for the time when their child, too, can leave home.

Governments only react to the demands of the electorate, and no government is going to make funds available for education or training or maintenance of a relatively small group of visually impaired children unless it is made acutely aware of the need by the people involved—parents, agencies, schools, concerned professionals, and the adult blind themselves.

More and more bright young students who are blind or partially sighted have been enrolling in universities and successfully earning their degrees in arts, music, science, education, and law. Some are now being admitted to courses from which they were previously excluded and are proving that normal sight is not essential in fields such as linguistics, electrical engineering, computer programming, teaching, practical nursing, real estate, insurance sales, and horticulture. As these competent young people move out into the sighted community, obtaining employment in their chosen field and participating in social and recreational activities with their sighted friends, they are proving, by their very presence and their demands for equal opportunities in all areas including education and employment, to be a most effective and forceful influence for changing the public's attitude toward the visually impaired.

Figure 12.2. Independent travel.

The greatest changes in the future for young people who are visually impaired will come as a result of new technological developments, many of which are already available, and from their further adaptations, some of which are already in the testing phase. By making use of a variety of computerized aids young adults who are blind or partially sighted are now enjoying successful careers in areas that formerly were considered impossible. Devices like scanners that can read print aloud or print it in braille or large type or regular print permit the reading and answering of personal or business correspondence without sighted help. Talking calculators and typewriters are widely used. Computers are able to search out information requested and either print it or read it aloud. Some secondary students who are blind have become computer whizzes and are writing their own programs. Computer literacy is an essential skill for the ambitious visually impaired student who wants to have a successful career in the sighted world.

Chapter 13

Where Are They Now?

$\blacklozenge \ \blacklozenge \ \blacklozenge \ \blacklozenge \ \blacklozenge \ \blacklozenge$

Parents often ask about what has happened to the boys and girls we wrote about in the first two editions of *Can't Your Child See?* and some newer parents also are interested in knowing how they turned out, so we decided to make some inquiries. The search proved to be very easy, as most of the families still live in the same metropolitan area, and many of them know other families' addresses and phone numbers. All the parents and young people we spoke to were delighted to talk to us and let us tell their stories. There were a few disappointments, but overall we were amazed at how well most of them had done, particularly the totally blind ones.

Unless otherwise stated the children had no useful vision. The pages on which they are mentioned in this edition are in brackets after each item.

Tom B. was a bright, active preschooler with a little partial sight who astounded the neighbors with his desire to try everything, including riding a bicycle. With little or no itinerant support services he found school frustrating and discouraging, particularly secondary school, where he had to work long hours at home to keep up. After working at a fast food outlet on weekends he went to work there full-time after he left school and is now a branch manager. His first love has always been radio and he has a part-time weekend job with the expectation of being hired full-time in a few months. He also is engaged to be married. [p. 4]

Cheryl graduated from college with a degree in music and has as many piano pupils as she can handle. She has her own apartment in her parents' home. [p. 9; Figure 6.7]

Betty worked for a year developing films and then attended college, where she graduated in honors French. She worked for several years teaching French at a junior college but has recently been put in charge of programs for all disabled students there. She is married with two sons. [pp. 19, 130]

Kenny, who has additional disabilities, went as far as the 10th grade and is now living in a group home with five other young people with disabilities. [p. 29; Figure 3.3]

Fernando, who can see print at 2″ but must use a cane to move around, has just enrolled in college. He has not yet decided whether to take law or computer science. He organized a small band in secondary school and still books and plays dates on weekends. [pp. 81, 169; Figures 3.6, 6.1]

Ian has finished secondary school but has not yet decided on a career. While he undergoes vocational counseling he is doing volunteer work at a youth counseling center. [p. 80]

Robin, who gained fairly good partial sight following eye surgery, is a good student and a good athlete. She was involved in horseback riding and swimming as a youngster and now at college is on the swim team and into cross country running and skiing. [Figures 5.2, 5.3, 5.4, 5.5]

Bobby moved to California with his family years ago, but friends say that he took up scuba diving as a youth and accompanied a group of divers to Norway one summer. He attended college and is now employed as an oceanographer. [p. 95]

Brian, an accomplished musician and linguist after graduating with honors, is currently working for the federal government in the North. He has a small goat farm several miles from his work site and either snowshoes, hitchhikes, or walks to and from work. He has built a windmill that provides power for his computer. [pp. 7, 119]

Barry P. played in a band in secondary school and now works full-time as a country-and-western musician. He is married for the second time. [pp. 61, 124]

Samantha moved with her family to another province, but we have learned she is in her final year of secondary school, despite her early poor prognosis. [p. 147; Figure 8.6]

Marilyn graduated with a degree in music and is a talented pianist and singer who works part-time as a professional musician. She is married with two small children, is active in the community, and was elected recently to the municipal school board. She also serves on the board of the agency for the blind. [p. 128]

Judy, with a degree in library science as well as a B.A., is the librarian at the university braille and tape library and recording facility for blind students in the region. She married a partially sighted administrator. [p. 183]

Patsy married at 16 to another partially sighted student. She has one son and operates a small neighborhood day-care center. She also is active at the local agency for the blind as a volunteer and board member. [Figure 10.2]

Robbie, with his bubbling personality and despite his cerebral palsy, founded and operates his own computer business. He is married and very active in his church and community. [pp. 40, 150]

Jean attended junior college but did not graduate. She lives in her own apartment near her parents and has a visiting homemaker. [p. 88]

Tina, after obtaining a master's degree in special education, had difficulty finding work but at last is working as an itinerant teacher and loving it. She has enough partial sight to read print up close. She plays guitar and sings at weddings, etc. [p. 64; Figures 11.8, 11.9]

Sandy, despite having to use crutches because of cerebral palsy, obtained a degree in music and now shares an apartment with two friends and teaches music. [pp. 146, 150]

Cory's family moved several times, so he attended several different schools. Each time he settled in quickly and soon became involved in school activities. He was on the student council in secondary school and very active socially. He is now attending college in the East. [pp. 97, 127; Figures 3.1, 6.3, 6.5, 9.4, 9.5]

Supplemental Readings

◆ ◆ ◆ ◆ ◆ ◆

SUGGESTED READINGS ABOUT VISUALLY IMPAIRED CHILDREN

Barraga, N. C., & Erin, J. N. (1992). *Visual handicaps and learning.* Austin, TX: PRO-ED.

Harrison, F., & Crow, M. (1993). *Living and learning with blind children.* Toronto: University of Toronto Press.

Lowenfeld, B. (1971). *Our blind children: Growing and learning with them.* Springfield, IL: Charles C. Thomas.

McInnes, J. M., & Treffry, J. A. (1982). *Deaf-blind infants and children.* Toronto: University of Toronto Press.

National Society for Parents of the Visually Impaired. *Awareness* magazine. Watertown, MA: Author.

Scott, E. P. (1982). *Your visually impaired student.* Austin, TX: PRO-ED.

Sonksen, P., & Stiff, B. (1991). *Show me what my friends can see.* London: Institute of Child Health.

SUGGESTED READING ABOUT
ALL CHILDREN

Brazelton, T. B. (1969). *Infants and mothers, toddlers and parents.* New York: Delacorte Press.

SUGGESTED READINGS ABOUT
OTHER DISABILITIES

Botshaw, M. L. (1991). *Your child has a disability: A complete source book of daily and medical care.* Boston: Little, Brown.

Featherstone, H. (1980). *A difference in the family: Life with a disabled child.* New York: Basic Books.

Finnie, N. R. (1990). *Handling the young cerebral palsied child at home* (3rd ed.). New York: E.P. Dutton.

Freeman, R. D., Carbin, C. F., & Boose, R. J. (1981). *Can't your child hear?* Austin, TX: PRO-ED.

Jan, J. E., Zieglrt, R. G., & Erba, G. (1992). *Does your child have epilepsy?* Austin, TX: PRO-ED.

Pader, O. F. (1981). *A guide and handbook for parents of mentally retarded children.* Springfield, IL: Charles C. Thomas.

Segal, M. (1988). *In time and with love: Caring for a special needs baby.* New York: Newmarket Press.

Appendix A

Common Eye Conditions

◆ ◆ ◆ ◆ ◆ ◆

In industrialized nations, the majority of children with visual impairments are born with their eye disorders (congenital disorders), while about one quarter of them develop their visual loss later in life. Severe visual impairment is uncommon in these countries, only approximately 6 to 8 children in 10,000 have this disability. Unfortunately, in recent years the prevalence of congenital ocular visual impairment has increased because of the reemergence of retinopathy of prematurity. Due to improved medical care, more markedly premature infants survive, and as a result more of them develop this still incompletely understood eye condition. In strong contrast, in nonindustrialized nations, childhood blindness is very common, but most children acquire their visual loss rather than being born with it. A recent United Nations study indicates that every year over 1 million children become blind in these countries, mainly because of infections, and most of them die. Poor hygiene, malnutrition, vitamin deficiencies, and lack of immunization predispose children to devastating eye infections.

It is important for parents to become familiar with the nature of their child's visual impairment, and, when old enough, the children themselves also must be given a satisfactory explanation. A series of questions should always be asked of ophthalmologists, pediatric

251

neurologists, developmental pediatricians, genetic clinicians, and others who assist children who are visually impaired. In recent years, a number of parent associations were formed to promote family education. Parents also could visit medical libraries, but the information is often complex and because these textbooks tend to concentrate on complications they could lead to unnecessary worries. Some of the more common eye conditions are described briefly below.

Optic Nerve Atrophy

Optic nerve atrophy (ONA) is one of the most common eye abnormalities leading to visual impairment. The optic nerve is a cable of nerve fibers that carries visual messages in the form of electrical impulses from the eyes to the brain and back. ONA occurs when this cable is significantly damaged by various medical disorders, such as temporary lack of oxygen at birth or in near drowning, bacterial or viral infections, accidental or nonaccidental injuries, slowly growing tumors, various brain and eye diseases (often inherited), ingestion of toxins such as methyl alcohol, and so on. Once ONA is noted on eye examination, careful investigations must be carried out because the treatment depends on the cause. Since the eye is a part of the brain, additional neurological problems commonly are seen in children with ONA, because whatever damages the optic nerve also often affects the brain. Therefore, epilepsy, cerebral palsy, hydrocephalus, developmental delay, hearing loss, endocrine deficiencies, and learning difficulties are commonly associated. Once there is optic nerve atrophy, regeneration of the damaged nerve fibers is rare, and thus the visual loss is permanent. Early treatment is critically important in children with neurological disorders that predispose them to ONA.

Optic Nerve Hypoplasia

Occasionally, some children are born with underdeveloped, small optic nerves and as a result have impaired sight. The ophthalmologist who examines the eyes with an ophthalmoscope sees a small optic nerve head with other characteristic features. Brain scanning also can reveal small optic nerves and, exceptionally rarely, the absence of optic nerves. Optic nerve hypoplasia (ONH) occurs when a variety of neurological insults damage the developing optic nerves. These can be maternal ingestion of drugs, severe prenatal alcohol intake, infections, and even tumors in the unborn fetus. Often the pregnancy is entirely normal and the parents never discover the cause. This disorder is almost never hereditary and the visual loss is not progressive. Once ONH is noted, neurological, endocrine, and developmental investigations must be done because multiple disabilities are common. The sense of smell also may be deficient in children with ONH. The visual loss varies depending on the severity of optic nerve involvement.

Cataracts

A cataract is an opacity or a cloudiness of the lens. The normal lens is clear and its function is to focus the light rays on the retina. If the lens becomes cloudy, passage of light to the back of the eye will be obstructed. In a normal eye the pupil appears to be black, in the same way that the uncurtained window of an unlighted house appears black from across the street. If you hang a white curtain behind the window it will appear white. Similarly, when the lens behind the pupil is opaque, the pupil appears to be grayish-white.

Most often cataracts are present at birth or appear very soon after in early infancy. If the opacity of the lens is very dense, the child will not be able to see and the lens will need to be removed. The surgery must be done immediately after diagnosis, because visual deprivation can cause permanent loss of sight. Without its own lens, the eye will not be able to focus, and the child will need to use special glasses or contact lenses. The latter are being used successfully on infants, and the parents very quickly learn to insert and remove them. Ophthalmologists can implant artificial lenses in adults, but in small children this procedure is still complicated and risky.

It is more difficult for an older child to accept contact lenses, and these children use glasses, as do those whose parents find the insertion and removal of a contact lens too difficult. The elastic band or harness commonly used to hold glasses on small children tends to be uncomfortable and can be replaced by ribbons tied across the back of the head, with another pair of ribbons tied over the top of the head. The ribbons make it more difficult for the glasses to come off accidentally or otherwise. Since their vision is markedly improved by glasses or contact lenses, most young children accept them very readily. It is a good practice to keep a spare set of contact lenses, because they can be lost or swallowed. Glasses can be sat on, rolled on, or stepped on, as well as lost.

Most frequently, cataracts are familial, therefore genetic counseling is advised. The child may have a parent with cataracts and in turn is apt to pass on the eye condition to his or her children. Children with hereditary cataracts usually do not have additional disabilities. Congenital cataracts can be caused by a disturbance to the developing eye during the mother's pregnancy. The eye is actually damaged as it is being formed. The rubella virus (German measles) is probably the best known cause of this type of cataract. In many cases the damage is not restricted to the eye, and these children may have severe hearing loss, heart defects, developmental problems, and other health difficulties. Fortunately rubella cataracts have become extremely rare, due to comprehensive immunization programs. Cataracts acquired during later childhood are very rare.

Most children with congenital cataracts retain their impaired vision, especially when they develop nystagmus (eye tremor) even with corrective lenses, and function as partially sighted.

Albinism

The diagnosis of albinism is made when the pigmentation of the skin, hair, and eyes is reduced, from birth. There are many different forms, but the two major clinical types are neurocutaneous and ocular albinism.

Children with neurocutaneous albinism have very blond hair, fair skin, and most often defective vision. The irises are usually pale blue and cannot screen the excess bright light from the eyes. As a result, these children are very sensitive to bright light (photophobic). Sunglasses, sunbonnets, and billed caps help to reduce the discomfort from the glare. If corrective lenses are prescribed, they are usually tinted. Special care should be taken to protect the skin from sunburn, either by sunscreen lotions or protective clothing. Skin cancer can develop without these protective measures. The various forms of albinism are familial, therefore genetic counseling is desirable.

Children with ocular albinism have reduced pigmentation only in their eyes. They also tend to be photophobic and frequently have defective vision. The diagnosis is not always easy or clear-cut. All children with albinism have differently formed visual pathways (the connections between the eyes and the visual centers in the brain), and special electrical tests can prove whether someone has albinism or not. The vision of children with albinism does not deteriorate later and they tend to do well in life.

Retinal Disorders

The congenital and acquired retinal disorders that can cause visual impairment in children are too numerous to be discussed here in detail. They cause about half of the visual losses in children, and many are genetic. They may be progressive or stationary. At times only the retina is affected, while at times the brain and other parts of the body are also involved in the disease process. Accurate diagnosis is frequently difficult because the appearance of the retina may not be fully characteristic of a specific retinal disorder. Therefore, usually detailed tests must be carried out, including electroretinograms, fluorescein angiography, and metabolic and genetic studies. In order to offer genetic advice to a family, the doctor must accurately identify the disease.

Retinopathy of Prematurity. Retinopathy of prematurity (ROP) was first diagnosed in the early 1940s and then was seen in epidemic proportions. The disorder was first called retrolental fibroplasia but later was given the more descriptive present term. Originally the cause was felt to be entirely due to the toxic effect of oxygen on the immature retinal blood vessels, and many physicians were sued for giving "too much oxygen." However, oxygen therapy could not be eliminated from the treatment of prematures because it prevented severe, permanent brain damage. The disorder may occasionally occur even when oxygen is not used, and now it is clear that a multitude of factors in addition to oxygen are responsible for ROP. It is not a genetic disorder. After the 1950s ROP was infrequent, but during the last few years it has again become common in markedly premature infants who, due to improved medical care, now survive.

Most infants with acute ROP recover without scarring of their retina, but unfortunately, for reasons as yet unknown, some do not. The occurrence of ROP is now confined almost exclusively to infants of less than 1,000 gm birth weight. Some infants with ROP have additional difficulties due to the various complications of prematurity;

therefore, they should all have regular, multidisciplinary developmental assessments.

Leber's Amaurosis.   Leber's amaurosis is a retinal disorder, present from birth and often with severe visual loss. On initial eye examination, the retina may have a normal or close-to-normal appearance, yet the electroretinogram is usually profoundly abnormal in a characteristic way. Later the retina shows progressive pigmentary changes. Leber's amaurosis is not a single entity because several neurologic and ophthalmic disorders can cause a congenital retinal abnormality. Therefore, detailed investigations are always required. These conditions are always hereditary.

Some, but not all, children with Leber's amaurosis are intense eye pressers, to the point where their globes are pushed back into their sockets, and it can be very difficult to stop their eye pressing. Severe hyperopia (far-sightedness) is occasionally seen, and corrective glasses might be quite helpful for those with residual sight.

Retinitis Pigmentosa.   Retinitis pigmentosa (RP) is a term used for retinal disorders characterized by night blindness (decreased vision in the dark), visual field loss, and abnormal electroretinograms. Occasionally RP is confined only to the eye; at other times it is part of a widespread disorder. These conditions are all hereditary, but the inheritance can differ depending on the exact type of RP. The appearance of the retina changes over the years. In most instances in children, the central vision is preserved until early adulthood. Generally, with a few exceptions, there is no treatment. Ophthalmologists often can predict the rate of progression.

Retinoblastoma.   Retinoblastoma, a tumor of the retina, when confined within the eye poses no threat to life. It is a curable condition. When it spreads to the brain through the optic nerves, or through the orbit, it can be fatal, unless the child receives extensive treatment. Enucleation (removal) of the affected eye is only rarely done nowadays because of more effective treatment.

If removal of the eye is necessary, the child can be fitted with a plastic artificial eye within a few weeks. The plastic eye is called a prosthesis, and it will look remarkably natural. An artificial eye is not round but rather is shaped like a cupped hand. The cupped side fits over a clump of muscles left in the socket, so the eye will have some movement. Insertion and removal for washing are very simple, and many children of 4 and 5 learn to do it themselves. As the child grows, it will be necessary to have the eye built up periodically to ensure a snug fit.

Retinoblastoma usually occurs as an accident of nature, in families without any history of that eye condition. The odds are very high, however, that the children of the person who has this condition will inherit it, and he or she should seek genetic counseling. For some unknown reason children with retinoblastoma are usually found to have superior intelligence and are often brighter than their brothers or sisters.

Coloboma

On rare occasions, infants are born with a developmental defect of any or all of the iris, ciliary body, choroid, and optic nerve (see Figure 2.1). Some of these children are visually impaired, but their visual loss is rarely severe. Genetic counseling is advised.

Glaucoma

Childhood glaucoma, which is caused by increased pressure within the eye, is exceptionally rare. The human eye is filled with clear fluid, which is normally manufactured and discharged at the same rate, keeping the pressure more or less constant. In glaucoma, the inflow of the fluid (secretion) is normal but the outflow (absorption) is impaired. Therefore the pressure builds up, and if not corrected it can cause permanent damage.

This eye condition is divided into two forms: primary and secondary. In primary glaucoma there is a developmental abnormality in the eye that interferes with the absorption, whereas in secondary glaucoma there is a disease process within the eye, resulting in the disturbance of the fluid circulation.

In infants with glaucoma, the corneas are often large and cloudy, with marked sensitivity to light and excessive tearing. In older children, glaucoma presents with pain and vomiting. The diagnosis is made by measuring the pressure within the eye. While there is successful treatment available, many children are visually impaired.

Glaucoma can be inherited in different ways. Accurate diagnosis of the cause is very important in order to offer sound genetic advice.

Aniridia

Aniridia is diagnosed when the iris fails to form (see Figure 2.1). These children are photophobic because the light can freely enter the eye. Glaucoma and cataracts can occur with aniridia but seldom do in childhood. Occasionally a rare kidney tumor (Wilm's tumor) develops during the first few years of life; therefore, for early detection children with aniridia all should have regular kidney ultrasounds during this period. Some children exhibit a specific abnormality of one of their chromosomes, in which case the Wilm's tumor is more frequent. Aniridia is a hereditary condition, and genetic counseling should be arranged.

Strabismus

Children with visual impairments frequently have strabismus (cross-eye or squint). The movement of each eye is controlled by six muscles that work in pairs. When one of these muscles contracts or tightens, its partner relaxes in any direction desired. It is important that both eyes move together. Sometimes, when one muscle is out of balance, the affected eye will not move in unison with the other. When the two eyes do not coordinate, the child may see double. Because double vision is confusing, the brain causes the image from the abnormal eye to be suppressed, and the young child will use just one eye. If the eye is not straightened early, the vision in the affected eye may be permanently damaged.

Appendix B

Cortical Visual Impairment

◆ ◆ ◆ ◆ ◆ ◆

The statement that "we see with our brain rather than with our eyes" should not be surprising to anyone. Like mobile cameras, the function of the eyes is to focus on an object of interest and then transmit that information to the brain. The visual centers, which are located in the occipital lobes (in the back of the head), receive and then transmit this information to different parts of the brain for analysis. Vision is a strong sense, and it is through vision that all the senses and all the incoming information are unified. When the visual centers or the pathways leading to them are damaged, cortical visual impairment (CVI) can result.

CVI, which was once considered to be rare, is seen significantly more often in recent years because improved medical care now allows many critically ill children with severe brain damage to survive. In fact, in many medical centers, CVI is the most common form of visual loss. The study of CVI is still in its infancy, and many comprehensive ophthalmology, pediatric, or neurology textbooks do not even discuss this topic.

Causes

The visual centers of the brain can be damaged before, during, or after birth. The causes can be infections, injury, lack of oxygen, toxins, tumors, or various neurological diseases. Almost all children with CVI have additional disabilities, such as slow development, seizures, cerebral palsy, and hearing loss. Simultaneous eye problems also can exist, especially optic nerve atrophy. In fact, brain damage is often widespread and severe.

Features

The visual behavior of children with CVI is so characteristic that the diagnosis can be strongly suspected just from talking to the parents. Most children do not appear blind, and they do not have fixation nystagmus (eye tremor on looking), which is the hallmark of severe visual loss due to eye conditions noted at birth or soon after. This type of nystagmus is only noted in CVI when there is simultaneous eye damage.

Children with CVI have a markedly short visual attention span. They see little and their vision appears to vary from minute to minute. They often blank out visually for short periods of time, as if they want to block out their visual environments. Unfamiliar places, the complexity of visual information, suboptimal lighting, poor contrast, innate processing factors, medications, and their own energy levels can all dramatically affect visual perception. This extreme variability is a common cause of confusion to the caregivers.

Children, even with severe CVI, are attracted to colors, especially yellow and red. Most children with CVI have some sight, therefore the term *cortical visual impairment* is used rather than *cortical blindness*. Like children with eye problems, they view objects at a close range in order to magnify what they see. However, through this mechanism they also can reduce visual information to simpler units and thus analyze them better.

Prolonged, compulsive light gazing, which was discussed earlier, is commonly noted. Mild light sensitivity also can present, although less frequently. Peripheral visual field loss (reduced side vision) is very common, and as a result they can bump into objects when walking. Some children seem to see stationary objects best, while others have a striking ability to detect movement. However, no one knows how children with CVI actually see.

Visual Recovery

Some degree of visual recovery is seen in the majority of cases, while visual recovery is more complete in others. Recovery tends to be gradual, but occasionally, even after several months of blindness, it may be surprisingly rapid. The improvement can continue for several years. The recovery of acuity (how far they see) is not the same as recovery of vision, which is a vastly complex function. Such children often remain visually inattentive and are weak visual learners, and their psychological tests show severe visual perceptual difficulties.

Doctors often find it difficult to give an accurate prognosis for visual recovery, although after careful investigations there are some clues. Overall, it is possible to state that with less severe damage to the visual centers, the prognosis for visual recovery is better.

Can We Help Children with CVI To Recover?

The developmental and educational intervention in this field is so new that professionals are still searching for satisfactory approaches. Children with CVI have different abilities and needs. Therefore successful intervention is based on detailed, multidisciplinary evaluations. Their habilitation is radically different from that of children with eye defects. With eye disorders, the vision is reduced but the analysis of information is sound. Thus, visual enrichment, many visual stimuli, and training to scan more efficiently are successful remediation techniques. For children with CVI this approach causes overloading. Therefore visual images need to be simple and presented in isolation.

The energy level of these multidisabled children is so minimal as they struggle to maintain their balance and posture that inappropriate seating arrangements, mild upper respiratory infections, or sedative drugs can readily interfere. Mainstreaming with regular students might result in some social benefits, but it also can have serious adverse consequences, because the multidisabled children so easily overload. In our view, one-on-one teaching by trained professionals, at the right time and in a controlled classroom environment, is clearly superior.

Appendix C

Common Tests

◆ ◆ ◆ ◆ ◆ ◆

Children with visual impairment commonly have medical tests to identify the cause and extent of the various disorders affecting the eyes, the brain, and the rest of the body. Some of these tests are briefly described below. They are not painful nor harmful, yet the parents should know something about them, because they need to prepare their children for these experiences. Machines that make buzzing noises, all the different lights in the examining rooms, the strange hospital smell, and the busy people who work there can unnecessarily frighten children. Hospitals and clinics almost always provide a description of these tests to the parents, and they also explain the procedures to the children.

Brain Wave Test

The "brain wave test" or electroencephalogram (EEG) is an important test for the investigation of visual impairment. It is often done during the initial diagnostic period. Most people are aware of the importance of electrical tests in heart disease, but they tend not to be aware of the existence of the EEG. The electrical activity of the brain can be recorded in the same way as is done for the heart (electrocardiogram) or muscle (electromyogram). The test is entirely painless. It usually lasts 60 to 90 minutes. The technician carefully measures the child's head and may make little colored marks with a pencil for accurate placement of wires (electrodes) on the scalp. Through them the electrical activity of the brain is picked up, magnified, and then recorded by special pens on moving paper. The EEG is continuously recorded when the child is awake or asleep, during periods of deep breathing (if they are cooperative), and under special types of bright, flickering light placed in front of their eyes.

The children should be prepared physically and emotionally for the EEG. Their hair should be washed thoroughly the day before so that the scalp is clean. They must know that the test does not hurt and their hair will not be shaved off. Most children are scared of wires and may think that the EEG machine might give them a shock. They need to be reassured that this is not true.

Children may be asked to stay up for most of the preceding night in order for them to be able to fall asleep naturally during the recording on the following day. Usually they are delighted to watch a movie or the late show on TV!

After the recording, the test is carefully analyzed. The EEG can be a valuable tool in the evaluation of visually impaired children. Children with normal EEGs are unlikely to develop epilepsy. If they have developmental problems, most likely they will be minor. Cortical visual impairment and field defects can be confirmed or ruled out. An abnormal EEG can alert the physician to carry out more investigations and even call for developmental evaluations.

CAT Scan

During the investigation of visual impairment, a doctor might order a head CAT scan (Computed Axial Tomography). This painless procedure is performed as the child lies comfortably on his or her back while a series of X rays disposed all around the head send in beams, each from a different angle. A computer measuring the amount of X ray in each single point of the brain pieces the images together, and the picture of a section of the head appears on a TV screen. The CAT scan usually lasts from 15 to 30 minutes. Occasionally a special dye is injected into the bloodstream in order to get a better view of certain parts of the brain. The child must lie quietly because movements blur the images, making this important test quite useless. Therefore, children who do not cooperate or are not able to hold their heads abso-

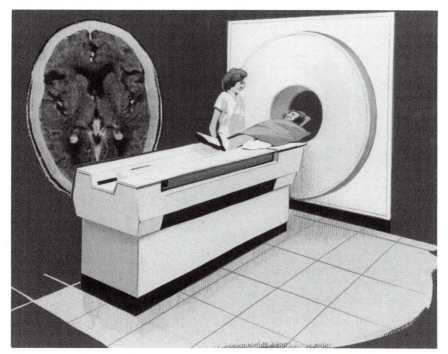

Figure A. A head CAT scan often is necessary in the investigation of visual loss. It is a painless test.

lutely still for a few minutes at a time require sedation or a brief period of anesthesia.

The images of the brain are developed immediately after the test and they are studied carefully. The reports go to the referring physician.

MRI

Magnetic Resonance Imaging (MRI Scan) is a new, informative technique that takes extremely precise pictures. The part of the body that needs to be scanned is placed in a large, powerful magnet. The human body is composed of atoms, within which protons randomly spin around. In the magnetic field, they line up together and spin in the same direction. Next a radio frequency signal is beamed into the magnetic field, which temporarily makes the protons move out of alignment. A receiver coil measures the energy released by the disturbed protons and also the time it takes them to return to their original aligned position. Using this information, a computer creates a TV image of the scanned body part. The image is then recorded on film or magnetic tape so that there is a permanent copy.

Before the scan, children may eat normally and take their usual medications. However, they have to remove objects such as jewelry, hair pins, and glasses. Children with metallic devices and implants, surgical clips, and plates cannot have this test. The child is comfortably positioned on a table, which is then moved inside the giant magnet. There is no discomfort. The total scanning time usually lasts from 30 to 90 minutes. Both the CAT and MRI scans can accurately show the structure of the brain and reveal many different abnormalities.

Electroretinogram

The electroretinogram (ERG) is a test similar to a brain wave test (EEG) or a heart test (ECG). All living tissues in the human body generate electrical activity. Electrodes (wires) are placed around the eyes or on the eyes, with the use of a contact lens, and the electrical activity from the retina is recorded in light and in darkness. Retinal disorders affect the electrical activity in different ways. When the test results are carefully analyzed, a specific diagnosis often can be made.

Visual Evoked Potential (VEP) Studies

When the child is exposed to various visual stimuli, the retina changes the signals to electrical currents, which then pass through the visual pathways to the visual centers. It is possible to measure the speed of conduction, the strength of these signals, whether or not they reach the visual centers, and what happens to them afterwards. This study can give a great deal of very useful medical information.

Blood Tests

Investigations of visual impairment occasionally include blood tests. The physician needs to know about the blood sugar, calcium, biochemical abnormalities, and whether infection was the cause of the visual problems. Whenever possible, it should be explained to the child how and when blood is taken. The parents should not say that it does not hurt, because it does, and then the child can become more frightened or distrustful. Usually a single sample is enough for all the tests. Blood is sometimes taken from the finger, but usually it is taken from the arm after a tourniquet is put on and the area is cleansed with alcohol. The pain resembles a mosquito bite and is quickly over.

About the Authors

♦ ♦ ♦ ♦ ♦ ♦

Eileen Scott, with a background of teaching and medical social work, has counseled the parents of hundreds of visually impaired children over many years. Her compassionate and optimistic approach and practical advice is a direct result of her association with these families. She has always been a firm believer in enhancing the services available to meet their special needs, and she actively recruited and taught professionals from many other fields to provide such services. She was actively involved in the planning and establishment of the first multidisciplinary center for visually impaired children and their families and served part-time on its staff. She has always been a strong parent advocate and is convinced that the best way to help a child who is visually impaired is to provide the parents with sound information and emotional support. Eileen Scott is well known to parents and professionals through her books and articles and her teaching and participation in many conferences and seminars.

Dr. James E. Jan, an internationally known pediatric neurologist, is full-time director of a unique multidisciplinary center offering a full range of services to the visually impaired children and their families in British Columbia. His research, based on his assessment and follow-up of over 3,000 children, is concerned with the neurological aspects of blindness and the effects of visual impairment on normal development and has been published in numerous articles in international

269

medical journals. His findings have created great interest and have resulted in frequent visits from concerned professionals from many countries to the center.

Dr. Roger D. Freeman is a child psychiatrist who specializes in treating children with chronic disabilities. He has been associated with the multidisciplinary program for visually impaired children since 1971. He has carried out two long-term studies concerned with the psychiatric problems of the visually impaired children he has examined and treated.

The three authors all reside in Vancouver, British Columbia, and worked together for years.

Index